BOOK [illegible]LEMENTS

THE HAUKSBÓK RECENSION OF *LANDNÁMABÓK*

Translated by

Matthias Egeler

VIKING SOCIETY FOR NORTHERN RESEARCH
UNIVERSITY COLLEGE LONDON
2022

VIKING SOCIETY TEXTS

General Editors

Alison Finlay
Carl Phelpstead

© Viking Society for Northern Research 2022
Printed by Short Run Press Limited, Exeter

ISBN: 978-1-914070-02-0

Cover design: Clive Tolley

The cover image represents the site of a contemporary settlement story. According to local tradition, the rock pinnacles of the Broddar ('Spikes') in the Strandir district of the Icelandic Westfjords mark the burial site of the primeval founding hero Broddi ('Mr Spike'), said to be the first settler at the farm of Broddanes ('Peninsula of the Spikes').

CONTENTS

For my grandfather, Johann Thür

INTRODUCTION

Place and Story in the Book of Settlements

The *Book of Settlements* is a book of tales half-told, untold, and told wrongly. In a retrospect of several hundred years, it presents an account of the first settlement of Iceland during the last third of the ninth and the early part of the tenth centuries. In doing so, it takes the reader on a journey clockwise once round Iceland and tells of the settlers who took land in the different parts of the country, outlining their land-claims, enumerating their descendants and in many cases enlivening the resulting lists of names and directions with copious anecdotal material. In the account thus created, the chronological distance between the scribe's present and the past of the Settlement Period shows itself in many different ways: there are both lacunae and historical 'mistakes', but more importantly, this chronological distance means that the formerly empty spaces and now-settled places of Iceland have, by the time when the *Book of Settlements* is composed, accrued a kaleidoscope of narrative associations built up during several centuries' worth of storytelling. The way in which the *Book of Settlements* presents a cross-section of these narrative associations of the Icelandic landscape is one of the most remarkable aspects of this text: however dubious its contents may be as history, the *Book of Settlements* provides us with a glimpse of the first associations that came to the mind of a high-medieval Icelander when making a mental circuit of the island.

In many cases, these associations are not spelled out in any detail—and frequently the underlying tales are told in so little detail that it becomes nearly impossible to see what is actually going on. Thus, when Þormóðr the Mighty and Óláfr Bench start to fight about the small and inaccessible valley system of the Hvanndalir in Northern Iceland and almost twenty people die, neither the *Book of Settlements* nor the remaining extant medieval literature of Iceland ever reveals what it was that sparked off this fight about land-rights, even though this fight demanded the highest blood-toll reported about any argument about land-rights during the whole, conflict-ridden time of the

Settlement Period.[1] This story, like many others, is half-told at best, and yet, overall, it is still one of the more elaborate tales in the *Book of Settlements*, for most of its stories remain entirely untold: we never hear what the feats of magic were that earned Þorkell Bound-Foot at the foot of the mountain Þríhyrningr, or Óláfr-with-Meeting-Eyebrows at Skeið, their reputations as men of great magical powers;[2] we never learn why Eyvindr Hrólfsson was called 'Oaken-Hook',[3] why Sigurðr at Kvenvágastrǫnd was called 'Pig-Head',[4] or why Ármóðr Þorbjarnarson was called 'the Red'.[5] Behind every single one of the countless nicknames mentioned in the *Book of Settlements* lurks a story, but of most of these stories no trace remains beyond the elusive one-word reflex they have found in the nicknames that memorialise them.

Perhaps most fascinating of all, however, are the stories told wrongly—fascinating not only in the spirit in which, in *Sturlunga saga*, King Sverrir called 'lying sagas' the most entertaining of all saga narratives.[6] One example of what I mean by 'stories told wrongly' may be provided by the tale of the settler Vilbaldr:[7]

> Vilbaldr was the name of a man, the brother of Áskell-of-the-Thread-Hook. They were the sons of Dofnak. He came from Ireland and had the ship which was called Kúði. He came into Kúðafljótsóss Estuary.

The semi-implicit message of this tale is that *Kúðafljótsóss*, the 'Estuary of Kúði's Water', was so named because it was the place where the ship called 'Kúði' reached Iceland. A gloss on this passage in the Skarðsárbók recension of the *Book of Settlements* claims *Kúði* to be an Irish word; yet this recension only stems from the seventeenth century and thus is too late a text to be authoritative. More likely may be Richard Cleasby and Gudbrand Vigfusson's idea that the place-name element *kúði-*, which is otherwise unattested in the Old Norse corpus, is a form of the noun

[1] Ch. 182. It is only local folklore recorded during the early modern period that suggests a possible explanation for the ferocity of this conflict, telling us that the Hvanndalir were believed to be a valley of immortality in which nobody was able to die (Heizmann 1998; Egeler 2015; Egeler 2018, 188–208).

[2] Chs 306, 332.

[3] Ch. 61.

[4] Ch. 68.

[5] Ch. 102.

[6] *Þorgils saga ok Hafliða*, ch. 10 (Brown, ed., 1952).

[7] Ch. 285.

kóð, which denotes the fry of trout and salmon. Yet if this is so, then *Kúðafljótsóss* means 'Fry-Stream-Estuary', implying that the story of the ship called 'Kúði' has been developed out of the place name rather than the other way round. A toponym thus seems to have been reinterpreted to provide it with a story—a story which may be 'wrong' from a factual historical point of view, but may well have been deeply meaningful for the contemporary local audience that lived at and worked this estuary and that viewed the coming of Vilbaldr in his ship as the arrival of an ancestral founder figure.

In the case of *Kúðafljótsóss*, if the suggestion made by Cleasby and Gudbrand Vigfusson is correct, the story of the ship 'Kúði' may have arisen when a form of the word for 'fry' fell out of use and was reinterpreted as a name, which in turn was interpreted as a foreign word.[8] Such reinterpretations of place-name elements may have happened more than once; another instance may be provided by the settlement story of a certain Galmr:[9]

> Galmr was the name of the man who took Galmansstrǫnd Coast between the rivers Þorvaldsdalsá and Reistará. His son was Þorvaldr, the father of Ormr, the father of Bjǫrn, the father of Þóroddr, the father of Þórunn, the mother of Dýrfinna, the mother of Þorsteinn the Smith, son of Skeggi. Hámundr[10] gave land to Þorvaldr between the rivers Reistará and Hǫrgá, but before that he had lived in Þorvaldsdalr 'Þorvaldr's Valley'.

The topography here becomes remarkably crowded, as according to the preceding chapter[11] the Galmansstrǫnd Coast (even though there it is spelled Gamlastrǫnd or Galmastrǫnd) had already been taken by a certain Hámundr and been sold on to one Þorvaldr. (The compiler of our text is aware of this problem and attempts to adress it by returning to the definition of Þorvaldr's property at the end of the paragraph, and perhaps by ascribing a son by the name of Þorvaldr to Galmr. In doing so, however, he ultimately just increases the problem: why should a son of the original settler have had to buy his father's land from Hámundr?) This apparent over-attribution of one and the same stretch of land to

[8] On the importance of sometimes highly localised language developments especially for toponymy cf. Robinson 1996, 157–58.

[9] Ch. 188.

[10] Manuscript: Helgi (which is inconsistent with the preceding chapter).

[11] Ch. 187.

both Hámundr/Þorvaldr and Galmr may be explained by an observation again already made by Cleasby and Vigfusson, who note that the name element *galm* only occurs in place names and may be related to Old English *gealm* 'din', suggesting that *Galmansstrǫnd* (or *Galmastrǫnd/ Gamlastrǫnd*) may be 'called so from the roaring of the surf'.[12] If this is so, then Galmr the person has been extrapolated purely from the place name, which would explain how his settlement came to be associated with a place already taken by not just one but two settlers. Here, we may be getting a glimpse of a process that may lie behind a number of the early settlers referred to in the *Book of Settlements*.

If in the two preceding examples a place story is 'wrong' arguably because a place-name element was misunderstood after a word had fallen out of use, other instances of place-name stories are suggestive, rather, of a conscious play on place names. The tale of how the wetland of Flugumýrr got its name may belong here:[13]

> Þórðr Dove's-Beak was a freedman of Oxen-Þórir. He brought his ship into Gǫnguskarðsáróss Estuary. At that time, the whole western part of the district was settled. At Landbrot Land-Slip he crossed the Jǫkulsá River in a northerly direction and took land between Glóðafeykisá River and Djúpá River and lived at Flugumýrr Moor. At that time, a ship came[14] out [to Iceland] into Kolbeinsáróss Estuary, and it was loaded with livestock, and they lost a foal in the Brimnesskógar Forests, and Þórðr Dove's-Beak bought the chance of finding it and did so. That was the fastest of all horses and was called Fluga ('Fly').
>
> Ǫrn was the name of a man who ranged from one end of the land to the other. He was versed in witchcraft. He waylaid Þórir in Hvinverjadalr Valley, when he was meant to be going southwards over Kjǫlr, and he made a bet with Þórir which of them owned the faster horse; for he had a very good stallion; and each of them staked a hundred pieces of silver. They both rode southwards over Kjǫlr until they came to the stretch of the road which is now called Dúfunefsskeið 'Dove's-Beak's Stretch of Road'; and the difference in speed between the horses was no smaller than that Þórir came back on his second lap to meet Ǫrn in the middle of the course on his first. Ǫrn bore the loss of his money so badly that he did not want to live any longer and went up to the foot of Arnarfell 'Ǫrn's/Eagle's Mountain' and killed himself there, and Fluga remained behind there, because she was very exhausted.

[12] Cleasby and Vigfusson 1874, *s.v.* 'galm'.

[13] Ch. 169.

[14] Missing in manuscript.

> And when Þórir went home from the Assembly,[15] he found a grey stallion with a remarkable mane by Fluga. She had conceived from him. Eiðfaxi was born to them, who went abroad and killed seven men at Mjǫrs on a single day, and there he himself died. Fluga was lost in a quagmire on Flugumýrr 'Fly Swamp'.

In this vividly recounted story the name of the moor Flugumýrr is explained, a moor which today gives its name to a farm and a large church and may well have been of similar toponymic importance at the time when our story was written down. In this tale, the name Flugumýrr 'Bog of the Fly' or 'Bog of the Gnat' is explained as being derived from the name of a horse called 'Fly/Gnat' that supposedly drowned there. There is, of course, no way of disproving this; in support of such a story one might even point to the Modern Icelandic idiom *eins og fluga* '[swift] as a fly',[16] which, if this usage is old, might suggest that *fluga* could indeed have served as a plausible name for a particularly fast horse, as the story claims. Yet this is not the only possibility. A *mýrr* is wetland, and wetland is an ideal breeding ground for flies and gnats; within Icelandic toponymy, the most well-known reflex of this is the name of the 'Fly-Lake' Mývatn, which is generally acknowledged to have been named for the masses of flies that breed in its waters. Thus one wonders whether the 'Fly's Bog' Flugumýrr might not have a similar ecological background.[17] Perhaps this was not the place where a horse named 'Fly' was drowned, but rather simply the wetland habitat of such masses of flies and gnats that these insects seemed the most appropriate element to refer to in the naming of the place. To later generations, however, the naming of their farm from the swarms of gnats that haunted it might have seemed unworthy, or at least a bit banal; and so, in narrative, the name-giving insect was turned into a horse with supernatural associations. This would not have rid the local landscape of the insects that were making a nuisance of themselves, but it would at least have made it more interesting from a narrative point of view.

[15] Probably the assembly at Þingvellir, which is in the area one reaches by going southwards over Kjölur.

[16] Cleasby and Vigfusson 1874, *s.v.* 'fluga'.

[17] For parallels to the formation of a place name with the genitive singular of a word for an animal forming the first element of the toponym cf. *Hvalshǫfði*, *Arnarfell*; a formation with the nominal stem without an ending or a genitive plural would be more common, however. Today, the name is pronounced locally as *Flúmýri*.

In accounts such as those of Kúðafljótsóss, Galmansstrǫnd or Flugumýrr, the place stories told by the *Book of Settlements* appear to take their starting point from the toponymy of the Icelandic landscape. Yet this is not the only way that place lore can be created: the materiality of the landscape, too, can become the basis of a narrative. An example may be the case of Ketill Steam. About him it is told:[18]

> A man was called Ketill Steam . . . Ketill took Rosmhvalanes Peninsula. There he spent the first winter at Gufuskálar 'Steam-Houses', and in spring he went further inland on the peninsula and spent the second winter at Gufunes 'Steam-Peninsula'. . . Ketill did not get a residence on the headlands, and he went further into Borgarfjord to find a residence for himself, and he spent the third winter at Gufuskálar 'Steam-Houses', on Gufá 'Steam River'. The fourth winter he spent at Gufuskálar on Snæfellsnes.

The lava field at Gufuskálar on Snæfellsnes.

This story claims that a multitude of places whose names include 'steam' are called so after their founder, who, strangely but fittingly, is called Ketill *gufa*: 'Cauldron Steam'. While there is no way of proving that there was no man of this name who founded places and named them after himself, this would perhaps not be the most economical explanation of

[18] Ch. 97.

this cluster of place names.[19] For, normally, *gufa* is not a feature of a person, but a feature of the materiality of the landscape: the steam from hot springs. The 'Cauldron Steam' who, according to the story, named places such as Gufuskálar (which, significantly, is the site of a lava field) was probably not a human founder who named places after himself; more likely, the other way round, he was created out of the landscape. In him, a person seems to have been extrapolated from toponyms which originally made reference to features of the materiality of the land. The 'steam' places were not named after a man; the man was created out of the 'steam' in their names—which makes it very fitting indeed that this creation of steam received the name Ketill 'cauldron'. Thus, here the physical landscape is the basis for toponyms which, in a second step, are reinterpreted in stories, and it is only this second step—the narrative reinterpretation rather than the historical origin of the place names—that finds a reflex in the *Book of Settlements*.

Another important aspect of the relationship between stories and the materiality of the landscape is aetiology: narratives explaining how a feature of the physical landscape, and its associated place name, came about. Here, at least on the imaginative level of the story's plotline, the thrust of the narrative is inverted in comparison to what seems to have been happening in the example of Ketill Steam: instead of topography leading to story at the cost of obscuring the connection between the two, in aetiological tales a story claims to tell how topography was created. In such narratives, the connection between the story and the land is emphasised rather than veiled. One instance of this is found in the account of the settlement of the Irish magician Dufþakr. The *Book of Settlements* tells us:[20]

> Dufþakr in Dufþaksholt Forest ... had great shape-shifting powers, and so did Stórólfr, son of [Ketill] Salmon. He lived then at Hváll Hill. They got into an argument about the grazing. One night, a man with second sight saw that a great bear came from Hváll Hill and a bull from Dufþaksholt Forest, and they met at Stórólfsvǫllr Field and, angry, set upon each other, and the bear was stronger. In the morning there was a valley left behind where they had met, as if the earth had been turned over, and that is now called Ǫldugróf 'Wave's Pit'. They were both injured and lay in bed.

[19] See Bandle 1977, 62.

[20] Ch. 309. For a detailed discussion see Egeler 2022.

This story takes its starting point from a pit which in its local topographical context was striking enough to deserve an individual name, being called Ǫldugróf 'Wave's Pit': a name suggestive of a hole that was not just deep but also wavy, as if the ground had been churned up by some inexplicable force. The inexplicable force hinted at by this topographical feature was then given shape in a narrative about a fierce fight fought by two magicians in the shape of mighty animals, a narrative capable both of 'explaining' the formation of the landscape as it could be observed by a contemporary and—perhaps more importantly—imbuing this landscape with connotations of something extraordinary. Thus, topography was given an aetiology, and a mere location was turned into a place filled with cultural meaning, a cultural landscape that people could be fascinated by and identify with.

That there was indeed a relationship between narrative, identity and the physical materiality of the landscape, is perhaps most clearly visible in the case of the farm on Snæfellsnes that was once visited by a water-horse:[21]

> Auðun the Stutterer, son of Váli the Strong, he married Mýrún, the daughter of Bjaðmakr, king of the Irish. He took all of Hraunsfjord above Hraun Lava Field between Lake Svínavatn and the ridge Trǫllaháls; he lived at Hraunsfjord. From him the Hraunfirðingar are descended. One autumn he saw that an apple-grey horse ran down from Lake Hjarðarvatn and to his stud-horses. It defeated the breeding stallion. Then Auðun went there and took hold of the grey stallion and yoked it to a two-ox sledge, and it gathered up all the hay from his home-field. The stallion was easy to manage until midday. Yet when the hour was advanced, it stamped into the hard ground up to the hoof-tufts; and after sunset it broke the whole harness and ran up to the lake. It has not been seen since.

This story tells of the settler Auðun the Stutterer, who was married to a daughter of the king of the Irish; elsewhere it is stated that Auðun's father had settled on the (Gaelic-speaking) Hebrides,[22] so his 'stuttering' may reflect a less-than-perfect command of Norse. This nickname thus may be a condensed version of a motif we also meet in the story of Haraldr *gilli* in *Magnússona saga*:[23] there, a man claims descent from

[21] Ch. 71. For a detailed discussion of this passage see Egeler 2018, 99–109.
[22] Ch. 60.
[23] Ch. 27.

the king of Norway but, having grown up in Ireland, he is laughed at for his weak Norse. Furthermore, given that Auðun had an Irish wife, the story seems to suggest that he and his family were largely Hibernicised. Now this Auðun founds a farm on Snæfellsnes, but one day a marvellous creature appears out of the local landscape: a grey, preternaturally strong horse emerges from a mountain lake above his farm, works for Auðun for a while, and ultimately returns to its mountain lake, never to be seen again.

The story of this grey water-horse emerging from a mountain lake ties in beautifully with Auðun's Gaelic family connections: exactly the type of water-horse that visits Auðun is also prominent in contemporary Irish heroic narrative.[24] The best-known example of such animals in early Irish literature is the Grey of Macha, the horse of the hero Cú Chulainn. Just like Auðun's water-horse, the Grey of Macha is (1) a preternaturally strong, (2) grey (3) stallion that has (4) emerged from and ultimately (5) returns to (6) a mountain lake. This horse played a prominent role in Irish heroic narrative throughout the Middle Ages and would have been well-known to any contemporary who had soaked up something of Gaelic culture, as Auðun seems to have done more than was good for his Norse. What the account in the *Book of Settlements* seems to be describing, therefore, is a strongly Hibernicised settler coming to Iceland and filling the new, empty land with Gaelic storytelling. Here, a Norseman for whom 'home' has become Gaelic turns the Icelandic landscape into the landscape of an Irish heroic fairy tale.

In Auðun's case as well, furthermore, this turning of a new, empty locality into a narrative landscape seems to be tied directly to the physical materiality of this landscape. What is important here is a little detail of the account:

> The stallion was easy to manage until midday. Yet when the hour was advanced, it stamped into the hard ground up to the hoof-tufts . . .

The mighty stallion stamping into 'hard ground' will have left hoofprints behind, imprinting himself into the physicality of the land and leaving a marker perpetually memorialising the story of his visit to the human world. Such a self-imprinting into the landscape, indeed, is a behavioural pattern of Irish water-horses that is also known from elsewhere. On Inishmore, the largest of the Aran Islands at the mouth of

[24] For detailed references see the literature quoted above, n. 21.

Galway Bay in the West of Ireland, about a third of a mile south-west of the medieval ruined church of Teampall Bheanáin and some forty paces inland from the cliffs framing the bay Poll Dick, there is a series of horseshoe-shaped ripple-marks in a bare sheet of rock. Local folklore identifies these ripple-marks as the hoof prints of a water-horse: they are attributed to a water-horse which, jumping up from the breakers of the Atlantic Ocean, somewhat misjudged its leap up to the clifftop, skidded over this rock-sheet, and in doing so left a permanent marker of its visit. A second series of horseshoe marks, furthermore, was left behind by the foal of this water-horse.[25]

The hoof-prints left by a water-horse and its foal on the rocky ground of the south-western coast of Inishmore.

There certainly is no direct historical connection between the water-horse hoof-prints on Inishmore and the story of the Snæfellsnes water-horse; rather, what we are observing here are two stories which are closely comparable only on a typological level. Yet nonetheless a comparison between the two is illuminating. In both cases, a supernatural horse emerges from a local body of water, enters the human world for a

[25] This piece of Aran folklore was collected by Tim Robinson in the 1970s or 1980s (Robinson 2008, 45–46). For somewhat earlier accounts of water-horses from Aran and Connemara, see Lady Gregory 1920, 7–8, 10, 15, 17, 23–25.

short span of time, and in that time leaves its mark on the materiality of the landscape. For, especially seen against the background of the Aran tale, this seems to be exactly what is happening in the tale of Auðun's water-horse: by 'stamping into the hard ground up to the hoof-tufts', the Snæfellsnes water-stallion must have created hoof-prints. In fact, this creation of hoof-prints is emphasised by the specific designation of the ground as 'hard': the water-horse did not leave a fleeting mark on squashy boggy ground, or on a soft meadow, but it imprinted itself into something firm—something like a rock surface. It is impossible to prove, but it seems eminently likely that somewhere within the boundaries of Auðun's farm on the Hraunsfjord there was a rock which showed some kind of strange, horseshoe-shaped marks, which at the time were shown and explained through the story that we meet today in the *Book of Settlements*.

The Recensions of the Book of Settlements

The tale of Auðun's water-horse brings us into immediate contact with the materiality of the Icelandic landscape, and with a strategy for creating 'home' through a welding-together of this materiality with a culturally specific narrative, giving a deeply Gaelic cultural significance to the 'hard ground' of Iceland. Yet this tale not only illustrates how closely narrative and real-world landscape can be intertwined, but also brings us to the problems of textual transmission. There is no single authoritative text of the *Book of Settlements*; rather, it is extant in three medieval and two early modern recensions. The medieval recensions are that preserved in Sturlubók, probably composed *c.*1275–80 and extant in a seventeenth-century copy; that of Hauksbók, compiled by the politician-cum-scholar Haukr Erlendsson at some point between the years 1302 and 1310 and partly extant in his autograph; and that of Melabók, from the early fourteenth century, of which only two sheets of a fifteenth-century vellum copy are extant. To this corpus, seventeenth-century scholars added two further versions: the Þórðarbók recension written by Þórður Jónsson, who died in 1670, and the Skarðsárbók recension by Björn Jónsson, which was composed at some point before the year 1636.

Of these various versions of the *Book of Settlements*, only the Sturlubók recension has until now been available in a complete translation.[26] This

[26] Hermann Pálsson and Edwards 1972; Boyer 1973. The translation by Baetke (1967) is abridged and selectively follows partly Sturlubók, partly Hauksbók.

recension takes precedence over the Hauksbók recension in two respects: chronologically, as it predates it; and stemmatically, as it was among the versions of the *Book of Settlements* that Haukr Erlendsson drew on in the composition of his own text, a fact that is clear both from the structure of Haukr's version and from the explicit statement which Haukr makes to this regard in his postscript to his text, where he writes:[27]

> Now a perusal has been made of the land-takings that there have been in Iceland, according to what wise men have written, first Ari the Priest the Learned, son of Þorgils, and Kolskeggr the Wise. And this book [I],[28] Haukr, son of Erlendr, have written, on the basis of the book which Sir Sturla the Lawspeaker had written, the most learned man, and on the basis of the second book, which Styrmir the Learned had written. And I took from each of the two that which explained more; and a great part was what they both said in agreement with each other. And therefore it is not surprising if this Book of Settlements is longer than any other.

In this postscript, Haukr states explicitly that he has directly drawn on the version written by Sturla the Lawspeaker, which today is extant as the Sturlubók recension of the *Book of Settlements*. In this sense, Haukr's version is secondary. Yet he also states that, drawing on a variety of different sources, he has expanded the *Book of Settlements* and created the longest and most detailed version in existence at the time.

That this can be highly important for the interpretation of the tales contained in it is illustrated not least by the tale of Auðun's water-horse. In Haukr's recension, from which the above quotation has been taken, it is stated that the water-horse stamps 'into the hard ground', which implies the creation of permanent marks in the landscape. The text of the Sturlubók recension is only slightly, but tellingly, different: there it is said merely that the water-horse stamped 'into the ground'. Here, this ground is not qualified as hard, and through this small divergence, the image created is a significantly different one. For, reading the Sturlubók account, the mental image created by the text is not that of hoofs imprinted in rock, but rather merely a stamping into something soft, yielding and flexible—sods of turf, a waterlogged meadow, marshy ground. There still is a momentary creation of hoofprints, but by omitting to qualify the medium in which these prints are created as a 'hard' one, the image loses

[27] Ch. 354.

[28] Later addition in the margin of the manuscript.

its permanence. The act of stamping into the ground is reduced from a shaping of the landscape to a display of temper; and thus, I would argue that, ironically, the oldest extant version of the account leaves out much of the tale's meaning, a meaning which is conveyed with much more clarity in Haukr's later but more detailed account.

The story of Auðun's water-horse is not the only case in which Haukr's version gives more detail than the Sturlubók recension, detail which can be crucial for understanding the material. Another illuminating instance is provided by the settlement account of Ørlygr Hrappsson.[29] This account tells how the Chrisian settler Ørlygr set out from the Hebrides to take land in Iceland. Before his departure, he asked for the advice of his foster-father, the (unhistorical) Bishop Patrick of the Hebrides, and Bishop Patrick gave Ørlygr building material and an iron bell for a church which Ørlygr was to build at the place where he took land in Iceland. When Ørlygr finally came within sight of the land where he was to settle, the church bell he had received from his episcopal foster-father fell overboard. It soon turned out, however, that no harm was done: where Ørlygr came ashore and took land, he found that the church bell had been washed up on the beach and was lying in a heap of seaweed.

What is important in the present context about the detail of the church bell is that, while there is also an account of Ørlygr's settlement in the Sturlubók recension of the *Book of Settlements*, the Sturlubók recension makes no mention of the strange occurrence of the church bell floating ashore onto Ørlygr's destined place of settlement. This occurrence, however, is crucial for contextualising the narrative. The motif that a church bell floats ahead of the ship of a Christian settler and indicates the place where a Christian settlement is to be founded finds a close parallel in the foundation legend of the monastic settlement of Ardmore in Munster in southern Ireland as it is presented in an Irish Life of St Declan; taken together with the Gaelic connection established by the figure of 'Bishop Patrick' of the (Gaelic-speaking) Hebrides, this suggests that the settlement account of Ørlygr Hrappsson has been substantially influenced by Irish hagiographic legend,[30] and perhaps—just as is the case with Auðun the Stutterer—uses Gaelic hagiographic legend to help a Gaelicised settler to establish 'home' in the emptiness of the new land. Yet this particular context of the narrative becomes visible only in the Hauksbók recension, not in the more concise Sturlubók recension, where the decisive detail has

[29] Ch. 15.

[30] Young 1936, 119–20; Egeler 2018, 110–27.

been omitted. Here, as in other instances, the Hauksbók recension gives us a substantially fuller picture than the only slightly earlier Sturlubók version. This makes it crucial to consult the Hauksbók recension for every narratological (or other) analysis of the text, since the Hauksbók recension not only acts as testimony to the specific approach and interests of its author Haukr Erlendsson,[31] but also as a potentially independent witness of local narrative lore.

Haukr Erlendsson

The Hauksbók recension of the *Book of Settlements* is one of the comparatively few cases in Old Icelandic literature in which we can grasp the specific person that stood behind the creation of a major literary work: Haukr, son of Erlendr 'the Strong', who was born sometime in the thirteenth century and died in Norway in 1334. Haukr was a descendant of one of the most prominent Icelandic families of the later Middle Ages and himself deeply involved in the politics of the late thirteenth and early fourteenth centuries. He makes his first appearance in the historical record in 1294, when he is mentioned as acting as a judge and the highest magistrate in a thing-district in south-eastern Iceland. Later in his life, he held judicial offices both in Oslo and in Bergen, where he acted as the Lawman of the Gulaþing in Western Norway, and even was raised to the rank of a knight; some of his correspondence from this time is extant. Even though he was to hold the office of a judge in Bergen at least as late as 1322, he spent the years 1306 to 1308 in Iceland, apparently on the king's business. As a whole, Hauksbók 'Haukr's Book' appears to have been composed between 1302 and 1310, with different sections written by various hands both Norwegian and Icelandic; judging from the prevalence of Icelandic hands in the manuscript, however, it seems that that most of the manuscript was written during Haukr's stay in Iceland in 1306–08. Originally, Hauksbók consisted of some 200 sheets of vellum, of which 141 are extant in the original. Much of the lost material survives in early modern copies, but the *Book of Settlements* is among those parts of the work which are not preserved in their entirety—though not much seems to be missing, and what is extant is in Haukr's own hand. At some point in its history, the manuscript was split into three codices, whose original sequence cannot any more be established beyond doubt. Already

[31] It might here be remembered, for instance, that Jakob Benediktsson called Haukr 'the first Celtomaniac in Iceland' (Jakob Benediktsson 1966–69, 290), though this much-quoted dictum is rather overstated.

in the early eighteenth century, however, Árni Magnússon noted that the codex begins with 'some fragments' from the *Book of Settlements*.

As a whole, Hauksbók was a library of learned works condensed into one large codex, with history and cosmology functioning as leading themes. Its contents ranged from native Icelandic historical works to continental European learned treatises, bringing together Icelandic, Norwegian and Danish history, early Arthurian literature (in its guise as early British history), natural history, mathematics and theology. It seems that the *Book of Settlements* was the first text in Hauksbók, forming its opening; this alone tells us much about the prestige that this text held for an Icelander of the time, especially given that much of the august political career of this particular Icelander was taking place in Norway: even for an Icelander who held high office in Norway, the beginning of learning, and perhaps the beginning of history itself, was the beginning of the settlement of Iceland as described in the *Book of Settlements*. At first glance one might wonder whether this is not simply, and perhaps more than anything else, reflective of an expatriate's yearning for home; but in a way the *Book of Settlements* itself shares this view of history in which history begins with the settlement of Iceland. For given the intense Icelandic interest in all things genealogical, it is striking that for many of the first settlers no patronymics are given:[32] not just the history of Iceland, but even genealogy, and thus human history itself, only begins with the arrival in Iceland. Even considering the encyclopaedic range of Hauksbók, it seems that Haukr himself would not have been too averse to subscribing to such a somewhat self-referred view of history, as he also appears to add his own share of self-centredness to the work. For not only does he begin the compilation of world learning that is 'Haukr's Book' with the history of his home country, but wherever he has the chance to do so he also describes this history as leading up to his own person: half a dozen times throughout the *Book of Settlements* he presents genealogies which end with 'Sir Erlendr, the father of Haukr', presenting himself and his family as the end-point (and culmination?) of the history of Iceland.

In the Hauksbók recension of the *Book of Settlements* we encounter a text which is both self-contained and part of a larger corpus of learning, which builds on a long-established tradition of writing about the Settlement and yet is deeply individualistic, and which is both self-involved

[32] Cf. the 'Table of Chapters' at the end of this book.

and yet broad enough in its scope to encompass the whole of the medieval Northwest Atlantic world. Yet ultimately, being all these things, the *Book of Settlements* in 'Haukr's Book' is first and foremost one thing: an individual's engagement with his place of origin, from its materiality to its people and from its local history to its international entanglements. Thus, it provides us with an invaluable glimpse of how a prominent Icelander in the service of the king of Norway viewed his origins, his history, and thus ultimately himself.

A note on the translation

This translation is based on the text of the Hauksbók recension of *Landnámabók* as edited in the form of the (more or less) diplomatic edition by Finnur Jónsson (1900). The more recent edition by Jakob Benediktsson (1968) has been consulted throughout, but it has not been made the basis of the translation. The reason for basing this translation on Finnur Jónsson's older text is simply that Jakob Benediktsson's edition does not present the reader with the full Hauksbók version: in those parts of the text where the Hauksbók and Sturlubók recensions are very similar, Jakob Benediktsson does not give both texts, but merely one text, and this text represents the wording of the Sturlubók recension; in such passages, only major deviations of Hauksbók from Sturlubók are pointed out in the notes. This editorial procedure makes it impractical to use Jakob Benediktsson's edition as the basis for a translation of the Hauksbók recension. In this translation, however, place names and personal names are not given in the forms found in Finnur Jónsson's diplomatic edition, but follow Jakob Benediktsson's normalised spelling (excepting of course those cases where Hauksbók gives different names entirely from those given in the Sturlubók text that forms the primary basis of Jakob Benediktsson's edition).

The emendations that Finnur Jónsson made in his edition of the Hauksbók recension of the *Book of Settlements* have on the whole been silently accepted here, but a number of his major emendations have been highlighted in the notes. This seemed necessary not least because Finnur Jónsson does not only emend clearly scribal and/or orthographic mistakes, but sometimes also what appear to be mistakes in content. Most importantly, he sometimes replaces 'incorrect' names with names which the wider context of the passage in question shows to be the 'correct' ones. It should, however, not be the task of the editor (or the translator) of a medieval text to hide the fact that even the medieval scribe sometimes lost track of the intricacies of the genealogical material he was handling.

The translations of the skaldic stanzas contained in the text eclectically draw both on the interpretations offered by Finnur Jónsson and on those proposed by Jakob Benediktsson.

Many Icelandic personal names, and virtually all Icelandic place names, have a meaning which would have been understood by the text's contemporary audience. This means that the translator has to face the awkward question of how to deal with the semantics conveyed by these names. If a name like, for instance, *Breiðafjǫrðr* (modern Breiðafjörður) is given in its Icelandic form, then it can be localised on a modern map; but at the same time, it loses the graphic force it would have had for a medieval (or modern) Icelandic audience, who would have understood it as meaning 'Broad Fjord' (which Breiðafjörður indeed is). There does not seem to be an ideal solution for this dilemma, or at least I have not been able to find it. A list of topographical names in Icelandic frequently constitutes a colourfully descriptive tableau encapsulating an account of the landscape as seen by a contemporary; but trying to provide an all-out translation nevertheless sounds somewhat strange to the modern reader, and furthermore would make it impossible to cross-reference the translated text either with modern maps or with other texts: a backwards translation by the reader might (perhaps) still work for the Broad Fjord, but, for example, connecting the name Hraunsáss with the translated name 'Lavafield Ridge' would be strictly a one-way street for any but the most deeply initiated. So an intermediate way has been attempted. Place names have generally been left untranslated, but in many cases their semantics have been indicated by adding a noun indicative of the main feature underlying the place name: 'Brynjudalr Valley' (*dalr* meaning 'valley'); 'Ǫlfusá River' (*á* meaning 'river'). This has not been done for all place names, but the aim was to give such indications of the main semantics of the toponymy widely enough to convey a feel of its general tendencies, and the underlying landscape perception, without overburdening the translated text. The decision when to make these kinds of additions has necessarily been subjective, but I hope I do not have to apologise for this, subjective decisions being an unavoidable part of any translation. The semantics of a number of toponyms furthermore have been indicated by making other kinds of smaller additions where there was no good one-word English equivalent; for instance, the toponym *Reynir* has been translated as 'the rowan-tree grove of Reynir' (*reynir* meaning 'rowan-tree'); *Melar* is translated as 'the gravel hills of Melar' (a *melr* being a hill, dune or bank of sand or gravel); *Blǫndukvíslir* has been rendered as 'Blǫndukvíslir, where the river forks' (a *kvísl* being the branching or forking of a river). With the many names ending in *-fjǫrðr* 'fjord', I have taken the shortcut of anglicising this element (Breiðafjord, Reyðarfjord, Hafnarfjord, etc.). In the case of the term *holt*, which originally seems to have denoted a wood or forest but later came to designate a hill with no further association with trees, I have chosen to translate as 'Forest', as this probably was the semantics which underlay the original naming of the places in question, even though it has nothing to do with either the later semantics of the term or the present-day appearance of the relevant places. In some cases, where the semantics of a place name are directly tied into a story and therefore crucial for understanding this story, place names have been given both in their Icelandic forms and in a full translation.

An aspect of Old Norse naming practice which is problematic for translation and which cannot easily be resolved is that Old Norse place names may not in all cases refer directly to the topographical features that they descriptively refer to. If it is stated, for instance, that one Valþjófr lived 'at Meðalfell Mountain' (*at Meðalfelli*, ch. 17), then it is not immediately clear whether 'Meðalfell' refers primarily to the mountain as such or the farm at its foot—though the latter is the more likely interpretation. Yet since in any case the farm is named after the mountain, this point, while it should be noted, never really impedes the understanding of the text. While the best way for handling this issue certainly could be disputed, I have decided here to write 'Meðalfell Mountain', even though it can be assumed that what is normally meant in such cases is 'Meðalfell farm'. As far as the use of prepositions is concerned, I generally translate with 'lived *at*', rather than following the Old Norse usage; i.e., *bjó í Þórólfsfelli* (ch. 300) is translated as 'lived at Þórólfsfell Mountain', rather than 'in Þórólfsfell Mountain', as the latter option would suggest a very different meaning from the one clearly intended: people lived in the farm of Þórólfsfell, not as troglodytes inside the mountain Þórólfsfell. Thus, in sum, generally it can be assumed that where the translation states that '[settler NN] lived at [place/mountain/river/brook/moor/waterfall/slope . . . NN]', the reference is to a farm named from a nearby landscape feature rather than the landscape feature as such.

Old Norse personal names have never been translated, with the exception of nicknames. Nicknames have been translated wherever it was possible; yet since many of them are *hapax legomena*, often this was not the case. Where I felt unable to provide a translation of a nickname, it has been given in italics in its Icelandic form. Among recurring epithets, *goði* has, for lack of better alternatives and to avoid ambiguity with Christian priests, been retained as *goði*, whereas *prestr* has been translated as 'priest'. Foreign personal names, such as those of foreign rulers, have been given in their current English form where the person in question is prominent and can be identified clearly; Irish names, however, have as a rule been left in their Icelandicised form, not least because in many cases of probable Irish names the identification of their Irish equivalent involves some insecurities, as the Icelandicised forms of Irish names are not always very close to their original forms.[33] The names of non-Icelandic places have been given in their modern English forms where the places in question are both easily identifiable and prominent, that is, where it can be assumed that the modern English form is more familiar to the Anglophone reader than the Old Norse form; thus, I write *Byzantium* and *Dublin* rather than *Miklagarðr* and *Dyflinn*, but keep *Agðir* rather than using the modern form *Agder*.

Most Icelanders do not use family names but patronymics. Where simply a patronymic is given, this most commonly takes the form *Flóki Vilgerðarson* 'Flóki, son of Vilgerðr', or *Helga Arnardóttir* 'Helga, daughter of Ǫrn'. In other cases, however, and especially when multiple generations are enumerated, other ways of presentation are used, e.g.: *Brandr, son Þorgríms Kjallakssonar*, 'Brandr, the son of Þorgrímr, Kjallakr's son'. Semantically, there does not seem to be any appreciable difference between the use of *son* or *dóttir* as an independent noun and its use as a suffix; nevertheless, at least to such an extent as this was possible without creating too many stylistic monstrosities, I have attempted to differentiate the two usages by using the English definite articles in different ways, following the pattern that the use of *son* or *dóttir* as an independent noun is reflected by the use of a definite article; thus, *Brandr Þorgrímsson* is translated as 'Brandr, son of Þorgrímr', whereas *Brandr, son Þorgríms* is translated as 'Brandr, *the* son of Þorgrímr', etc.

[33] For a detailed new study of Irish names in the *Book of Settlements* see now Etchingham et al. 2019, 272–319.

Acknowledgements

This research was funded by the Deutsche Forschungsgemeinschaft (DFG, German Research Foundation)—project no. 453026744. All photographs included in this volume are my own, and have been expertly prepared for publication by Clive Tolley.

My project was hosted by the Institut für Nordische Philologie of the Ludwig-Maximilians-University in Munich, where I would like to thank Wilhelm Heizmann and Joachim Schiedermair for their hospitality and Johanna Schreiber for her support with all matters administrative. For help at various stages in the preparation of this translation, I would like to thank Ármann Jakobsson, Hafdís Sturlaugsdóttir, and, in particular, the late Thorsten Andersson, who gave me generous advice on the linguistic side of toponymy and encouraged me in my slightly oblique perspective on it. To the editors of the Viking Society's Texts Series I am grateful for accepting this book for publication. I owe particular thanks to Alison Finlay, who has edited and revised the text, investing what must have been tremendous amounts of time into turning my 'English' translation into something which actually might be reconisable as English by a native-speaker of the language. What merit this translation has, it owes to her help; what mistakes it still contains are entirely my own.

Bibliography

Editions

Brown, Ursula, ed., 1952. *Þorgils saga ok Hafliða.* Oxford: Oxford University Press.

Finnur Jónsson, ed., 1900. *Landnámabók I–III. Hauksbók. Sturlubók. Melabók.* København: Thieles bogtrykkeri.

Finnur Jónsson and Eiríkur Jónsson, eds, 1892–96. *Hauksbók. Udgiven efter de Arnamagnæanske håndskrifter no. 371, 544 og 675 4to samt forskellige papirshåndskrifter.* 3 parts. København: Thieles bogtrykkeri.

Jakob Benediktsson, ed., 1968. *Íslendingabók. Landnámabók.* Íslenzk fornrit 1, Reykjavík: Hið íslenzka fornritafélag.

Jón Helgason, ed., 1960. *Hauksbók. The Arna-Magnæan Manuscripts 371 4to, 544 4to, and 675 4to.* Manuscripta Islandica 5. Copenhagen: Munksgaard. (Facsimile.)

Secondary literature

Bandle, Oskar 1977. 'Die Ortsnamen der Landnámabók'. In *Sjötíu ritgerðir helgaðar Jakobi Benediktssyni 20. júlí 1977.* Rit 12. Reykjavík: Stofnun Árna Magnússonar, 47–67.

Cleasby, Richard and Gudbrand Vigfusson 1874. *An Icelandic–English Dictionary.* Oxford: Clarendon Press.

Egeler, Matthias 2015. *Avalon, 66° Nord. Zu Frühgeschichte und Rezeption eines Mythos.* Ergänzungsbände zum Reallexikon der Germanischen Altertumskunde 95. Berlin and Boston: de Gruyter.

Egeler, Matthias 2018. *Atlantic Outlooks on Being at Home: Gaelic Place-Lore and the Construction of a Sense of Place in Medieval Iceland.* Folklore Fellows Communications 314. Helsinki: Suomalainen Tiedeakatemia (Academia Scientiarum Fennica).

Egeler, Matthias 2022. 'Crossing Borders between Literature and Toponymy: The Narrative Landscape of Hvolsvöllur and its Implications'. In *Crossing Disciplinary Borders in Viking Age Studies.* Ed. Daniel Sävborg. Turnhout: Brepols, 111–26.

Etchingham, Colmán, Jón Viðar Sigurðsson, Máire Ní Mhaonaigh and Elizabeth Ashman Rowe 2019. *Norse–Gaelic Contacts in a Viking World. Studies in the Literature and History of Norway, Iceland, Ireland, and the Isle of Man.* Medieval Texts and Cultures of Northern Europe 29. Turnhout: Brepols.

Gregory, Lady 1920. *Visions and Beliefs in the West of Ireland.* Collected and arranged by Lady Gregory. With two essays and notes by W. B. Yeats. New York and London: G. P. Putnam's Sons.

Heizmann, Wilhelm 1998. 'Hvanndalir – Glæsisvellir – Avalon. Traditionswanderungen im Norden und Nordwesten Europas'. *Frühmittelalterliche Studien* 32, 72–100.

Hempel, Annette 2001. 'Die *Hauksbók* – eine enzyklopädische Sammelhandschrift des 13./14. Jahrhunderts'. In *Arbeiten zur Skandinavistik.* Ed. Annegret Heitmann. Texte und Untersuchungen zur Germanistik und Skandinavistik 48. Frankfurt am Main: Peter Lang, 401–09.

Jakob Benediktsson 1966–69. '*Landnámabók.* Some Remarks on its Value as a Historical Source'. *Saga-Book* 17, 275–92.

Robinson, Tim 1996. *Setting Foot on the Shores of Connemara and other Writings.* Dublin: The Lilliput Press.

Robinson, Tim 2008. *Stones of Aran. Pilgrimage.* Introduction by Robert Macfarlane. London: Faber and Faber.

Schnall, Jens Eike 2009. 'Haukr Erlendsson – Hauksbók'. In *Kindlers Literatur Lexikon* 3, völlig neu bearbeitete Auflage, ed. Heinz Ludwig Arnold. Stuttgart and Weimar: Verlag J. B. Metzler 2009. (Kindlers Literatur Lexikon Online – Aktualisierungsdatenbank: www.kll-online.de, accessed 09/06/2016.)

Young, Jean 1937. 'Some Icelandic Traditions showing Traces of Irish Influence'. *Études Celtiques* 3, 118–26.

LANDNÁMABÓK

BOOK OF SETTLEMENTS

This is the prologue to this book

1. In the *Book of the Course of the World* which the Holy Priest Bede wrote, the island is mentioned which is called Thule, [and][1] in books it is said to lie six days' sailing north of Britain. There, he said, there is no day in winter nor night in summer when the day [is][2] longest. For this reason wise men believe that Iceland is called Thule, because it is the case in the land far and wide that the sun shines during the night[3] when the day is longest; and it is often the case during the days when the night is longest that one does not see the sun. And Bede the Priest died 735 years after the incarnation of our Lord Jesus Christ, according to what is written, more than one hundred years before Iceland was settled by the Northmen. And before Iceland was settled by the Northmen, there were the men there whom the Northmen call *Papar*. They were Christians, and people believe that they must have been from the British Isles, because after their disappearance Irish books, bells and croziers and even more things were found, which made it possible to understand that they were from the British Isles. These things were found to the east in Papey and in Papýli. It is also mentioned in English books that during that time there was traffic between the lands.

Here the Book of Settlements begins, and tells in the first chapter what is at the shortest distance from Iceland

2. At the time when Iceland was discovered and settled from Norway, Adrian was Pope in Rome, and John—the one who was the fifth of this name in this seat.[4] And Louis, son of Louis,[5] was emperor north of the mountains;[6] and Leo and his son Alexander over Byzantium.[7] At that time, Haraldr Finehair was king over Norway; and Eiríkr, son of Eymundr, and his son Bjǫrn, over Sweden; and Gormr the Old in

[1] Missing in the manuscript.

[2] Missing in the manuscript.

[3] Hauksbók here has *vetr* 'winter', which both the context and the other recensions show to be a scribal mistake for *netr* 'night'.

[4] *Recte* John VIII.

[5] Louis the German.

[6] Probably referring to the Alps.

[7] Leo VI and his brother(!) Alexander.

Denmark; Ælfred the Great in England and his son Játvarðr; and Kjarvall[8] in Dublin; Jarl Sigurðr the Great in Orkney.

Well-informed men say that it is seven days' sailing from Norway, from Staðr, to Horn in eastern Iceland; and from Snjófjallsnes[9] four days' sailing to Hvarf in Greenland. From the Hernar[10] off Norway one must sail always to the west to Hvarf in Greenland; and then one has sailed north of Shetland, so that it can only be seen when visibility is good;[11] and south of the Faeroe Islands so that the sea is in the middle of the mountain slopes;[12] and in such a way south of Iceland that they can catch fowl and whale from it.[13] From Reykjanes Peninsula in southern Iceland it is three[14] days at sea to Jǫlduhlaup[15]

'. . . from Langanes Peninsula in northern Iceland it is four days at sea northwards to Svalbard in the polar sea . . .' *The coast of Langanes.*

[8] Cerball.

[9] Snæfellsnes.

[10] Today's Hennøya Islands.

[11] The translation of this sub-clause is uncertain, but this seems to be its general meaning.

[12] That is, half the height of the mountains is visible above the horizon.

[13] That is, are not further from the coast than the water-fowl nesting there flies out to sea.

[14] Manuscript: íij, but *recte* probably *v*, as stated in the Sturlubók recension.

[15] Slyne Head in Connemara.

in Ireland in the south; and from Langanes Peninsula in northern Iceland it is four days at sea northwards to Svalbard in the polar sea; and it is a day's sailing to the wastelands in Greenland from Kolbeinsey Island in the north.

About Garðarr

3. A man was called Garðarr, the son of Svávarr the Swede. He had estates in Sjóland, but he had been brought up in Sweden. He went to the Hebrides to claim the paternal inheritance of his wife; but when he sailed through the Péttlandsfjord, a storm carried him off course and drove him westwards into the ocean. He reached land east of Horn.[16] Then there was a harbour. Garðarr sailed round the land and understood that it was an island. He came to the fjord which he called Skjálfandi, the 'Shaking'. There they launched a dinghy and his slave Náttfari went into it. Then the rope broke, and he came into Náttfaravík 'Náttfari's Bay', beyond Skuggabjǫrg Cliffs. But Garðarr came to the other side of the fjord and spent the winter there; therefore he called that place Húsavík 'Bay of Houses'. Náttfari remained behind together with his slave and maidservant; therefore that place is called Náttfaravík 'Náttfari's Bay'. Garðarr sailed back eastwards and praised the land a lot and called it Garðarshólm 'Garðarr's Island'.

About Naddoddr

4. A man was called Naddoddr, the brother of Oxen-Þórir, a relative by marriage of Ǫlvir Children's-Man. He was a great Viking; he took up his abode on the Faeroe Islands for the reason that nowhere else was he really left in peace. He set off from Norway and wanted to get to the islands and was driven off course towards Garðarshólm 'Garðarr's Island', and came into Reyðarfjord in the Eastern Fjords; and there they climbed the highest mountain to find out whether they could see any dwellings or smoke; but they saw no sign. And when they sailed away from the land, there was a heavy snowfall. Therefore he gave it the name Snæland 'Snow-Land'. They praised the land a lot.

[16] That is, on the south coast of Iceland.

'Naddoddr . . . set off from Norway and wanted to get to the Islands and was driven off course towards Garðarshólm "Garðarr's Island", and came into Reyðarfjord in the Eastern Fjords; and there they climbed the highest mountain to find out whether they could see any dwellings or smoke; but they saw no sign.' *Reyðarfjörður.*

About Flóki

5. A great Viking was called Flóki, son of Vilgerðr. He got himself ready to set out from Rogaland to search for Snjóland 'Snow-Land'; they lay in the Smørsund channel. He held a big sacrifice and offered sacrifices to three ravens which were to show him the way, because at that time sailors in the northern lands did not have a compass. They piled up a cairn at the place where the sacrifice had been held and called it Flókavarða 'Flóki's Cairn'. That is at the place where Hǫrðaland and Rogaland meet.

First he went to Shetland and lay in Flókavágr 'Flóki's Bay'. There his daughter Geirhildr perished in Geirhildarvatn 'Geirhildr's Lake'. With Flóki on his ship were the free farmer who was called Þórólfr, and another [by the name of] Herjólfr, and Faxi, a man from the Hebrides. From there, Flóki sailed to the Faeroe Islands and there he gave his daughter in marriage. From her, Þrándr in Gata was descended. From there he sailed out into the ocean with those three ravens that he had offered sacrifices to in Norway. And when he set the first raven free, it flew back over the stern. The second flew up into the air and back to the ship. The third flew forwards over the stem in the direction in which they found land. They came from the east to Horn; then they sailed south of the land. And when they sailed westwards around Reykjanes Peninsula and the fjord opened up so that they saw Snæfellsnes Peninsula, Faxi said: 'This must be a big country that we have found. Here the water-courses are big.' That has since been called Faxaóss 'Faxi's Estuary'.

'And when they sailed westwards around Reykjanes Peninsula and the fjord opened up so that they saw Snæfellsnes Peninsula, Faxi said: "This must be a big country that we have found. Here the watercourses are big."'
The southern coast of Snæfellsnes at Arnarstapi.

Faxi and his people sailed westwards over Breiðafjord and took land at the place which is called Vatsfjord by Barðastrǫnd Coast. The whole fjord was full of animals that could be caught and, occupied with the hunting and fishing, they did not pay attention to making hay, and all their livestock died during the winter. Spring was quite cold. Then Flóki went northwards onto a mountain and saw a fjord full of sea ice. Therefore they called the land Ísland 'Iceland'. They went away during the summer and were late in getting ready for departure. One can still see the ruin of their house there inland from Brjánslœkr[17] Brook, and also their boatshed and likewise their cooking pit. They did not manage to tack around Reykjanes Peninsula, and there their dinghy broke away from them, with Herjólfr in it. He came into Herjólfshǫfn 'Herjólfr's Harbour'. Flóki came into Hafnarfjord 'Harbour's Fjord'; they found a whale on one island out beyond the fjord and called the place Hvaleyrr

[17] Manuscript: *Bians-*.

‘Whale Gravel-Bank’. There Herjólfr and his companions were found. During the summer they sailed to Norway. Flóki spoke very critically about the country; but Herjólfr said good and bad things about the country; and Þórólfr said that butter was dripping from every blade of grass in the country that they had found. Therefore he was called Þórólfr Butter.

About Ingólfr and Hjǫrleifr

6. A man was called Bjǫrnólfr, and another Hróaldr. They were sons of Hrómundr Gripsson. They left Telemark because of acts of manslaughter, and they took up residence in Dalsfjord in Fjalir. The son of Bjǫrnólfr was Ǫrn, the father of Ingólfr and Helga, and Hróaldr’s son was Hróðmarr, the father of Leifr.

The foster-brothers Ingólfr and Leifr went raiding with the sons of Jarl Atli the Thin of Gaular: Hásteinn and Hersteinn and Hólmsteinn. They got along well with them, and when they came home, they agreed to go on a joint trip the next summer. And during winter, the foster-brothers held a feast for the sons of the jarl. At that feast, Holmsteinn took the vow that he would have Helga, daughter of Ǫrn, or else no other woman. The men did not like this vow, and Leifr reddened, and he and Hólmsteinn had little to say to each other when they parted.

The following spring the foster-brothers made themselves ready to go raiding and expected to meet up with the sons of Jarl Atli. They met at Hísargafl, and there Hólmsteinn and his brothers started a battle against the foster-brothers. And when they had fought for a while, Ǫlmóðr the Old, the son of Kári-of-the-Hǫrðar, a relative of Leifr, came along and helped Ingólfr and his companions. Hólmsteinn fell in this battle, and Hersteinn fled. Then Leifr and his companions went raiding. And the following winter, Hersteinn attacked Leifr and his companions and wanted to kill them. But they received word of his coming and went to meet him and they fought and Hersteinn fell there. After that men were sent to Jarl Atli and Hásteinn to offer a peace settlement. And what they settled on was that Leifr and his men yielded up their lands to father and son. The foster-brothers fitted out a big ship and sailed to search for the land that Raven-Flóki had found, which was then called Iceland. They found the land and were in the Eastern Fjords in the Southern Álptafjord. The land seemed better to them in the south than to the north. They were in the land for one winter and then went back to Norway. After that, Ingólfr invested their money in the move to Iceland, but Leifr went raiding in the British Isles. He raided in Ireland

and there found a large underground room. He went into it, and it was dark until a light shone from the weapon that the man held in his hand. Leifr killed this man and took the sword and much other wealth. After that he was called Hjǫr-Leifr 'Sword-Leifr'. Hjǫrleifr plundered widely in Ireland and got much booty there. He took ten slaves there, who had the following names: Dufþakr and Geirrøðr, Skjaldbjǫrn, Halldórr and Drafdrit. No others are named. After that Hjǫrleifr went to Norway and there met his foster-brother Ingólfr. Earlier, he had married Helga, daughter of Ǫrn, Ingólfr's sister.

About Ingólfr and Hjǫrleifr

7. That winter, Ingólfr held a great sacrifice and sought good omens for his destiny. But Hjǫrleifr never wanted to sacrifice. The oracle pointed Ingólfr towards Iceland. Afterwards, each of the two relatives fitted out his ship for Iceland. Ingólfr had their joint property in his ship, and Hjǫrleifr his plunder. They put to sea when they were ready and sailed out.

'Ingólfr took land at the place which is now called Ingólfshǫfði "Ingólfr's Headland".' *Ingólfshǫfði seen from the east.*

The Killing of Hjǫrleifr

8. In the summer that Ingólfr and his men went to settle Iceland, King Haraldr Finehair had been king in Norway for twelve years. At that time, 6073 winters had elapsed since the beginning of this world and since the time when Adam was created. And since the incarnation of our Lord

Jesus Christ 800 years and 74 winters. They sailed together until they saw Iceland. Then they parted. And when Ingólfr saw land, he threw his high-seat pillars overboard for luck. He made a solemn declaration that he would settle at the place where the pillars came ashore. Ingólfr took land at the place which is now called Ingólfshǫfði 'Ingólfr's Headland'. But Hjǫrleifr was driven westwards along the coast. They ran short of water. Then the Irish slaves resolved to knead flour and butter together and considered that thirst-quenching. They gave it the name *minnþak*. And when it was ready, there was a heavy shower of rain, and then they collected water from tarpaulins. And when the *minnþak* started to moulder, they threw it overboard, and it drifted ashore at the place which is now called Minnþakseyrr '*minnþak*-Gravel-Bank'. Hjǫrleifr took land at Hjǫrleifshǫfði 'Hjǫrleifr's Headland'. And there was an inlet, and its inner end pointed towards the headland. Hjǫrleifr had two

'Hjǫrleifr took land at Hjǫrleifshǫfði "Hjǫrleifr's Headland".'
The view from Hjörleifshöfði over the plain of black sand surrounding it today.

houses built there. And the ruin of one is eighteen fathoms long, and of the other nineteen. Hjǫrleifr spent the winter there. And in spring he wanted to sow. He only had one ox, and he made the slaves pull the plough. And when Hjǫrleifr and his men were indoors, Dufþakr made a plan that they should kill the ox and say that a brown bear had killed it. And then they should attack Hjǫrleifr and his men when they were searching for the bear. After that they told this to Hjǫrleifr. And when they went to search for the bear and scattered through the wood, the slaves killed every single one of them and murdered them all, just as many as themselves. They ran away with their women and livestock and the boat. The slaves went to the islands that they saw out to sea in the southwest and settled there for a while.

Vífill and Karli were the names of slaves that Ingólfr owned. These he sent westwards along the coast to search for his high-seat pillars. And when they came to Hjǫrleifshǫfði Headland, they found Hjǫrleifr dead. Then they went back and told Ingólfr these tidings, and he expressed his displeasure about it. After this, Ingólfr went west to Hjǫrleifshǫfði. And when he saw Hjǫrleifr dead, he said: 'Here a good man has come to a bad end, being killed by slaves. And I see it happening in this way to everyone who does not want to sacrifice.' Ingólfr had a funeral held for Hjǫrleifr and his men and looked after their ship and possessions.

Ingólfr then went up onto the headland and saw islands lying out to the sea to the southwest. It came to his mind that they would have run away to that place, as the boat had disappeared. And they went to search for the slaves. And they found them in the place in the islands that is called Eið. They were just sitting over a meal when Ingólfr descended on them. They were gripped by terror, and each of them ran his own way. Ingólfr killed them all. The place where Dufþakr died is called Dufþaksskor 'Dufþakr's Cleft'. Some of the others jumped over the cliff, which has ever since been named after them. The place where they were killed has ever since been called Vestmannaeyjar 'Islands of the Western Men', because they were men from the west. Ingólfr and his men took the women of those who had been murdered with them. Then they went back to Hjǫrleifshǫfði. Ingólfr stayed there for another winter. And the following summer he went westwards along the coast. He spent the third winter at the foot of Ingólfsfell 'Ingólfr's Mountain', west of Ǫlfusá River, [where some people say that he is buried].[18] That year Vífill and Karli found his high-seat pillars at Arnarhváll Hill below the heath.

About Ingólfr's Settlement

9. In spring, Ingólfr went down across the heath. He made his home where the high-seat pillars had come ashore. He lived in Reykjarvík Bay.

[18] Addition in brackets after Þórðarbók; Hauksbók has a lacuna here.

There, those high-seat pillars are still in the heated hall. And Ingólfr took land between Ǫlfusá River and Hvalfjord beyond Brynjadalsá River[, the land between it and Hramnagjá River, and the whole peninsula out from there][19]. Then Karli said: 'For something bad did we go over good lands if we must settle on this outlying headland.' He disappeared, and a maidservant with him. To Vífill Ingólfr gave his freedom, and he lived in Vífilsstaðir. Vífilsfell 'Vífill's Mountain' is named after him. He lived there for a long time and was an upright man. Ingólfr had a house built on Skálafell, the 'Mountain of the House'. From there he saw smoke at Ǫlfusvatn Lake and there found Karli.

Family Account

10. Ingólfr is the most famous of all settlers, because he came here to the empty land and was the first to settle the land, and other settlers then followed his example. He married Hallveig, daughter of Fróði, the sister of Loptr the Old. Their son was Þorsteinn, who had the assembly established on Kjalarnes Peninsula before the General Assembly was established. His son was the law-speaker Þorkell Moon, who was one of the highest in conduct of the pagan men in Iceland. When he was terminally ill, he had himself carried into the rays of the sun and handed himself over into the hands of that god who was supposed to have created the sun. His life had been as pure as that of the best-conducted Christian men. His son was Þormóðr, who was the law-speaker of the General Assembly when the Christian faith came to Iceland. His son was Hamall, the father of Már and Þormóðr and Torfi. Sigurðr was Már's son, father of Hamall, father of Guðmundr, father of Þormóðr Skeiða-*goði*.

About Þórðr Shaggy

11. Bjǫrn the Ungartered was the name of a powerful and famous chieftain in Norway. He was [the son][20] of chieftain Weather's-Grímr from Sogn; Grímr married Hervǫr, the daughter of Þorgerðr, daughter of King Eylaugr. Bjǫrn married Vélaug, the sister of Vémundr the Old. They had three sons: one was Ketill Flat-Nose, the second Helgi, the third Hrappr. These were famous men, and about their descendants much is said in this book, and from them almost all great people in Iceland are

[19] Hauksbók has the misreading *ok millim Hranna giollnes*.

[20] Missing in the manuscript.

descended. Hrappr married Þórunn Snow-Grouse-of-Grœningr. Their son was Þórðr Shaggy. He married Vilborg, daughter of King Óswaldr and Úlfrún the Unborn, the daughter of Játmundr, king of the English. Þórðr first settled for ten or fifteen years in Lón towards the east, but when he got word of his high-seat pillars being in Leiruvágr Bay, he sold his lands to Úlfljótr. He was the son of Þóra, daughter of Kári-of-the-Hǫrðar. And he went westwards with all his possessions and on the advice of Ingólfr took land between Úlfarsá River and Leiruvágsá River and then lived at Skeggjastaðir. His daughter was Helga, who was married to Ketilbjǫrn the Old at Mosfell Mountain. From Þórðr many important people in Iceland are descended.

About Hallr's Settlement

12. A man was called Hallr, son of Þórir the Godless, son of Ormarr. He was the brother of Hildr, daughter of Ormarr, who was married to Þorbjǫrn-the-Man-from-Gaul, who had the same father—and she had the same mother—as Þórðr Shaggy. Father and son did not want to sacrifice and believed in their own strength. Hallr went to Iceland and took land between Mógilsá River and Leiruvágsá River and lived at Múli Crag. His son was Helgi, who married Þuríðr, daughter of Ketilbjǫrn. Their son was Þórðr at Álfsnes Peninsula, who married Guðný, daughter of Hrafnkell.

Why Ketill Flat-Nose was banished from the land

13. Haraldr Finehair was on a military expedition to the British Isles, as is written in his saga. He brought all the islands of the Hebrides under his control so far to the west that the possessions of no king of Norway since have reached further, with the exception of King Magnús Bareleg. And when he sailed back from the west, Vikings invaded the Hebrides, men from Scotland and Ireland, and plundered and looted widely. And when King Haraldr heard of this, he sent Ketill Flat-Nose, the son of Bjǫrn the Ungartered, to the west to win the islands back. Ketill married Yngvildr, the daughter of Chieftain Ketill Storm of Hringaríki. Their sons were Bjǫrn the Easterner and Helgi *bjóla*. Auðr the Deep-Minded and Þórunn Edge were their daughters. Ketill sailed to the west and left his son Bjǫrn behind. He brought all the islands of the Hebrides under his control and made himself their chieftain, but did not pay taxes to King Haraldr as was expected. Then King Haraldr brought Ketill's lands in Norway under his control and drove his son Bjǫrn away.

Here it tells about Helgi bjóla

14. Helgi *bjóla*, the son of Ketill Flat-Nose, went to Iceland from the Hebrides. He spent the first winter with Ingólfr and on his advice took the whole Kjalarnes Peninsula between the rivers Mógilsá and Mýrdalsá. He lived at Hof 'Temple'. His sons were Manslaughters-Hrappr and Eyvindr Guard, the father of Kollsveinn, father of Eyvindr, who married Þorlaug, daughter of Klœngr; their daughter was Þorgerðr, mother of Þóra, who was married to Þorkell, the son of Ásgeirr Pincers. Their son was Ǫgmundr, the father of Bishop Jón the Holy.

About Ørlygr

15. Ørlygr was the name of a son of Hrappr, son of Bjǫrn the Ungartered. He was in fosterage with Bishop Patrick the Holy on the Hebrides. He wanted to go to Iceland and asked Bishop Patrick to help him. The bishop obtained timber for a church for him and asked him also to take with him a plenarium and an iron bell and a gold penny and blessed earth that he was to put under the corner post by way of consecration, and he was to dedicate [this church] to Saint Columba. Then Bishop Patrick said:

'Wherever you take land, only settle where you see three mountains from the sea and a fjord can be seen between all the mountains and a valley in each mountain. You shall sail to the southernmost mountain. There will be a forest there, and to the south under the mountain you will find a clearing and three piled-up or erected stones; there you shall erect a church and dwell there.'

Ørlygr put to sea, and on the second ship was the man who was called Kollr, his foster-brother; they sailed together. Together with Ørlygr on the ship was the man who was called Þorbjǫrn Sparrow; a second was Þorbjǫrn Whale-Bone; a third Þorbjǫrn Dusk. They were sons of Bǫðvarr Bladder-Baldhead. And when they came near the land, a great storm broke out over them, and it drove them westwards around Iceland. Then Ørlygr called upon Bishop Patrick, his foster-father, that they might reach land, and he would name after him the place where he reached land. They did not wait a long time after that before they saw land. He came with his ship to Ørlygshǫfn 'Ørlygr's Harbour', and therefore he named the fjord Patreksfjord. But Kollr called upon Thor; they were separated in the storm, and he came to the place called Kollsvík 'Kollr's Bay', and there he lost his ship. There they spent the winter. Some of his oarsmen took land there, as will be

'And when they came near the land, a great storm broke out over them, and it drove them westwards around Iceland. Then Ørlygr called upon Bishop Patrick, his foster-father, that they might reach land, and he would name after him the place where he reached land. They did not wait a long time after that before they saw land. He came with his ship to Ørlygshǫfn "Ørlygr's Harbour", and therefore he named the fjord Patreksfjord.'
The inner part of Patreksfjörður.

related further. And in spring Ørlygr got his ship ready and sailed off with all his possessions. And when he came south past Faxaóss, there he recognised those mountains to which he had been pointed. Then the iron bell fell over board and sank, and they sailed inland along the fjord and took land at the place now called Sandvík Bay on Kjalarnes Peninsula. Then the iron bell was lying there in a heap of seaweed. On the advice of his relative Helgi *bjóla* he lived at the foot of Esjuberg Cliff and took land between Mógilsá River and Ósvífrslœkr Brook. He built a church by Esjuberg Cliff, as he had been told. His wife was called Hjálp; their son was Valþjófr, who came to Iceland with Ørlygr when he was already grown up. Later, Ørlygr married Ísgerðr, the daughter of Þormóðr, son of Bresi; their son was Geirmundr, the father of Halldóra, who was married to Þjóstólfr, the son of Bjǫrn Gold-Bearer; their son was Þorleifr, who lived at the Esjuberg Cliff after his grandfather Geirmundr. They believed in Saint Columba, even though they were not baptised. Þorleifr had uncanny powers and nevertheless accepted Christianity; many men are descended from him. The daughter of Ørlygr and Ísgerðr was Vélaug, who was married to Gunnlaugr Snake-Tongue the Old, and their daughter was Þuríðr *dylla*, the mother of Illugi the Black.

Here it tells about Svartkell

16. A man was called Svartkell. He went to Iceland from England and took land inland from Mýdalsá River and between it and Eilífsdalsá River and lived first at Kiðjafell Mountain and then at Eyrr Gravel-Bank. His son was Þorkell, the father of Glúmr, who as an old man accepted Christianity; he prayed thus before the cross:

'Something good always for old men, something good always for younger men.'

His son was Þórarinn, the father of Glúmr at Vatnlausa. Svartkell's sister was called Arnleif, who was married to Þórólfr Wish-Hostage, the father of Kleppjárn the Old from Flókadalr Valley. Their daughter was Hallgerðr, who was married to Bergþór, son of Kollr.

About Valþjófr

17. Valþjófr, who has been mentioned earlier, the son of Ørlygr at Esjuberg Cliff, took all of the Kjós Hollow and lived at Meðalfell Mountain. His son was called Þorbjǫrn Pate, the father of Hallveig, who was married to Þórðr Lamb; that is the Valþýflingar family. Valþjófr's daughter was called Signý, after whom Signýjarstaðir is named; she was married to Grímkell, the son of Bjǫrn Gold-Bearer. Their sons were Hǫrðr, who was killed on Geirshólmr Island, and Gnúpr, the father of Birningr, father of Gnúpr, father of Bishop Eiríkr of the Greenlanders. Another son of Valþjófr's was called Valbrandr, the father of Torfi, who was the first to live at Mǫðruvellir Fields. Father and son had a joint enterprise with Tongue-Oddr; that is why thenceforth they lived on Breiðabólstaðr in the northern Reykjardalr Valley. Torfi was the father of Þorkell on Skáney Island, who married Arngerðr, the daughter of Þorkell, son of Svartkell.

About Hvamm-Þórir

18. Hvamm-Þórir took land between the rivers Laxá and Forsá and lived in Hvammr 'Grassy Slope'. He argued with Refr about the cow which was called Brynja and after which Brynjudalr 'Brynja's Valley'

is named. Þórir had lost this heifer for a long time, but it was found in Brynjudalr Valley, where Refr owned land, and together with her there were forty heads of cattle which all were descended from her and had been grazing without a shepherd. Therefore each of them claimed the cattle as his own, and Þórir attacked Refr with eight men on that occasion when they fought at the hills which ever since have been called Þórishólar 'Þórir's Hills'.

About Sǫlmundr

19. Þórólfr Butter, who has been mentioned earlier, was the son of Þorsteinn Snow-Ice, son of Grímr, the man who owing to his popularity received sacrifices after his death and was called *kambann*. The son of Þórólfr Butter was Sǫlmundr, the father of Þorsteinn, who took land in Brynjudalr Valley between the rivers Bláskeggsá and Forsá. He married Þorbjǫrg *katla*, the daughter of Helgi Cormorant, son of Geirleifr, who took Barðastrǫnd Coast. Their son was Refr in Brynjudalr Valley, father of Halldóra, who was married to Sigfúss, son of Ship-Grímr. Their daughter was Þorgerðr, mother of Sigfúss, the father of Priest Sæmundr the Wise.

Chapter

20. A man from Ireland was called Ávangr, who was the first man to live at the head of the fjord in Botn, and lived there his whole life. At that time there was such a large forest there that he built a seagoing ship there, and loaded it at the place which is now called Hlaðhamarr 'Load-Cliff'. His son was Þorleifr, father of Þuríðr, who was married to Þormóðr, son of Þjóstarr. Their son was Bǫrkr, father of Þórðr, father of Auðun in Brautarholt Forest.

21. Þormóðr the Old and Ketill, sons of Bresi, went from Ireland to Iceland and took the whole Akranes Peninsula between the rivers Aurriðaá and Kalmansá. They were Irishmen. Kalman, after whom the river is named, was also Irish, and was the first to live on Katanes Peninsula. These brothers divided the lands between themselves in such a way that Þormóðr had [the lands] south of the rowan-tree grove Reynir and as far as Kalmansá River and lived at Inner-Hólmr Island, and his brother Ketill had [the lands] west of Reynir and north of Akrafell Mountain as far as Aurriðaá River. His son was called Bersi, father of Þorgestr, father of Starri at Hólmr Island, father of Knǫttr, father of Ásdís, who

was married to Klœngr, son of Snæbjǫrn, [son][21] of Harbour-Ormr. Geirlaug was the daughter of Þormóðr the Old, mother of Tongue-Oddr. Jǫrundr the Christian was the son of Ketill, son of Bresi; he lived in Jǫrundarholt Forest; that is now called 'in Garðar Yards'. To his dying day he held well to the Christian faith and in his old age he was a hermit. Jǫrundr's son was Kleppr, father of Einarr, father of Narfi. Another son of Kleppr's was called Hávarr, the father of Þorgeirr. Eðna was the name of the daughter of Ketill, son of Bresi. In Ireland she was married to the man who was called Konáll. Their son was Ásólfr *alskik*, who went from Ireland to Iceland during that time and came to the Eastern Fjords. They came from the east as a group of twelve, until they came to the farm of Þorgeirr the Hǫrðalander in Holt Forest under the Eyjafjǫll Mountains and put up their tent there. And his three companions then fell ill. They died there, and Priest Jón, son of Þorgeirr, father of Grímr in Holt Forest, found their bones and brought them to a church. Then Ásólfr built himself a house, close to what is now the church corner at Ásólfsskáli Hall, on the advice of Þorgeirr, because Þorgeirr did not want to have them by his house. A river flowed past Ásólfr's own house. That was an early winter. The river immediately became full of fish. Þorgeirr said that they were on his fishing ground. Then Ásólfr went away from there and built another house to the west by another river. That [river] is called Írá 'Irishmen-River' because they were Irish. And when men came to the river, it was so full of fish that the men thought they had never seen such a marvel; and everything was gone from the eastern river. Then the men of the area drove them away from there, and he went then to the house further west. Everything happened the same way. The farmers called them sorcerers, but Þorgeirr said that he thought that they were good men. In spring they went away and to the west to Akranes Peninsula. He built a farm at Hólmr Island at Kirkjubólstaðr. His son was Sǫlvi, father of Þórhildr, who married Brandr, the son of Þorgrímr, son of Kjallakr; their son was Þorleifr, father of Bárðr, father of Jófríðr, who was married to Árni, son of Torfa. Their daughter was Helga, who was married to Arngrímr, son of Guðmundr.

And when Ásólfr got old, he became a hermit. His cell was where the church is now. There he died and was buried there at Hólmr Island. And when Halldórr, son of Illugi the Red, lived there, a dairymaid had the habit of wiping her feet on the mound which was on Ásólfr's grave.

[21] Missing in the manuscript.

She dreamed that Ásólfr rebuked her for wiping her dirty feet on his house. 'And we will be reconciled,' he says, 'when you tell your dream to Halldórr.' She told him, and he did not ascribe significance to what the woman dreamed, and paid no attention to it. And when Bishop Hróðólfr went away from Bœr Farm, where he had lived, three monks remained behind. One of them dreamed that Ásólfr spoke to him:

'Send your farmhand to Halldórr at Hólmr Island and buy the mound from him which is on the cattle trail, and pay a mark of silver.'

The monk did so. The farmhand was able to buy the mound, and dug the earth from it and found there the bones of a man; he picked them up and went home with them. The following night, Halldórr dreamed that Ásólfr came to him and said that he would make both his eyes burst from his skull unless he bought his bones for the same price he had sold them for. Halldórr bought Ásólfr's bones and had a wooden shrine made and set over the altar. Halldórr sent his son Illugi abroad for timber to build a church; but when he was coming back to Iceland and came between the peninsulas Reykjanes and Snæfellsnes, then he was, because of the ship's owners, unable to go ashore where he wanted. Then he threw all the timber for the church overboard and prayed that it would go where Ásólfr wanted. And the Norwegians came west to Vaðill. And three nights later the timber reached the Kirkjusandr 'Church's Beach', at Hólmr Island, except that two trees came to Raufarnes Peninsula in Mýrar Moors. Halldórr had a church built measuring thirty [ells?] and roofed with wood, and dedicated it to Columba together with God.

22. Kolgrímr the Old, the son of the chieftain Hrólfr and of Unnr, daughter of Hákon, son of Jarl Grjótgarðr, after whom the Grjótgarðshaugr burial mound south of Agðanes is named, went to Iceland from Trondheim and took the Lower Hvalfjarðarstrǫnd Coast from Bláskeggsá River as far as Laxá River and out to the brook that runs out from Saurbœr Farm, and he lived at Ferstikla. His son was Þorhalli, father of Kollgrímr, father of Steinn, father of Kvistr, father of Kali; Bergþóra, who was married to Refr in Brynjudalr Valley, was Kolgrímr's daughter.

23. Finnr the Rich, the son of Halldórr, son of Hǫgni, went to Iceland from Stavanger; he married Þórvǫr, daughter of Þorbjǫrn from Mosfell Mountain, son of Hraði. He took land south of Laxá River as far as Kalmansá River. He lived at Miðfell Mountain. His son was Þorgeirr, father of Hólmsteinn, father of Þórunn, mother of Guðrún, mother of Sæmundr, father of Bishop Brandr. Skeggi in Skógar Forests was Þórunn's son, father of Styrmir and Bolli in Skógar.

24. A man was called Bekan, who took land inland from Berjadalsá River as far as Aurriðaá River and lived at Bekansstaðir within Ketill's land-claim. Hallkell, who took Hvítársíða Riverside, first lived on Akranes Peninsula at Hallkelsstaðir, before the sons of Bresi drove him away. And when he went after his cattle, which had been out grazing without a shepherd there, he was killed and is buried in a mound there.

25. Harbour-Ormr went to Iceland from Stavanger and took all lands around Melahverfi outwards as far as the rivers Aurriðaá and Laxá and inwards as far as Andakílsá River and lived in Hǫfn Harbour. His son was Þorgeirr Cut-Cheek, father of Þórunn, the mother of Þórunn, mother of Jósteinn, father of Sigurðr, father of Bjarnheðinn.

Two brothers lived within the land-claim of Finnr and Ormr: Hróðgeirr the Wise at Saurbœr Farm and Oddgeirr at Leirá River; and Finnr and Ormr bought them out, because it felt too cramped for them. The brothers then took Hraungerðingahreppr, and Hróðgeirr lived in Hraungerði Garth, and Oddgeirr in Oddgeirshólar Hills. He married the daughter of Ketill Steam.

Harbour-Ormr is buried in a mound there on the headland in front of the farmstead at Hǫfn Harbour, where he took land . . . .[22]

26. Rauðr was the name of a man who took land upwards from Rauðsgil 'Rauðr's Glen', as far as the glen of Gil, and lived at Rauðsgil. His sons were Úlfr at Úlfsstaðir and Auðr at Auðsstaðir to the north of [the river, whom Hǫrðr killed],[23] and from that the *Saga of Hǫrðr, son of Grímkell, and of Geirr* was made.

About Grímr

27. Grímr was the name of a man who took the more southerly land upwards from the glen of Gil as far as Grímsgil 'Grímr's Glen', and lived at Grímsgil. His sons were Þorgils Puddle at Augastaðir 'Puddle-Steads', and Hrani at Hranastaðir, the father of Grímr, who was called Stern-Grímr. He lived at Stafngrímsstaðir 'Stern-Grímr's-Steads'. That is now called Sigmundarstaðir. Opposite there, north of Hvítá River on that same river, is his burial mound. There he was killed.

[22] Here there is a lacuna in the manuscript which may reflect the loss of a leaf from the original.

[23] Finnur Jónsson's emendation of a major dittography.

About Þorkell

28. Þorkell Grain-Hill took the rocky ridge of Southern Áss from Kollslœkr Brook as far as Deildargil Glen and lived at Áss Ridge. His son was Þorbergr Grain-Hill, who married Álǫf Ship-Shield, daughter of Ófeigr and Ásgerðr, the sister of Þorgeirr *gollnir*. Their children were Eysteinn and Hafþóra, who married Eiðr, son of Skeggi, who later lived at Áss. There Miðfjord-Skeggi died, and his burial mound is there below the farm. Another son of Skeggi's was Kollr, who lived at Kollslœkr Brook. The sons of Eiðr were Eysteinn and Illugi.

About Úlfr

29. Úlfr, the son of Grímr the Hálogalander and of Svanlaug, the daughter of Þormóðr from Akranes Peninsula, the sister of Bersi—this Úlfr took land between Hvítá River and the south glacier and lived at Geitland. His sons were Hrólfr the Rich, the father of Halldóra, who was married to Gizurr the White; their daughter was Vilborg, who was married to Hjalti, son of Skeggi. Another son of his was Hróaldr, the father of Hrólfr the Younger, who married Þuríðr, daughter of Valþjófr, son of Ørlygr the Old. Their children were Kjallakr at Lundr Grove in Syðradalr Valley, the father of Kollr, father of Bergþórr. Another was Sǫlvi at Geitland, the father of Þórðr in Reykjaholt Forest, father of Sǫlvi, father of Þórðr, father of Magnús, father of Þórðr, father of Helga, mother of Guðný, the mother of the [sons][24] of Sturla: Sighvatr and Þórðr and Snorri. The son of Sighvatr was Sturla, father of Þuríðr, who was married to Sir Hrafn. Their children were Jón Raven, Hallkatla and Valgerðr and Þorgerðr. The sons of Hallkatla and Jón, son of Pétr, were Sturla and Pétr, and the daughter was Steinunn, who was married to Guðmundr, son of Þorsteinn, son of Skeggi. Hrólfr's third son was Illugi the Red, who first lived at the rocky ridge of Hraunsáss. He then married Sigríðr, the daughter of Þórarinn the Bad, the sister of Bǫlverkr-of-the-Mice.[25] He [Illugi] gave that dwelling-place to Bǫlverkr, and Illugi then went to live at Hofstaðir 'Temple-Steads', in Reykjardalr Valley, because the people of Geitland had to maintain that temple half-and-half with Tongue-Oddr. Lastly, he lived at Inner-Hólmr Island on Akranes Peninsula, because he swapped [everything] with Hólm-Starri,

[24] Manuscript: 'father'.

[25] *Mús* can mean both 'mouse' and 'bicep'; hence, the name might also be translated as 'Bǫlverkr Strongarms'.

lands and wives and all lifestock. Then Illugi got Jórunn, the daughter of Þormóðr, son of Þjóstarr of Álptanes Peninsula; but Sigríðr hanged herself in the temple, because she did not want the husband-swapping. Hrólfr the Younger gave his daughter Þorlaug the Priestess to Oddi, son of Ýrr. Therewith he moved west as far as Ballará River and lived there for a long time and was called Hrólfr of Ballará.

Here begins the Settlement in the Western Fjords

30. Here begins the settlement in the Quarter of the People of the Western Fjords, which many great men have inhabited. A man was called Kalman the Hebridean. He went to Iceland and reached Hvalfjord and spent the winter at Kalmansá River. Two sons of his drowned there in Hvalfjord. And then he took land west of Hvítá River, between it and Fljót Water, the whole Kalmanstunga, and thus all towards the east under the glaciers as far as grass grows, and lived in Kalmanstunga. He drowned in Hvítá River when he had gone south into the lava-field to meet his lover. And his burial mound is on Hvítárbakki Bank, in the south. His son was Sturla the *goði*, who first lived at Sturlustaðir up there at the foot of Tungufell Mountain, above Skáldskelmisdalr Valley, and later lived in Kalmanstunga. His son was Bjarni, who argued with Hrólfr the Younger and his son about Little-Tunga; then Bjarni vowed to accept Christianity; after that the Hvítá River broke through the channel that it is now flowing in. Then Bjarni acquired Little-Tunga up there around Grindr and Sǫlmundarhǫfði Headland.

A brother of Kalman's was called Kýlan. He lived below Kollshamarr Rock. His son was Kári, who quarrelled with Karli, son of Konáll, at Karlastaðir, a freedman of Hrólfr from Geitland, over an ox, and it turned out in such a way that Karli got it. Then Kári egged on his slave to kill Karli. The slave pretended to be mad and ran south over the lava-field. Karli was sitting on the threshold. The slave dealt him his death blow. Then Kári killed the slave. Þjóðólfr, the son of Karli, killed Kýlan, son of Kári, at Kýlanshólmar Islands. Then Þjóðólfr burned Kári in his house, at the place which is now called 'at the Burning'.

Bjarni, son of Sturla, had himself baptised and lived at Bjarnastaðir in Little-Tunga and had a church built there.

About Hallkell

31. A famous man was called Þrándr *nefja*, father of Þorsteinn, who married Lopthœna, the daughter of Chieftain Arinbjǫrn from the Fjords.

Lopthœna's sister was Arnþrúðr, who was married to Chieftain Þórir, son of Hróaldr, and their son was Chieftain Arinbjǫrn. The mother of Arnþrúðr and Lopthœna was Ástríðr Slender-Lad, the daughter of the poet Bragi and of Lopthœna, the daughter of Erpr the Bowing. The son of Þorsteinn and Lopthœna was Hrosskell, who married Jóreiðr, daugher of Ǫlvir, son of Finni, son of King Mǫttull.[26] Their son was called Hallkell. Hrosskell went to Iceland and came into Grunnafjord, and at first he lived on Akranes Peninsula; there, Ketill and his brothers took exception to him. Then he took Hvítársíða Riverside between Kjarrá River and Fljót Water; he lived at Hallkelsstaðir, and [likewise] his son Hallkell after him, and he married Þuríðr *dylla*, the daughter of Gunnlaugr from Þverárhlíð Mountainside and of Vélaug, daughter of Ørlygr from Esjuberg Cliff. Hrosskell gave land to Þorvarðr, father of Smiðkell, father of Þórarinn and of Auðun, who ruled over the cave men. He lived at Þorvarðsstaðir and had the whole Fljótsdalr Valley up there by Fljót Water. Hrosskell gave land to Þorgautr, a man from his ship's crew, down at Síða Waterside. He lived at Þorgautsstaðir. His sons were both called Gísli.

The children of Hallkell and Þuríðr were Þórarinn and Finnvarðr, Tindr and Illugi the Black and Gríma, who was married to Þorgils, son of Ari. Þórarinn slew Bǫlverkr-of-the-Mice when he lived at the rocky ridge of Hraunsáss. Then he had a fort built there and diverted the Hvítá River against the ridge, whereas before it had flown down through Melrakkadalr Valley. Illugi and Tindr attacked Bǫlverkr in the fort.

Chapters

32. Ásbjǫrn the Rich, son of Hǫrðr, bought land south of the Kjarrá River, up at Sleggulœkr Brook as far as Hvítbjǫrg Ciffs; he lived at Ásbjarnarstaðir. He married Þorbjǫrg, the daughter of Miðfjord-Skeggi. Their daughter was Ingibjǫrg, who was married to Illugi the Black.

33. Ǫrnólfr [was the name of a man][27] who took the valleys Ǫrnólfsdalr and Kjarradalr in the north up as far as the Hvítbjǫrg Cliffs. Ketill *blundr* bought from Ǫrnólfr all the land north of the cliff and lived in Ǫrnólfsdalr Valley. Ǫrnólfr then established a farm upp in Kjarradalr Valley. The place there is now called Ǫrnólfsstaðir. Above the cliff it is called Kjarradalr 'Brushwood Valley', because there were shrubs and

[26] *Recte* probably S: 'daugher of Ǫlvir, son of Mǫttull, king of the Finns'.

[27] Missing in the manuscript.

small woods between the rivers Kjarrá 'Brushwood River' and Þverá 'Side-River', so one could not live there. Blund-Ketill was a mightily rich man. In the forests, he had land extensively cleared and settled.

34. Hrómundr was the name of a man, the brother of Grímr the Hálogalander. He came with his ship to Hvítá River. He took Þverárdalr Valley and Þverárhlíð Mountainside up there as far as Hallarmúli Crag and further to the Þverá River. He lived at Hrómundarstaðir, at the place which is now called Karlsbrekka Slope. His son was Gunnlaugr Snake-Tongue, who lived at Gunnlaugsstaðir south of Þverá River. He married Vélaug, as has been written earlier. A man from the crew of Hrómundr's ship was called Hǫgni. He lived at Hǫgnastaðir. His son was Helgi at Lake Helgavatn, the father of Arngrímr the Good, who was at Blund-Ketill's burning. Hǫgni was the brother of Finnr the Rich.

35. The brothers Ísleifr and Ísrøðr took land downwards from Sleggjulœkr Brook between the rivers Ǫrnólfsdalsá and Upper-Hvítá as far as Rauðalœkr Brook, and the more southerly land downwards to Hǫrðahólar Hills. Ísleifr lived at Ísleifsstaðir, but Ísrøðr [lived at] at Ísrøðarstaðir and had the more southerly land by Hvítá River. He was the father of Þorbjǫrn, father of Ljótr at Veggir, who fell in the Fight of the Heath.

About Ásgeirr

36. Ásgeirr was the name of a man from the crew of Hrómundr's ship, who lived at Hamarr Crag, above Lake Helgavatn. He married Hildr Star[, the daughter of Þorvaldr, son of Þorgrímr][28] Foul-Taste. Their sons were Steinbjǫrn the Strong and the Great Blow and Þorvarðr, the father of Mæva, who was married to Hrifla; the third was Þorsteinn; the fourth Helgi, father of Þórðr, the father of Poet-Helgi.

About Arnbjǫrg

37. A woman was called Arnbjǫrg. She lived at Arnbjargarlœkr Brook. Her sons were Eldgrímr, who lived on the long ridge above Arnbjargarlœkr Brook at Eldgrímsstaðir, and Þorgestr, who received his death wound when he and Hrani fought at the place which is now called Hranafall 'Hrani's Fall'. Þórunn lived in Þórunnarholt Forest. She had land down as far as Víðilœkr Brook and up as far as the point where it bordered on the land of the seeress Þuríðr, her sister, who lived in Grǫf.

[28] Missing in the manuscript, supplied from the Sturlubók recension.

After her, Þórunnarhylr 'Þórunn's Deep Place' in Þverá River is named, and from her the Hamarbyggjar are descended.

38. Þorbjǫrn, the son of Arnbjǫrn, son of Óleifr Long-Neck, was the brother of Lýtingr in Vápnafjord. Þorbjǫrn took Stafaholtstunga between the rivers Norðrá and Þverá. He lived in Arnarholt Forest. His son was Teitr in Stafaholt Forest, the father of Einarr.

About Þorbjǫrn blesi

39. Þorbjǫrn *blesi* took land in Norðrárdalr Valley to the south above Krókr Corner, and the whole Hellisdalr Valley, and lived at Blesastaðir. His son was Gísli at the gravel hills of Melar in Hellisdalr Valley. After him, Gíslavatn is named: 'Gísli's Lake'. Blesi's second son was Þorfinnr at Þorfinnsstaðir, the father of Þorgerðr Heath-Widow, the mother of Þórðr *erra*, the father of Þorgerðr, the mother of Helgi at Lundr Grove.

About Geirmundr

40. Geirmundr, the son of Gunnbjǫrn Enchantment, took Tunga between the rivers Norðrá and Sandá and lived at Tunga. His son was Brúni, father of Þorbjǫrn at Steinar, who fell in the Fight of the Heath.

41. Ǫrn the Old took the valleys Sanddalr and Mjóvadalr and likewise Norðrárdalr down from Krókr Corner as far as Arnarbœli Farm, and lived at Háreksstaðir.

About Bjǫrn-of-the-Bog-Ore

42. Bjǫrn-of-the-Bog-Ore took Bjarnardalr Valley and those valleys which branch off from it, and had another farm running down from Mælifellsgil Glen, and another down in the district, as is written.

43. Karl took Karlsdalr Valley running up from Lake Helgavatn and lived at the foot of Karlsfell Mountain. He had land down to Jafnaskarð and up to where it bordered on the land of Grímr.

About Gríss and Grímr

44. Gríss and Grímr were the names of freedmen of Baldhead-Grímr's. He gave them land up on the mountain: to Gríss, Grísartunga Tongue-of-Land, and to Grímr, Grímsdalr Valley.

45. A man was called Bálki, the son of Blæingr, son of Sóti of Sótanes Peninsula. He fought against King Haraldr in Hafrsfjord; therefore he went to Iceland and took the whole of Hrútafjord and lived at Bœr Farm. His son was Bersi the Godless, who took Langavatsdalr Valley and lived at Torfhvalastaðir. His sister was Geirbjǫrg, who was married to Þorgeirr *meldún* at Tungufell Mountain. Their son was Véleifr the Old, the father of Duel-Bersi. Bersi the Godless married Þórdís, the daughter of Þórhaddr from Hítardalr Valley, and she brought Hólmslǫnd Lands as her dowry with her, and he then lived there. Their son was Arngeirr, who married Þórdís, the daughter of Þorfinnr the Torrential. Their son was Bjǫrn Champion-of-the-Hítdœlir. Þuríðr's[29] mother was Sæuðr, the daughter of Baldhead-Grímr.

46. Sigmundr was the name of a freedman of Baldhead-Grímr's. To him he gave land between the rivers Gljúfrá and Norðrá. He lived at Haugar Mounds, before he moved to Munoðarnes Peninsula. After him Sigmundarnes Peninsula is named.

47. Bjǫrn-of-the-Bog-Ore bought land from Baldhead-Grímr between the rivers Gljúfrá and Gufá. He lived at Rauða-Bjarnarstaðir 'Bog-Ore-Bjǫrn's-Steads', above Eskiholt Forest. His son was Þorkell Rag at Skarð and Helgi at Hvammr 'Grassy Slope', in Norðrárdalr Valley, and there he is buried in a mound; and Gunnvaldr, the father of Þorkell, who married Helga, the daughter of Þorgeirr of Víðimýrr Moor.

48. To the brothers Þorbjǫrn *krumr* and Þórir *beigaldi* Baldhead-Grímr gave land beyond the Gufá River. Þorbjǫrn lived in Hólar Hills, and Þórir at Beigaldi.

49. To Þórðr Giant and Þorgeirr Earth-Long and their sister Þorbjǫrg Pole Baldhead-Grímr gave land south of Langá River. Þórðr lived at Þursstaðir 'Giant-Steads', and Þorgeirr at Jarðlangsstaðir 'Earth-Long's-Steads', and Þorbjǫrg at Stangarholt 'Pole-Forest'.

50. Áni was the name of a man to whom Grímr gave land between Langá River and Háfslœkr Brook. He lived at Ánabrekka Slope. His son was Ǫnundr *sjóni*, father of Steinarr and Dalla, the mother of Kormakr.

51. Þorfinnr the Hard was the name of the standard-bearer of Þórólfr, son of Baldhead-Grímr. To him Baldhead-Grímr gave his daughter Sæuðr and land beyond Langá River as far as Leirulœkr Brook and up to the

[29] That is, 'Þórdís's': probably a mistake in the manuscript.

mountain and as far as Álptá River. He lived at Fors Waterfall. Their daughter was Þórdís, the mother of Bjǫrn Champion-of-the-Hítdœlir.

52. A man was called Yngvarr, the father of Bera, who was married to Baldhead-Grímr. To him Grímr gave land between Leirulœkr Brook and Straumfjord; he lived on Álptanes Peninsula. Another daughter of his was Þórdís, who was married to Þorgeirr Lamb at Lambastaðir 'Lamb's-Steads', the father of Þórðr, whom the slaves of Ketill Steam burned in his house.

53. Steinólfr was the name of the man who took both the Hraundalr valleys, everything between the rivers Álptá and Hvítá and up as far as Grjótá River, and lived in southern Hraundalr Valley. His son was Þorleifr, from whom the Hraundœlir are descended. Steinólfr's daughter was called Þórunn, who was married to Þorbjǫrn, son of Vífill, the father of Þorgerðr, the mother of Ásmundr, the father of Sveinbjǫrn, the father of Oddr, the father of Gróa, the mother of Oddr on Álptanes Peninsula.

54. A famous man was called Þórhaddr, the son of Steinn the Swift-Sailing, son of Vígbjóðr, son of Bǫðmóðr from Cargo Hold. He took the whole Hítardalr Valley down as far as Grjótá River in the south, and in the north everything between the rivers Hvítá and Kaldá as far as the sea. His son was Þorgeirr, the father of Hafþórr, the father of Guðný, the mother of Þorlákr the Rich, the father of Þorleifr the Bitter, [the father][30] of Þorleikr, the father of Ketill, the father of Valgerðr, the mother of the sons of Narfi, Þorlákr and Þórðr.

55. Þorgils *knappi*, a freedman of Kolli, son of Hróaldr, took Knappadalr Valley. His sons were Ingjaldr, Þórarinn and Þórir, who lived at Akrar Ploughlands and took possession of all the land between the rivers Hítá and Álptá and up to where it bordered on the land of Steinólfr. Þórir's son [was][31] Þrándr, who married Steinunn, the daughter of Hrútr of Kambsnes Peninsula. Their sons were Þórir and Skúmr, the father of Torfi, the father of Tanni. His son was Hrútr, who married Kolfinna, the daughter of Illugi the Black.

Now have been listed the men who settled within Baldhead-Grímr's land claim. Baldhead-Grímr's son was Egill, the father of Þorsteinn, the father of Hrifla, the father of Skúli, the father of Þórðr, the father of

[30] Missing in the manuscript, which here has a lacuna; added from other recensions.

[31] Missing in the manuscript, added from a different recension.

Bǫðvarr, the father of Þórðr the Priest, the father of Bǫðvarr, the father of Þórðr, the father of Járngerðr, who was married to Sir Erlendr the Strong. Their daughter was Valgerðr.

About Seal-Þórir

56. A man was called Grímr, son of Ingjaldr, son of Hróaldr from Haddingjadalr Valley, the brother of Ási the chieftain. He went to Iceland in search of land and sailed to the northern part of the land. He spent the winter on Grímsey Island on Steingrímsfjord. His wife was called Bergdís, and a son Þórir. In winter, Grímr rowed out to fish with his slaves, and his son was with him, and when the boy started to feel cold, they dressed him in a sealskin bag and pulled it up to his neck. Grímr caught a merman. Grímr said:

'Predict our life-stories, and long lives, otherwise you don't go home.'

'That's not worth knowing for any of you except the boy in the sealskin bag, for you will be dead before spring comes, and your son will live and take land at the place where Skálm, your mare, lies down under her burden.'

And later that winter Grímr died and is buried there in a mound.

In spring, Bergdís and Þórir left Grímsey Island and went westwards over the heath to Breiðafjord. Skálm led the way the whole summer and never lay down. The second winter they spent on Skálmanes Peninsula in Breiðafjord, and the following summer they turned south. Then Skálm led the way until they came from the heath south to Borgarfjord, to a place where there were two red gravel hills; there Skálm lay down under her burden under the outer gravel hill. There Þórir took land south of the Gnúpá River as far as the rivers Kaldá, below Knappadalr Valley, and Laxá, everything between the mountain and the foreshore. He lived at Rauðamelr ytri 'Outer Red Gravel Hill'.

Þórir was already old and blind when he came out late one evening and saw that a man was rowing in from the sea in an iron dinghy into the mouth of Kaldá River. He looked big and vicious and went ashore there, up to the farm which was called 'in Hrip', and there he started digging under the gate of the milking-shed. And during the night volcanic fire welled up there and a lava-field erupted. The farm was at the place where the outcrop of rock is now. Seal-Þórir's son was Þorfinnr, who married Jófríðr, the daughter of Tongue-Oddr. Þorfinnr's daughter was Þuríðr, who was married to Þorbrandr in Álptafjord. Seal-Þórir and his pagan relatives died into Þórisbjǫrg 'Þórir's Cliffs'. Þorgils and Þorkell, the sons of Þorfinnr, were both married to Unnr, the daughter of Álfr in Dalir Valleys. Skálm died in Skálmarkelda 'Skálm's Morass'.

57. Kolbeinn Damaged-Head, son of Atli, from Atley off Fjalir, went to Iceland and bought all lands between the rivers Kaldá and Hítará below Sandbrekka Slope and lived at Kolbeinsstaðir. His sons were Finnbogi in Fagraskógr Forest, and Þórðr the Poet.

58. Þormóðr the *goði* and Þórðr the Stooping, the sons of Oddr the Dog, son of Þorviðr, son of Freyviðr, son of Álfr of Vǫrs, these brothers went to Iceland and took land between the rivers Laxá and Straumfjarðará. Þórðr had Gnúpudalr Valley and lived there, and later his son Skopti, the father of Hjǫrleifr the Good and of Finna, who was married to Refr the Big. Their son was Dálkr, father of Steinunn, mother of Poet-Refr. Þormóðr lived at Rauðkollsstaðir; he married Gerðr, the daughter of Kjallakr the Old. Their son was Guðlaugr the Rich. He married Þórdís, the daughter of Svarthǫfði, Bjǫrn Gold-Bearer's son, and of Þuríðr, daughter of Tongue-Oddr, who then lived at Hǫrgsholt Forest. Guðlaugr the Rich saw that Rauðamelslǫnd Lands were better than other lands there in the district. He demanded lands from Þorfinnr and challenged him to a duel. They both became incapacitated on the fighting ground, and Þuríðr, daughter of Tongue-Oddr, healed them and reconciled them.

59. Guðlaugr then took land from the Straumfjarðará River as far as the Fura[32] between the mountain and the foreshore and lived in Borgarholt Forest. From him the Straumfirðingar are descended. His son was Guðleifr, who had one trading ship, and another was owned by Þórólfr, the son of Loptr the Old of Eyrarbakki Bank, when they fought against Jarl Gyrðr, son of Sigvaldi, in the Meðalfarssund Sound and held on to their possessions. About that Guðleifr composed the *Stanzas about Gyrðr*. Another son of Guðlaugr's was Þorfiðr, the father of Guðlaugr, the father of Þórdís, the mother of Þórðr, the father of Sturla the Old in Hvammr 'Grassy Slope'.

60. Váli the Strong was the name of a liegeman of King Haraldr Finehair. He committed manslaughter on holy ground and was outlawed. He went to the Hebrides, and three sons [of his][33] went to Iceland. Their mother was Hlíf the Horse-Gelder. One was called Atli;

[32] *Sic*; a river.

[33] Missing in the manuscript, added after the other recensions.

the second Álfarinn; the third Auðun the Stutterer. Atli, son of Váli, and his son Ásmundr took land from the Fyra to the Lýsa.[34] Ásmundr lived at Langaholt Forest at Þórutóptir Ruins; he married Langaholt's-Þóra. And when Ásmundr grew old, he broke up with Þóra because of the number of visitors and went to Qxl to live until his dying day. There Ásmundr was buried in a mound and laid in a ship and his slave together with him, the one who killed himself and did not want to live any longer after Ásmundr's death; he was laid in the other end of the ship. A little later Þóra dreamed that Ásmundr said to her that the slave was causing him discomfort. The place where he is buried is called Ásmundarleiði 'Ásmundr's Grave'. This stanza was heard in his mound:

> Alone I inhabit the place of stones,
> the prow-room of Atall's raven;
> there is no man-throng on deck,
> I dwell in the steed of bent parts.
> Space is better for the battle-wise—
> I can steer the surf-animal;
> that will live with chieftains
> longer—than bad company.

Place of stones = the grave mound. Atall's raven = the raven of the sea-king = the ship. Steed of bent parts = steed of frames = ship. Surf-animal = ship. Live with = be remembered by.

After that, people sought out the mound and the slave was taken out of the ship.

Þóra had a house built at right angles across a main road and always had a table standing there, and she sat outdoors on a chair and asked everybody who wanted food to eat. Atli was the son of Ásmundr, the father of Surtr, the father of Guðleifr, the father of Guðbrandr, the father of Surtr the Smith, the father of Priest Eyjólfr the Monk.

61. Hrólfr the Fat, the son of Eyvindr Oaken-Hook, brother of Illugi Mountain-*goði*, from Síða in the east, took land from the Lýsa as far as Hraunhafnará River. His son was Helgi at Hofgarðar Yards, the father of Finnbogi and Bjǫrn and Hrólfr. Bjǫrn was the father of Gestr, the father of Poet-Refr.

[34] *Sic*; a river.

62. Sǫlvi was the name of the man who took land between Hellishraun Lava-field and Sleggjubeinsá River. He lived first in Brenningr and then on Sǫlvahamarr Crag, because he thought that it would be advantageous to more[35] people there.

63. Sigmundr, the son of Ketill Thistle, the one who had taken Þistilsfjord 'Thistle-Fjord', he married Hildigunnr. He took land between the lava-fields Hellishraun and Beruvíkrhraun. He lived at Laugarbrekka Slope and is buried there in a mound. He had three sons. One was Einarr, who later lived there at Laugarbrekka Slope. Father and son sold Lónland to the Einarr who later lived there. He was called Lón-Einarr. A whale was washed up on his foreshore and he carved a slice off it. A storm pushed it out to sea again and it was washed ashore on the land of Einarr, son of Sigmundr. Lón-Einarr declared that the witchcraft of Hildigunnr had caused that, and when the whale had been washed out to sea from Lón-Einarr['s land] he went to search [for it] and came up just as Einarr, son of Sigmundr, was cutting up the whale together with his farmhands. Immediately he dealt one of them a death-blow. Einarr of Laugarbrekka Slope asked his namesake to leave, 'because it will be of no avail to you to attack'. Lón-Einarr went away because he had too few men. Einarr, son of Sigmundr, brought the whale home, and one time when he was not at home, Lón-Einarr went to Laugarbrekka Slope with seven men and summoned Hildigunnr to court on a charge of witchcraft. She was the daughter of Beinir, son of Már, son of Naddoddr from the Faeroe Islands. Einarr came home when Lón-Einarr had just left. Hildigunnr told him this news and handed him a newly made tunic. Einarr took his shield and sword and a work horse and rode after them, causing the horse to break down at Þúfubjǫrg Cliffs. Then Einarr ran as fast he could, and when he came past the Drangar Rock Towers, he saw a troll sitting up there and swinging his legs so that they touched the surf, and he banged them together so that it made the sea foamy, and he spoke a stanza:

> I was there, where fell from a mountain
> a flood-grain of the giant's mother,
> out of the high sky of the mountain-giants,
> . . .

[35] In the sentence *hann þottiz þar vera fleri manna gagn*, the form *fleri* appears to be ungrammatical (one would expect *flera*), but Finnur Jónsson has highlighted it as the correct manuscript reading.

The giant succeeds in making
on the plain of the rowing bench
. . .
more boats hull-soaked than I.[36]

Flood-grain = cliff, rock. Sky of the mountain-giants = mountain. Plain of the rowing bench = the sea. Hull-soaked = by being swamped and sunk.

Einarr paid no attention to this. They met at the place which is called Mannafallsbrekkur 'Slopes of the Fall of Men' and fought there, but the weapons did not bite Einarr's outer garment. Four of Lón-Einarr's men fell, and two fled from him. The namesakes fought for a long time, until the belt of Lón-Einarr's trousers broke, and when he grasped it his namesake dealt him his death-blow. Furthermore, Hreiðarr, a slave of Einarr, son of Sigmundr, saw him [his master] run quickly and hurried after him. Then he saw Lón-Einarr's slaves fleeing. He then ran after them and then killed them both in Þrælavík 'Bay of Slaves'. For that Einarr gave him his freedom and as much land as he would be able to get done in three days.[37] The place where he lived is now called Hreiðarsgerði Garth. Einarr lived then at Laugarbrekka Slope, and he is buried in a mound not far from Sigmundarhaugr 'Sigmundr's Mound', and his mound is always green, winter and summer.

The son of Lón-Einarr was called Þorkell. He married Gríma, daughter of Hallkell, before Þorgils, son of Ari. The daughter of Einarr of Laugarbrekka Slope was Arnóra, who was married to Þorgeirr, son of Vífill. Their daughter was Yngvildr, who was married to Þorsteinn, the son of Snorri the *goði*; their daughter was Inguðr, who was married to Ásbjǫrn, son of Arnórr.

64. A man was called Grímkell, the son of Úlfr Crow, son of Hreiðarr, brother of Gunnbjǫrn, after whom the Gunnbjarnarsker 'Gunnbjǫrn's Skerries' are named. He took land from Beruvíkrhraun Lava-Field as far as Neshraun Lava-Field and out across Ǫndvertnes Peninsula and lived at Saxahváll Hill. He chased Saxi, son of Álfarinn, son of Váli, away from there, and he lived then at Hraun Lava-Field near Saxahváll

[36] The interpretation of this stanza is highly uncertain. It seems to represent the troll reminiscing about having been around supernaturally-caused rock-falls in which open boats were sunk.

[37] The meaning of 'getting land done' is obscure.

Hill. Grímkell married Þorgerðr, the daughter of Valþjófr the Old; their son was Þórarinn Grain. He had great shape-shifting powers and lies in Kornahaugr 'Grain Mound'. Þórarinn Grain married Jórunn, the daughter of Einarr in Stafaholt Forest. Their daughter was Járngerðr, who was married to Úlfr, son of Uggi. Another son of Grímkell was called Klœngr. He married Oddfríðr, the daughter of Helgi of Hvanneyrr Gravel-Bank. Their son was Kolli.

65. Álfarinn, son of Váli, had first taken the peninsula between Beruvíkrhraun Lava-Field and Enni Precipice. His sons were Hǫskuldr, who lived at Hǫskuldsár 'Hǫskuldr's Rivers'; and Ingjaldr, who lived at Ingjaldshváll 'Ingjaldr's Hill'; and Goti at Gotalœkr 'Goti's Brook'; and Hólmkell at Fors 'Waterfall', by Hólmkelsá River.

66. A man was called Óláfr the Elder who took land inland from Enni Precipice as far as Fróðá River and lived in Óláfsvík Bay.

'A man was called Óláfr the Elder who took land inland from Enni Precipice as far as Fróðá River and lived in Óláfsvík Bay.'
The view across Óláfsvík towards the village of Óláfsvík.

67. A man was called Ormr the Thin, who came with his ship to Fróðáróss Estuary and lived for a few years at Brimisvellir Fields. He drove Óláfr the Elder away and took the whole of Old-Vík Bay[38] between Enni Precipice and Búlandshǫfði Headland and then lived at

[38] Óláfsvík, which took its name from Óláfr the Elder.

Fróðá River. His son was Þorbjǫrn the Fat, who fought with Þórarinn the Black and fell himself, and three men together with him. About that Þórarinn composed *Máhlíðingi's Stanzas*, [which are named] after the man who recites them in *Eyrbyggja saga*. This is one:

> The wolf-bitch's joy will be told to me
> for deadly hatred, Hroptr's ember-diminisher!—
> already in the past in front of Enni
> I was able to make a weapon bite well—
> if the battle-wise(?) accuse me
> of a Valkyrie's ember-argument—
> I am egged on to what is proper—that I struck
> my goddess of the costly weavings.

Wolf-bitch's joy = fight. Hroptr's ember-diminisher = warrior. Valkyrie's ember-argument = fight. My goddess of the costly weavings = my wife.

Because of these words they fought a second time. Þorbjǫrn married Þuríðr, daughter of Bǫrkr the Fat, son of Þorsteinn Cod-Biter. Their son was Ketill Champion, and he was abroad at that time. He was the father of Hróðný, who was married to Þorsteinn, son of Manslaughter-Styrr.

68. Sigurðr Pig-Head was a great champion. He lived at Kvenvágastrǫnd Coast. His son Herjólfr was eight years old when he killed a brown bear because it had eaten his goat. About that, this has been composed:

> Bear Burnt-Arse
> ate a goat of Herjólfr's;
> Herjólfr Gnarled-Arse
> avenged the goat on Bear.

Herjólfr was twelve years old when he avenged his father. He was the most extraordinary man. In his old age, Herjólfr went to Iceland and took land between Búlandshǫfði Headland and Kirkjufjord. His son was Þorsteinn Coal-Beard, the father of Þórólfr, the father of Þórarinn the Black Máhlíðingi and Guðný, who was married to Vermundr the Thin. Their son was Brandr the Open-Handed, and Þorfinna, who was married to Þorsteinn, son of Kuggi.

69. Vestarr, the son of Þórólfr Bladder-Baldhead, he was married to Spana, daughter of Herrøðr. Their son was Ásgeirr. Vestarr went to Iceland together with his very old father and took Eyrarland and the

land between Kirkjufjord and Kolgrafafjord and lived at Ǫndverðeyrr Gravel-Bank. Both Þórólfr and his son are buried in a mound on Skallanes Peninsula. Ásgeirr, son of Vestarr, married Helga, daughter of Kjallakr. Their son was Þorlákr. His sons were Steinþórr, and Þórðr the Staring, who married Otkatla, daughter of Þorvaldr, and Þormóðr, who married Þorgerðr, the daughter of Þorbrandr from Álptafjord. The fourth was Bergþórr, who fell at Vigrafjord. Steinþórr married Þuríðr, the daughter of Þorgils, son of Ari. Their son was Gunnlaugr, who married Þuríðr the Wise, the daughter of Snorri the *goði*.

70. Kolr was the name of the man who took land from the west from Fjarðarhorn as far as Trǫllaháls Ridge and out over Berserkseyrr Gravel-Bank as far as Hraunsfjord. His son was Þórarinn, and Þorgrímr; after them, Kolssonafell 'Mountain of Kolr's Sons' is named. Father and sons all lived at Kolgrafir. From them, the Kolgreflingar are descended.

71. Auðun the Stutterer, son of Váli the Strong, he married Mýrún, the daughter of Bjaðmakr, king of the Irish. He took all of Hraunsfjord above Hraun Lava-Field between Lake Svínavatn and the ridge Trǫllaháls; he lived at Hraunsfjord. From him the Hraunfirðingar are descended. One autumn he saw that an apple-grey horse ran down from Lake Hjarðarvatn[39] and to his stud-horses. It defeated the breeding stallion. Then Auðun went there and took hold of the grey stallion and yoked it to a two-ox sledge, and it gathered up all the hay from his home-field. The stallion was easy to manage until midday. Yet when the hour was advanced, it stamped into the hard ground up to the hoof-tufts; and after sunset it broke the whole harness and ran up to the lake. It has not been seen since. Auðun's son was Steinn, the father of Helga, who was married to Án at Hraun Lava-Field. Their son was Már, the father of Guðríðr, the mother of Kjartan and Án at Kirkjufell Mountain. Ásbjǫrn was the name of another son of Auðun's; a third was called Svarthǫfði; and a daughter Þuríðr, who was married to Ásgeirr on Eyrr Gravel-Bank; their son was Þorlákr.

72. Bjǫrn was the name of the son of Ketill Flat-Nose and Yngvildr, the daughter of chieftain Ketill Storm of Hringaríki. Later, Bjǫrn had his residence on the property of his father, when Ketill went to the Hebrides. And when Ketill withheld the taxes from King Haraldr Finehair, the king drove his son Bjǫrn from his property and appropriated it to

[39] Manuscript: *Hardnsvatn.*

himself. Then Bjǫrn went west over the sea [to the British Isles] and did not want to settle down there and did not want to accept the Christian faith like Ketill's other children. Therefore he was called Bjǫrn the Easterner. He married Gjaflaug, daughter of Kjallakr, the sister of Bjǫrn the Strong. Bjǫrn the Easterner went to Iceland and took land between Hraunsfjord and Stafá River and lived at Bjarnarhǫfn Harbour at Borgarholt Forest and had mountain grazing rights up as far as Sel and had a fine estate. He died at Bjarnarhǫfn and was buried in a mound by Borgarlœkr Brook. The son of Bjǫrn and Gjaflaug was Kjallakr the Old, who lived at Bjarnarhǫfn after his father, and Óttarr, the father of Bjǫrn, the father of Vigfúss at Drápuhlíð Mountainside, whom Snorri the *goði* caused to be killed.

Another son of Óttarr's was Helgi. He raided in Scotland and there he acquired as plunder Níðbjǫrg, the daughter of King Bjólan and of Kaðlín, the daughter of Walk-Hrólfr. He married her, and their son was Ósvífr the Wise and Einarr Scales-Tinkle, who drowned at the skerry Einarssker in the Selasund Sound, and his shield was washed up on Skjaldey 'Shield Island', and his cloak on the islet Feldarhólmr 'Cloak Holm'. Einarr was the father of Þorgerðr, the mother of Herdís, the mother of Steinn the Poet. Ósvífr married Þórdís, the daughter of Þjóðólfr from Hǫfn Harbour. Their children were Óspakr (the father of Úlfr the Marshal, the father of Jón at Reyrvǫllr Field, the father of Erlendr Laggard, the father of Archbishop Eysteinn), and Þórólfr, Torráðr, Einarr, Þorkell, Þorbjǫrn—they were outlawed for the killing of Kjartan, son of Óláfr—and Guðrún, the mother of Þorleikr and Bolli and Gellir. Vilgeirr was the name of the son of Bjǫrn the Easterner. Kjallakr the Old [married Ástríðr],[40] the daughter of chieftain Hrólfr and of Ǫndótt, the sister of Ǫlvir Children's-Man. Their son was Þorgrímr the *goði*. His sons were Manslaughter-Styrr and Vermundr the Thin and Brandr, the father of Þorleikr. The daughter of Kjallakr the Old was Gerðr, who was married to Þormóðr the *goði*, and Helga, who was married to Ásgeirr of Eyrr Gravel-Bank.

73. Þórólfr, the son of Ǫrnólfr Fish-Flotsam, lived on Mostr; therefore he was called Beard-of-Mostr. He was a great sacrificer, and he trusted in Thor. He went to Iceland because of the tyranny of King Haraldr and sailed past the southern part of the land. And when he came to the west off Breiðafjord, he threw his high-seat pillars

[40] Missing in the manuscript.

overboard. Thor was carved on them. He made a solemn declaration that Thor should come ashore where he wanted Þórólfr to settle. Therefore he vowed to dedicate all his settlement area to Thor and to name it after him. Þórólfr sailed into Breiðafjord and gave the fjord its name. He took land in the south near the middle of the fjord. There he found Thor washed ashore on the headland. That place is now called Þórsnes 'Thor's Peninsula'. They went ashore there further inland in the small bay which Þórólfr called Hofsvágr 'Small Bay of the Temple'. There he built his farm and erected a large temple there and dedicated it to Thor. The place is now called Hofstaðir 'Temple-Steads'. At that time, the fjord was almost unsettled. Þórólfr took land from Stafá River inland as far as the Þórsá 'Thor's River', and called it all Þórsnes 'Thor's

'Þórólfr . . . had such a great belief in the mountain which stood on the headland and which he called Helgafell "Holy Mountain", that no man must turn his gaze there unwashed. And there was such a great holy peace there that one must do no harm to anything there on the mountain, either animals or men, unless they went away of their own accord. It was the belief of Þórólfr and his relatives that they would all die into the mountain.' *Helgafell on Þórsnes.*

Peninsula'. He had such a great belief in the mountain which stood on the headland and which he called Helgafell 'Holy Mountain', that no man must turn his gaze there unwashed. And there was such a great holy peace there that one must do no harm to anything there on the mountain, either animals or men, unless they went away of their own accord. It was the belief of Þórólfr and his relatives that they would all die into the mountain. There on the headland where Thor came ashore Þórólfr had all courts of justice held and there the district assembly was set up with the counsel of all the men of the district. And when people were there for the assembly, they must not relieve themselves on land, and for that a skerry was assigned, the one that they called Dritsker 'Guano Skerry',[41] because they did not want to let such a holy field be defiled.

And when Þórólfr was dead and his son Þorsteinn was young, Þorgrímr, son of Kjallakr, and his relative Ásgeirr did not want to go to the skerry to do their business, and the Þórsnes folk would not tolerate their defiling of their holy field. Therefore Þorsteinn Cod-Biter and Þorgeirr Bend fought about the skerry with Þorgrímr and Ásgeirr there at the assembly, and several men fell there, and many were wounded, before they were separated. Þórðr Yeller effected a compromise between them. And because neither of them was willing to change their stance, and the field was then desecrated by bloodshed, the decision was made to move the assembly away from there and further inland into the peninsula, to the place where it is now. That was then a very holy place. There stands Thor's Stone on which they broke the people that they sacrificed, and there nearby is the judgement-ring, where they condemned people to be sacrificed. There Þórðr Yeller established the Quarter Assembly with the counsel of all the men of the quarter.

The son of Þórólfr Beard-of-Mostr was Hallsteinn Þorskafjord-*goði*, the father of Þorsteinn Black the Wise. Ósk was the mother of Þorsteinn Black, the daughter of Þorsteinn Red. Another son of Þórólfr was Þorsteinn Cod-Biter; he married Þóra, the daughter of Óláfr *feilan*, the sister of Þórðr Yeller. Their son was Þorgrímr, the father of Snorri the *goði*, and Bǫrkr the Fat, who was the father of Sámr, whom Ásgeirr slew.

74. Geirrøðr was the name of a man who went to Iceland, and together with him Finngeirr, the son of Þorsteinn Snow-Shoe, and Úlfarr Champion. They went to Iceland from Hálogaland. Geirrøðr took land inland from Þórsá River as far as Langadalsá River; he lived on Eyrr Gravel-Bank. Geirrøðr gave land to his boatman Úlfarr on two sides of Úlfarsfell Mountain and on the highland. Geirrøðr gave land to Finngeirr around Álptafjord; he lived at the place which is now called 'on Kársstaðir'. He

[41] The term *drit* denotes animal and especially bird excrement, in modern Icelandic specifically the watery excrement of large sea-birds. (Not, for instance, the more solid excrement of geese.) The following story tied to it is consciously grotesque, playing on the tension between a place name denoting a guano-covered islet and a story of human excrement and pointless, escalating violence that claims to explain this toponym.

was the father of Þorfinnr, the father of Þorbrandr on Álptafjord, who married Þorbjǫrg, the daughter of Þorfinnr, son of Seal-Þórir.

Geirríðr was the name of a sister of Geirrøðr, who had been married to Bjǫrn, the son of Bǫlverkr Blind-Man's-Snout. Their son was called Þórólfr. He and Geirríðr went to Iceland after the death of Bjǫrn and spent the first winter on Eyrr Gravel-Bank. In spring, Geirrøðr gave his sister a residence in Borgardalr Valley, and Þórólfr went abroad and took up raiding. Geirríðr was not sparing in giving people food and had her house built at right angles across a main road. Þórólfr went to Iceland after the death of Geirríðr. He demanded lands from Úlfarr and challenged him to a duel. Úlfarr was old and childless. He fell on the duelling-ground and Þórólfr was wounded in the foot and walked with a limp forever after. Therefore he was called Twist-Foot. After the death of Úlfarr, Þórólfr took some of the lands, and Þorfinnr took some on the Álptafjord, and he settled his freedmen Úlfarr and Ørlygr on them.

Geirrøðr at Eyrr Gravel-Bank was the father of Þorgeirr Bend, who moved the farm from the island up under the mountains. He was the father of Þórðr, the father of Atli. Þórólfr Lame-Foot was the father of Arnkell the *goði* and of Geirríðr, who was married to Þórólfr at Mávahlíð Mountainside, the father of Þórarinn. The sons of Þorbrandr at Álptafjord, the [son][42] of Þórfinnr, were Þorleifr *kimbi* and Þóroddr, Snorri, Þorfiðr, Illugi, Þormóðr. They fought with Arnkell the *goði* about the inheritance of his freedmen and together with Snorri the *goði* they were at his killing at Ørlygsstaðir. After that Þorleifr *kimbi* went abroad. Then Arnbjǫrn, the son of Ásbrandr from Breiðavík Bay, hit him with a porridge-ladle. Kimbi took it as a joke. Þórðr the Staring confronted him with it at the Þórsnes Assembly, when he courted his sister. Then Kimbi had the Staring hit with a sandy sod of turf. From this came the conflicts between the inhabitants of Eyrr Gravel-Bank and the sons of Þorbrandr and Snorri the *goði*. They fought at the landing-place of Geirvǫr and at Álptafjord and Vigrafjord.

75. Þorbergr was the name of a man who went from Íafjord to Iceland and took both Langadalr valleys and lived in the outer one. His son was Áslákr, who married Arnleif, the daughter of Þórðr Yeller. Their children were Illugi the Mighty and Gunnhildr, who was first married to Breiðr and later to Halldórr on Hólmslátr. Illugi the Mighty married Guðleif, the daughter of Ketill Workshop-Log. Their sons were Eyjólfr

[42] Manuscript: 'father'.

and Kollr, and a daughter was Herþrúðr, who was married to Þorgrímr, son of Vermundr the Thin; and Friðgerðr, who was married to Oddr, son of Drafli; and Guðríðr, who was first married to Bergr, son of Þormóðr, and later to Jǫrundr in Skorradalr Valley; and Jódís, who was married to Már, the son of Illugi, son of Ari; and Arnleif, who was married to Kollr, the son of Þórðr the Staring. From Illugi the Langdœlir are descended.

76. Steinn the Swift-Sailing, the son of Vígbjóðr, the brother of Þórir Autumn-Darkness, took the Skógarstrǫnd Coast-Land up to the place where it bordered on the land of Þorbergr and further in as far as Laxá River. He lived at Breiðabólstaðr. His son was Þórhaddr, who took Hítardalr Valley, and Þorgestr, who married Arnóra, the daughter of Þórðr Yeller. Their son was Steinn the Law-Speaker and Ásmundr and Hafliði and Þórhaddr.

'Eiríkr then moved away from the north and cleared land in Haukadalr Valley. He lived at Eiríksstaðir near Vatshorn.'
Haukadalur with the reconstruction of the hall of Eiríkr the Red.

77. Þorvaldr, the son of Ásvaldr, son of Úlfr, son of Oxen-Þórir, and his son Eiríkr the Red left Jaðarr because of cases of manslaughter and took land on Hornstrandir Coast-Lands and lived at Drangar Rock Towers. Þorvaldr died there. Eiríkr then received Þjóðhildr in marriage, the daughter of Jǫrundr, son of Atli, and of Þorbjǫrg Ship-Chest, who was then married to Þorbjǫrn the Haukadalr-Man. Eiríkr then moved away from the north and cleared land in Haukadalr Valley. He lived at Eiríksstaðir near Vatshorn.

Then Eiríkr's slaves brought an avalanche down on the farm of Valþjófr at Valþjófsstaðir, and Eyjólfr Dirt, his relative, killed the slaves at Skeiðsbrekkur Slopes above Vatshorn. Because of that Eiríkr killed Eyjólfr Dirt. He also killed Duel-Rafn at Leikskálar Hollows. Geirsteinn and Oddr at Jǫrvi Gravel, relatives of Eyjólfr, brought the case of his killing to court. Eiríkr was then driven from Haukadalr Valley.

He took then the islands Brokey and Øxney, and he spent the first winter at Tǫður Infields on Suðrey Island. Then he handed partition-beams over to Þorgestr. Next Eiríkr went to Øxney Island and lived at Eiríksstaðir. Then he claimed his partition-beams back and did not get them. Eiríkr went to fetch the partition-beams from Breiðabólstaðr, and Þorgestr went after him; they fought not far from the farm at Drangar Rock Towers. There two of Þorgestr's sons fell, and a few other men. After that, each of the two summoned armed men. Styrr supported Eiríkr, and likewise Eyjólfr from Svíney Island and the sons of Þorbrandr from Álptafjord and Þorbjǫrn, son of Vífill; and Þorgestr was given support by the sons of Þórðr Yeller and Þorgeirr from Hítardalr Valley, Áslákr from Langadalr Valley and his son Illugi.

At the Þórsnes Assembly, Eiríkr and his men were outlawed. He fitted out a ship in the little bay Eiríksvágr, and Eyjólfr hid him in Dímunarvágr Bay, while Þorgestr and his men searched for him on the islands. Þorbjǫrn[43] and Eyjólfr and Styrr followed Eiríkr out around the islands. He said to them that he wanted to search for that land which Gunnbjǫrn, the son of Úlfr Crow, saw when he was driven westwards past Iceland, on the occasion when he found Gunnbjarnarsker 'Gunnbjǫrn's Skerries'. He said that he would come back to his friends if he found the land. Eiríkr sailed away from below Snæfellsjǫkull Glacier and came from Iceland to Miðjǫkull Glacier,[44] to the place which is called Bláserkr. He sailed westwards past Hvarf and spent the first winter on Eiríksey Island near Eystri byggð, the 'Eastern Settlement'. The following spring he went to Eiríksfjord and gave names to many places. He spent another winter on the Eiríkshólmar Islets by Hvarfsgnípa Peak. And the third summer he went all the way to the north to Snæfell, the 'Snow Mountain', and into Hrafnsfjord; then he said that he had reached the longitude of the deepest part of Eiríksfjord. Then he turned back and spent the third winter on Eiríksey Island off the mouth of Eiríksfjord. The following summer he went to Iceland, to Breiðafjord. He spent this winter at Hólmslátr

[43] Manuscript: Þorgeirr.

[44] In Greenland.

with Ingólfr. In spring, Eiríkr and Þorgestr fought, and Eiríkr suffered a defeat. After that they were reconciled. That summer, Eiríkr went to settle the land he had found, and he called it Greenland, because he said that the fact that the land had a good name would do much to encourage people to go there.

78. Ari, son of Þorgils, says that that summer twenty-five ships set sail for Greenland from Borgarfjord and Breiðafjord, and fourteen reached their destination abroad. Some were driven back, and some were lost. That was sixteen winters before the Christian faith was adopted by law in Iceland.

79. Herjólfr was the name of a man, son of Bárðr, son of Herjólfr. He went to Greenland with Eiríkr. With him on the ship was a Christian man from the Hebrides, who composed the *Poem in Praise of the Hafgerðingar*. It contains this refrain:

> I pray to the monks' blameless examiner
> to support my journey.
> The lord of the high hall of the earth
> hold the hawk's pedestal over me.

The monks' blameless examiner = Christ. The high hall of the earth = the sky. Hawk's pedestal = arm; hold his arm over me = protect me.

Herjólfr took Herjólfsfjord and lived on the Herjólfsnes Peninsula. He was a most respected man. Eiríkr the Red took Eiríksfjord and lived at Brattahlíð Mountainside, and his son Leifr after him. The following men then took land in Greenland and went out to it with Eiríkr: Ketill took Ketilsfjord; Hrafn, Hrafnsfjord; Sǫlvi, the Sǫlvadalr Valley; Snorri, son of Þorbrandr, Álptafjord; Þorbjǫrn *glóra,* Siglufjord; Einarr, Einarsfjord; Hafgrímr, Hafgrímsfjord and Vatnahverfi Village; Arnlaugr, Arnlaugsfjord; and some went to Vestribyggð, the 'Western Settlement'.

80. A man was called Þorkell Travelling-Jacket, a cousin of Eiríkr the Red. He went with Eiríkr to Greenland and took Hvalseyjarfjord[45] and the land between Eiríksfjord and Einarsfjord and lived on Hvalseyjarfjord. From him the Hvalseyjarfirðingar are descended. He was very, preternaturally, strong. On one occasion, when he wanted to entertain

[45] Manuscript: *Hvalseyjar*, which should probably be emended to *Hvalseyjarfjord* (Finnur Jónsson).

his relative Eiríkr and no seaworthy boat was at home, he swam out to Hvalsey Island after an old wether and brought it to the mainland on his back; that is a distance of half a nautical mile. Þorkell is buried under a cairn in the hay field on Hvalseyjarfjord and has ever since taken care of the work there.

About Ingólfr

81. Ingólfr the Strong and Þorvaldr, the sons of Áni, son of Ávaldr Narrowness-in-Heart, took land inland from Laxá River as far as Skrámuhlaupsá River and lived at Hvallátr.[46] The son of Þorvaldr was Þorleifr, the father of Halldórr, who later married Gunnhildr, the daughter of Áslákr, son of Hróarr from Langadalr Valley. Their son was Þórir, who married Hallveig, daughter of Tindr, son of Hallkell. Their son was Brandr, who married Þorgerðr, daughter of Brandr. Their son was Halldórr, who married Þorkatla, daughter of Þorgrímr. Their son was Prior Brandr the Wise, who has written most about the kindred of the Breiðfirðingar.

82. Óleifr the White was the name of a warlord. He was the son of King Ingjaldr, son of Helgi, son of Óláfr, son of Guðrøðr, son of Hálfdan White-Leg, king of the Upplendingar. Óleifr the White was raiding on the British Isles and conquered Dublin in Ireland, and the shire of Dublin, and made himself king there. He received Auðr the Deep-Minded in marriage, the daughter of Ketill Flat-Nose. Their son was called Þorsteinn the Red. Óleifr fell in battle in Ireland, and Auðr and Þorsteinn then went to the Hebrides. There, Þorsteinn received Þuríðr in marriage, the daughter of Eyvindr the Westman,[47] the sister of Helgi the Skinny. They had many children. Óleifr *feilan* was the name of their son. Their daughters were Gróa and Ólǫf, Ósk and Þórhildr, Þorgerðr and Vigdís. Þorsteinn established himself as a warlord and joined forces with Jarl [Sigurðr][48] the Rich, the son of Eysteinn Rattler. They conquered Caithness and Sutherland, Ross and Moray, and more than half of Scotland. Þorsteinn was king there before the Scots betrayed him, and he fell there in battle. Auðr was in Caithness when she received the news of Þorsteinn's death. Secretly, she had a trading ship built in the forest, and when it was ready, she sailed out to Orkney. There she married off Gróa,

[46] *Recte*: Hólmslátr.

[47] *Recte* probably: Eastman (i.e. Norwegian).

[48] Missing in the manuscript.

a daughter of Þorsteinn the Red; she was the mother of Grélǫð, who was married to Þorfinnr Skull-Cleaver. After that Auðr went to search for Iceland. She had twenty free men with her on the ship.

83. Kollr was the name of a man, son of Wether-Grímr, son of Ási the chieftain. He acted as Auðr's steward and was held in highest esteem by her. Kollr married Þorgerðr, the daughter of Þorsteinn the Red. A freedman of Auðr's was called Erpr. He was a son of Meldún, jarl of Scotland, the one who fell by Jarl Sigurðr the Great. Erpr's mother was Myrgjol, the daughter of Gljómall, King of the Irish. Jarl Sigurðr took them as plunder and enslaved them. Myrgjol was the maidservant of the jarl's wife and served her faithfully. She had many skills. She guarded the queen's unborn child[49] while she was taking a bath. Afterwards, Auðr bought her for a high price and solemnly promised her freedom to her if she served Þuríðr, the wife of Þorsteinn the Red, in the same way in which she had served the queen. Myrgjol and her son Erpr went to Iceland with Auðr.

84. Auðr first went to the Faeroe Islands and there married off Ólǫf, the daughter of Þorsteinn the Red. From there the Gǫtuskeggjar are descended. Then she went to search for Iceland and came to Vikarsskeið and was shipwrecked there. She went to Kjalarnes Peninsula to her brother Helgi *bjóla*. He invited her there with half of her entourage. But that seemed to her to be too shabby an invitation, and she said that he would long be a mean little man. She went westwards then to Breiðafjord to her brother Bjǫrn. He went to meet her with his farmhands and he said that he knew how noble his sister was and invited her with all her people. She accepted that. The following spring Auðr and her people went into Breiðafjord in search of land. They ate breakfast south of Breiðafjord at the place which is now called Dǫgurðarnes 'Breakfast Peninsula'.[50] Then they went [deeper] into [the fjord] across the Eyjarsund, the 'Island Sound'. They came ashore on the peninsula where

[49] The statement that Myrgjol 'had many skills' (*var margs kunnandi*) has undertones of supernatural powers, which may explain how she was able to guard an unborn child, possibly providing magical protection against miscarriage.

[50] A common class of Icelandic place names refers to the times of the day (including breakfast time), i.e. a place is named from the time at which the sun is standing above it as seen from the farm buildings. Dǫgurðarnes therefore could also be translated as '9 a.m. Peninsula'.

Auðr lost her comb. She called it Kambsnes 'Comb Peninsula'.[51] Auðr took all Dalalǫnd Lands . . .

Here there is a major lacuna in the text

---

85. <After that the sons of Kjallakr caught Ljótólfr and Þorsteinn in a subterranean house in the Fellsskógar, the 'Moutain-Forests', and Eilífr[52] found a second opening; he came from behind them and killed them both. Hrafsi entered Orrastaðir Farm, where Kjallakr sat by the fire at a banquet. Hrafsi was in women's clothes. He struck at Kjallakr, but he threw his shield over himself, and the bone of the one man's forearm broke, but the other man was not wounded. Hrafsi went through the door which was in the exterior walls and slew Ásbjǫrn, and then he got away. The sons of Kjallakr paid Þórðr, son of Vífill, to get Hrafsi into a situation where they would have a good chance. He says to Hrafsi that his ox was stuck in a bog. Þórðr carried his shield, and when he saw the sons of Kjallakr, he threw the shield to them. Hrafsi seized Þórðr and threw him down the cliff, and that was the death of him. The sons of Kjallakr did not manage to overpower him[53] until they threw a mast at him. Eilífr stood by idly while they overpowered him.>[54]

About Geirmundr and Hámundr

86. King Hjǫrleifr of the Hǫrðar, who was called 'the Womaniser', he married Æsa the Fair. Their son was Ótryggr, the father of Óblauðr, the father of Hǫgni the White, the father of Úlfr the Squint-Eyed. Another son of Hjǫrleifr was King Hálfr, who commanded Hálfr's Warriors. His mother was Hildr the Thin, the daughter of Hǫgni of Njarðey Island. King Hálfr was the father of King Hjǫrr, the one who avenged his father together with Sǫlvi, son of Hǫgni. King Hjǫrr raided in Bjarmaland.

[51] This place-name story is based on a word play which is not translatable in English: *kambr* (like German *Kamm*) denotes both a 'comb' and a 'mountain ridge'; thus, a 'Mountain Ridge Peninsula' can be explained by a story about a lost comb.

[52] Manuscript: Eyjólfr.

[53] That is, Hrafsi?

[54] This passage is not in the Hauksbók manuscript, but is attributed to it in Skarðsárbók and inserted into his edition of H by Finnur Jónsson.

There he got as plunder Ljúfvina, the daughter of the king of the Bjarmians. She remained behind in Rogaland when King Hjǫrr went to war. Then she gave birth to two sons. The one was called Geirmundr and the other Hámundr. They were very dark. Then her maid gave birth to a son. He was called Leifr, son of the slave Loðhǫttr. Leifr was fair. Therefore the queen swapped boys with the maid and appropriated Leifr to herself.

Yet when the king came home, he spurned Leifr and said that he was puny. Next time the king was out raiding, the queen invited the poet Bragi home and asked him to have a look at the boys. At that time they were three years old. She locked them into one room with Bragi and hid herself on the gallery. Bragi spoke this:

> Two are in here,
> I trust both of them well,
> Hámundr and Geirmundr,
> born to Hjǫrr,
> and Leifr is the third,
> son of Loðhǫttr;
> give food to that one, woman,
> another year he will be worse.

He banged a staff against the gallery where the queen was. When the king came home, she told this to him and showed him his sons. He said that he had never seen such hell-skin. Both brothers have been called that ever since.

Geirmundr Hell-Skin was a warlord. He went raiding in the British Isles, but had his realm in Rogaland. And when he came back from a raiding expedition, when he had been away for a long time, then King Haraldr Finehair had fought in Hafrsfjord with King Eiríkr of the Hǫrðar and Súlki, the King of Rogaland, and Kjǫtvi the Rich, and had gained victory. He had brought all Rogaland under his control and had driven many men from their hereditary land there. Geirmundr then saw no possibility of obtaining a position of honour there. Then he made the decision to go in search of Iceland. With him on the journey went his relative Úlfr the Squint-Eyed, and Steinólfr the Short, the son of Hrólfr the chieftain of Agðir and of Ǫndótt, the sister of Ǫlvir Children's-Man. [Also] Þrándr Thin-Legged and his people.

They sailed together and each of them steered a ship of his own. They reached Breiðafjord and lay at Elliðaey Island. There they learned that the southern part of the fjord was [already] settled, and the western part little or not at all. Geirmundr steered inwards to the Meðalfellsstrǫnd

Coast-Land and took land from Fábeinsá River as far as the Klofasteinar Rocks. He came ashore in Geirmundarvágr Bay and spent the first winter in Búðardalr Valley. Steinólfr took land inland from Klofasteinar Rocks, and Úlfr to the west of the fjord, as will now be told. Þrándr took the islands west of Bjarneyjaflói Bay and lived on Flatey Island. He married the daughter of Gils Ship-Nosed. Their son was Hergils Tight-Arse, who lived on Hergilsey Island. Hergils's daughter was Þorkatla, who was married to Már at Reykjahólar Hills. Hergils married Þórarna, the daughter of Ketill Flat-Footed, son of Ingjaldr. Their son was [Ingjaldr][55] who lived on Hergilsey Island and gave help to Gísli, son of Súrr. For that, Bǫrkr the Fat took the islands away from him, and he bought Hlíð Mountainside on the Þorskafjord. His son was Þórarinn, who was married to Þorgerðr, the daughter of Glúmr, son of Geiri; and their son was Helgu-Steinarr. Þórarinn was in Svínadalr Valley together with Kjartan on the day when he fell.

'Þrándr took the islands west of Bjarneyjaflói Bay and lived on Flatey Island.' *On the island of Flatey.*

Þrándr Thin-Legged lived on Flatey Island when Oddr *skrauti* and his son Þórir came out [to Iceland]. They took land on Þorskafjord. Oddr lived in Skógar, and Þórir went abroad on a raiding expedition. He acquired much gold in Finnmǫrk. He was accompanied by the son of Hallr of Hofstaðir, and when they came to Iceland, Hallr raised a claim on the gold, and great arguments arose about that. The *Saga of the Þorskfirðingar* deals with that. Gold-Þórir lived at Þórisstaðir. He married Ingibjǫrg, the daughter of Gils Ship-Nosed. Their son was Sigmundr.

[55] Missing in the manuscript.

87. Geirmundr went westwards to Strandir Coast-Lands and took land from the west in Rytagnúpr Peak as far as Horn and from there eastwards to Straumnes Peninsula. There he founded four farms. One in Aðalvík Bay; his steward supervised that one. Another in Kjaransvík Bay; his slave Kjaran supervised that one. A third one on the western commons; his slave Bjǫrn supervised that one, he who was convicted for sheep theft when Geirmundr was dead. His confiscated property became a common. The fourth farm Geirmundr had at Barðsvík Bay; his slave Atli supervised that one, and he had twelve slaves under him. And when Geirmundr travelled between his farms, he always had eighty men [with him]. He was very rich in movable property and had a great number of livestock. People say that his pigs grazed on Svínanes 'Peninsula of the Pigs', and his sheep on Hjarðarnes 'Peninsula of the Flock', and he had grazing rights in Bitra. Some say that he also owned a farm in Selárdalr Valley at Geirmundarstaðir on the Steingrímsfjord. Wise men say that he was the noblest of all early settlers in Iceland. And rarely did he have arguments with people here, because he came out [to Iceland] when he was already rather old. He and Kjallakr argued over the land which lay between the Klofningar Cloven Mountain and Fábeinsá River, and they fought on the tilled fields beyond Klofningar; both of them wanted to sow there. Geirmundr got the better of it then. Bjǫrn the Easterner and Vestarr of Eyrr made peace between them. On that occasion, when he went to the meeting, Vestarr came ashore on Vestarsnes Peninsula. Geirmundr hid a lot of property on Andarkelda Moor below Skarð. He married Herríðr, the daughter of Gautr, son of Gautrekr the Generous. Their daughter was Ýrr, who was married to Ketill, their sons Þórhallr and Oddi, the father of Hallvǫr, who was married to Bǫrkr, the son of Þormóðr, son of Þjóstarr. Geirmundr died at Geirmundarstaðir, and there he is buried in a mound in a ship outside the farm enclosure. Geirmundr gave a dwelling place at Ballará River to his friend Hrólfr, son of Kjallakr. His sons were Illugi the Red and Sǫlvi, the father of Þórðr, the father of Magnús, the father of Sǫlvi, the father of Priest Páll in Reykjaholt Forest.

About Steinólfr

88. Steinólfr the Short, the son of Chieftain Hrólfr of Agðir, took land inland from Klofasteinar Stones as far as Grjótvallarmúli Crag and lived in Fagradalr Valley at Steinólfshjalli Mountain-Ledge. He went into the mountains there. In the mountains, he saw a valley, large

and all covered in forest. He saw a clearing in that valley. There he had a farm built and called it Saurbœr 'Mud-Farm', because it was very muddy there, and thus he named the whole valley. The place where the farm was built is now called Torfnes 'Peat Peninsula'. Steinólfr married Eirný, daughter of Þiðrandi. Their son was Þorsteinn the Farmer, and Arndís the Rich was their daughter, the mother of Þórðr, the father of Þorgerðr, who was married to Oddr. Their son was Hrafn the Limerick-Farer, who married Vigdís, the daughter of Þórarinn *fylsenni*. Their son was Snǫrtr, the father of Jódís, who was married to Eyjólfr, son of Hallbjǫrn. Steinólfr lost three pigs. They were found two years later in Svínadalr 'Pigs' Valley', and there were thirty of them altogether then. Steinólfr also took Steinólfsdalr Valley on Króksfjord.

89. A man was called Lowlands-Bjǫrn. He married Þuríðr, the daughter of Steinólfr the Short. On the advice of Steinólfr he took the western valley at Saurbœr. He lived at Sléttu-Bjarnarstaðir 'Lowlands-Bjǫrn's Steads', above Þverfell Mountain. His son was Þjóðrekr, who married Arngerðr, the daughter of Þorbjǫrn, son of Shields-Bjǫrn. Their sons were Manslaughters-Sturla, who built the farm at Staðarhóll Hill, and Knǫttr, the father of Ásgeirr, and Þorbjǫrn and Þjóðrekr, after whom the rock outcrop on Kollafjarðarheiði, the 'Heath of Kollafjord', is named. At Saurbœr Farm it seemed too crowded to Þjóðrekr, son of Lowlands-Bjǫrn. Therefore he moved to Ísafjord. There the saga about Þorbjǫrn and Hávarðr the Lame takes place.

90. Óláfr Hide, whom Ormr the Thin drove away from Óláfsvík, took Belgsdalr 'Hide Valley', and lived at Belgsstaðir 'Hide-Steads', until Þjóðrekr and his people drove him away. Then he took land inland from the jutting crag of Grjótvallarmúli and lived in Óláfsdalr 'Óláfr's Valley'. His son was Þorvaldr, the one who handed a case of sheep theft against Þórarinn the Yelling over to Ǫgmundr, son of Knucklebone-Steinn. For that he slew Ǫgmundr at the Þorskafjord Assembly.

91. Gils Ship-Nose took Gilsfjord between Óláfsdalr Valley and the jutting crag of Króksfjarðarmúli; he lived at the stepped cliffs of Kleifar. His son was Heðinn, the father of Halldórr Garpsdalr-*goði*, the father of Þorvaldr in Garpsdalr Valley, who married Guðrún, daughter of Ósvífr.

Chapter

92. Þórarinn Angle took Króksdalr Valley 'Angle Valley', as far as the Hafrafell Mountain from Króksfjarðarnes 'Angle-Fjord Peninsula'.[56] He fought with Steinólfr the Short about Steinólfsdalr Valley and rowed after him with twenty men when he went from the shieling together with seven men. They fought at the mouth of Fagradalsá River on the sand banks. Then men from a house arrived at the scene to help Steinólfr. Then Þórarinn Angle fell together with three of his men and seven of Steinólfr's men. Their mounds are there.

93. Ketill Flat-Footed, the son of Þorbjǫrn Whale-Bone, took Berufjord. His daughter was Þórarna, who was married to Hergils Tight-Arse, as was written above.

94. Úlfr the Squint-Eyed, the son of Hǫgni the White, took the whole Reykjanes Peninsula between Þorskafjord and the Hafrafell Mountain. He married Bjǫrg, the daughter of Eyvindr the Eastman, a sister of Helgi the Skinny. Their son was Atli the Red, who married Þorbjǫrg, the sister of Steinólfr the Short. Their son was Már at Hólar Hills, who married Þorkatla, the daughter of Hergils Tight-Arse. Their son was Ari. He was driven off his course[57] to Hvítramannaland. Some call that Greater Ireland. That lies in the sea to the west, near Vínland the Good. It is said to lie six days' sailing west of Ireland. Ari was not able to sail back from there and was baptised there. Hrafn the Limerick-Farer, who had long been in Limerick in Ireland, was the first to tell about this. Þorkell, son of Gellir, declared that men from Iceland said, when they had heard Jarl Þorfinnr tell[58] of it in Orkney, that Ari had been recognised in Hvítramannaland and was not able to sail back from there, but was highly valued there. Ari married Þorgerðr, the daughter of Álfr from Dalir. Their sons were Þorgils and Guðleifr and Illugi. That is the family of the Reyknesingar.

[56] The topographically descriptive nature of the place names jars with their derivation from the nickname of a person, strongly suggesting that the connection of a man by the name of 'Þórarinn Angle' with the angular features of the local landscape is a secondary explanation, rather than the origin, of the toponyms of this story.

[57] *sæhafi* (*sic leg.*); the manuscript reading *sæfari* is certainly wrong (Finnur Jónsson).

[58] Missing in the manuscript.

95. Hallsteinn, the son of Þórólfr Beard-of-Mostr, took the Þorskafjarðarstrǫnd Coast-Land and lived at Hallsteinsnes Peninsula. He sacrificed to Thor that he might send him high-seat pillars, and for that he gave his son. After that, a tree was washed ashore on his land. That was sixty-three ells long and two fathoms thick. It was used for high-seat pillars, and from it the high-seat pillars on nearly every farm around the side-branch of the fjord were made. The place where the tree was washed ashore is now called Grenitrésnes 'Pine Tree Headland'. Hallsteinn had plundered in Scotland, and there he captured those slaves whom he had brought from abroad. Hallsteinn married Ósk, the daughter of Þorsteinn the Red. Their son was Þorsteinn, who invented the intercalary week.

96. A man was called Þorbjǫrn Thread-Loop, the son of Bǫðmóðr from Skut. He went to Iceland and took Djúpafjord and Grónes Peninsula as far as Gufufjord 'Steam Fjord'. His son was Þorgils at Þorgilsstaðir in Djúpafjord, the father of Kollr, who married Þuríðr, daughter of Þórir, son of Jarl Hallaðr. Their son was Þorgils, who married Otkatla, the daughter of Jǫrundr, son of Atli the Red. Their son was Jǫrundr. He married Hallveig, the daughter of Oddi, son of Ýrr and Ketill Steam. Snorri was a son of Jǫrundr; he married Ásný, the daughter of Manslaughter-Sturla. Their son was Gils, who married Þordís, daughter of Guðlaugr and of Þorkatla, daughter of Halldórr, son of Snorri the *goði*. And Gils' son [was Þórðr],[59] who married Vigdís, daughter of Svertingr. Their son was Hvamm-Sturla.

97. A man was called Ketill Steam, the son of Ørlygr, son of Bǫðvarr, son of Vígsterkr. Ørlygr married Signý, daughter of Óblauðr, and sister of Hǫgni the White. Their son Ketill came out [to Iceland] late in the time of the settlements. He had been plundering in the British Isles and had brought Irish slaves from Ireland. One was called Þormóðr, another Flóki; Kóri and Svartr and two named Skorri. Ketill took Rosmhvalanes Peninsula. There he spent the first winter at Gufuskálar 'Steam-Houses', and in spring he went further inland on the peninsula and spent the second winter at Gufunes 'Steam-Peninsula'. Then Skorri the Elder and Flóki ran away together with two women and a lot of livestock. They were in hiding in Skorraholt 'Skorri's Forest'; but they were killed in Flókadalr 'Flóki's Valley' and Skorradalr 'Skorri's Valley'. Ketill did not get a residence on the headlands, and he went further into Borgarfjord to

[59] Missing in the manuscript.

find a residence for himself, and he spent the third winter at Gufuskálar 'Steam-Houses', on Gufá 'Steam River'. The fourth winter he spent at Gufuskálar on Snæfells- nes. Early in spring he went deeper into Breiðafjord to find a residence for himself. There he was at Guðmundarstaðir 'Guðmundr's Steads', and asked for the hand of Ýrr, the daughter of Guðmundr, and got her.

Geirmundr then pointed Ketill to lands west of the fjord. Ketill's slaves ran away from Snæfellsnes Peninsula and in the night appeared at Lambastaðir 'Lambi's Steads'. At that time, Þórðr, the son of Þorgeirr *lambi*, lived there. The slaves then set fire to the buildings and burned Þórðr and all the members of his household inside. Then they broke into a storage shed and took a large amount of movable property and turned in the direction of Álptanes Peninsula. In the morning, when they had just gone away, Lambi the Strong, the son of Þórðr, came from the assembly. He went after them and had men with him; and when the slaves saw that, everyone ran his own way. They caught Kóri on Kóranes 'Kóri's Peninsula', and some went into the water. They took Svartr on Svartssker 'Svartr's Skerry', and Skorri on Skorrey 'Skorri-Island',[60] and Þormóðr on Þormóðssker 'Þormóðr's Skerry'. That is a nautical mile away from the land.

Ketill Steam took Gufufjord 'Steam Fjord', and Skálanes Peninsula as far as the Kollafjord. Oddi was the son of Ketill and Ýrr; he married Þorlaug, daughter of Hrólfr from Ballará River and of Þuríðr, the daughter of Valþjófr, son of Ørlygr from Esjuberg Cliff.

98. Temple-Kolli, son of Hróaldr, took Kollafjord and Kvígandisfjord and sold his land claim to various men, but he went to the Laxárdalr Valley to Hǫskuldsstaðir. He was called Kollr-of-the-Valleys. His son was Hǫskuldr, who married Hallfríðr, the daughter of Bjǫrn, who took Bjarnarfjord north of Steingrímsfjord. Their son was Þorlákr, the father of Bolli, who married Guðrún, daughter of Ósvífr.

99. Knútr, the son of Þórólfr Sparrow, is called Knútr-of-the-Peninsulas; he took the whole peninsula from Kvígandafjord as far as the Barðastrǫnd Coast. He married Eyja, the daughter of Ingjaldr, son of Helgi the Skinny. Their children were Einarr, the father of Steinólfr

[60] Since *skorri* is also the name of a kind of bird (the oystercatcher?), the story of the slave caught there is likely to be yet another instance of a consciously fanciful story invented to 'explain' a semantically clear place name in a deliberately grotesque way.

Trout, the father of Salgerðr, the mother of Bárðr the Black; and Eyjólfr, who was the stepfather of Þorbjǫrg Charcoal-Brown, daughter of Glúmr, about whom Þormóðr made a poem—and Þorgrímr was a son of Eyjólfr, the father of Yngvildr, who was married to Úlfheðinn at Víðimýrr Moor; and Þóra, the mother of Moor-Knjúkr in Dýrafjord. He was the father of Þorgautr, the father of Steinólfr, the father of Þorkell and of Halla, the mother of Steinunn, the mother of Hrafn, son of Sveinbjǫrn, and of Herdís, who was married to Hallr, son of Gizurr the Law-Speaker. The daughter of Hrafn was Steinunn, the mother of Sir Hrafn and of Halla and of Herdís, who was married to Svarthǫfði, son of Dugfúss. Their son was Óli, who married Salgerðr, daughter of Jón. Their daughter was Steinunn, who was married to Haukr, son of Erlendr.

100. Geirsteinn Jaw, with the advice of Knjúkr, took Kjálkafjord 'Jaw's Fjord', and Hjarðarnes Peninsula. His son was Þorgils, the father of Steinn the Dane, the father of Vigdís, the mother of Þórunn, the mother of Þorgeirr, the father of Abbot Þorfinnr.

101. Geirleifr, the son of Eiríkr, son of Hǫgni the White, took the Barðastrǫnd Coast-Land between Vatsfjord and Berghlíð Mountainside. He was the father of Oddleifr and Helgi Cormorant. Oddleifr was the father of Gestr the Wise and of Þorsteinn and of Æsa, who was married to Þorgils, the son of Grímr on Grímsnes. Gestr's children were Þórðr and Halla, who was married to Snorri, son of Álfr of Dalir Valleys. Their son was Þorgils. Another daughter of Gestr was Þórey, who was married to Þorgils. Their son was Þórarinn, the father of Jódís, the mother of Illugi, the father of Birna, the mother of Eyvindr, the father of Steingrímr, the father of Helga, the mother of Jórunn, the mother of Haukr, son of Erlendr. Geirleifr married Jóra, the daughter of Helgi. Þorfiðr was the name of Geirleifr's third son; he married Guðrún, daughter of Ásólfr. Þorsteinn, son of Oddleifr, was the father of Ísgerðr, who was married to Bǫlverkr, the son of Eyjólfr the Grey. Their son was the law-speaker Gellir. Vénŷ was a daughter of Þorsteinn's, the mother of Þórðr Crow-Nosed.

Chapter

102. Ármóðr the Red, son of Þorbjǫrn, the fosterbrother of Geirleifr, took Rauðasandr 'Red Sand-Plain'. His sons were Ǫrnólfr and Þorbjǫrn, the father of Hrólfr *hinn rauðsenzki*.

103. Þórólfr Sparrow came out [to Iceland] together with Ørlygr and

took Patreksfjord in the west and the Víkr Bays west of Barð with the exception of Kollsvík Bay; there lived Kollr, the foster-brother of Ørlygr. Þórólfr also took Keflavík Bay south of Barð. Knjúkr-of-the-Peninsulas and Ingólfr the Strong and Geirþjófr were the sons of Þórólfr Sparrow. A daughter of Ingólfr's was Þórarna, who was married to Þorsteinn, son of Oddleifr.

104. Þorbjǫrn Whalebone and Þorbjǫrn Dusk, the sons of [Bǫðvarr][61] Bladder-Baldhead, came out [to Iceland] together with Ørlygr. They took half of Patreksfjord and the whole of Tálknafjord as far as Kópanes Peninsula.

105. Ketill Flat-Footed, the son of Þorbjǫrn Whalebone, took all the Dalir Valleys, from Kópanes Peninsula as far as Dufansdalr Valley. He gave his daughter Þórarna to Hergils Tight-Arse. Then Ketill moved southwards into Breiðafjord and took Berufjord near Reykjanes Peninsula.

106. A famous man was called Ǫrn. He left Rogaland because of the tyranny of King Haraldr. He took the whole of Arnarfjord.[62] He spent the winter on Tjaldanes Peninsula, the 'Peninsula of the Tents', because there the sun did not disappear during the short midwinter days.

107. Ánn the Red-Natured, the son of Grímr Woolly-Cheeks from Hrafnista and of Helga, the daughter of Án Bow-Bender, fell out with King Haraldr and therefore left the land to go on a raiding expedition to the British Isles. He plundered in Ireland and there got Grélǫð, the daughter of Jarl Bjartmarr. They went to Iceland and came to Arnarfjord a year later than Ǫrn. Ánn spent the first winter in Dufansdalr Valley. There it seemed to Grélǫð that bad smells came out of the earth. Ǫrn got news that Hámundr Hell-Skin, his relative, was northwards on Eyjafjord. Therefore he sold all the lands between Langanes Peninsula and Stapi Rock Steeple to Ánn the Red-Natured. He founded a farm at Eyrr Gravel-Bank. There it seemed to Grélǫð that a scent of honey came from the grass. To his slave Dufann, Ánn gave Dufansdalr Valley.

Ánn's son was Bjartmarr, the father of two Végestrs and of Helgi, the father of Þuríðr and of Arnkatla. Bjartmarr's daughter was Þórhildr, who was married to Vésteinn, son of Végeirr, and Auðr and Vésteinn were their children. Hjallkárr was a freedman of Ánn's; his son was Bjǫrn,

[61] Missing in the manuscript.

[62] 'Ǫrn's Fjord' or 'Eagle-Fjord'.

a slave of Bjartmarr's. He gave Bjǫrn his freedom. Then he[63] became well-off. Végestr objected to that and pierced him with a spear, but Bjǫrn beat him to death with a spade.

108. Geirþjófr, son of Valþjófr, furthermore took land on Arnarfjord, Forsfjord, Reykjarfjord, Trostansfjord, Geirþjófsfjord, and all the way to Langanes Peninsula, and lived on Geirþjófsfjord. He married Salgerðr, the daughter of Úlfr the Squint-Eyed. Their son was Hǫgni, the father of Atli, the father of Hǫskuldr, the father of Atli, the father of Bárðr the Black, the father of Sveinbjǫrn, the father of Hrafn, the father of Steinunn, the mother of Sir Hrafn.

109. Eiríkr was the name of the man who took Keldudalr Valley south of Dýrafjord and Sléttanes Peninsula as far as Stapi Rock Steeple on Arnarfjord and as far as Outer-Háls Ridge on Dýrafjord. He was the father of Þorkell, the father of Þórðr, the father of Þorkell, the father of Steinólfr, the father of Þórðr, the father of Þorleif, the mother of Þóra, the mother of Guðmundr Piglet, who married Solveig, the daughter of Jón, son of Loptr. Their children were Magnús the *goði* and Þorlákr, the father of Bishop Árni, and Þóra, the mother of Jarl Gizurr.

'Vésteinn, the son of Végeirr, the brother of Vébjǫrn Champion-of-Sogn, took land between the Hálsar Mountain Ridges on Dýrafjord and lived in Haukadalr Valley.' *The view up Haukadalur valley.*

[63] That is, Bjǫrn.

110. Vésteinn, the son of Végeirr, the brother of Vébjǫrn Champion-of-Sogn, took land between the Hálsar Mountain Ridges on Dýrafjord and lived in Haukadalr Valley. He married Þórhildr, daughter of Bjartmarr. Þorbjǫrn Sourly came out to [Iceland to find] a fully settled land. Vésteinn gave half of Haukadalr Valley to him. His children were Gísli, who married Auðr, daughter of Vésteinn; and Þorkell, who married Sigríðr, daughter of Lowlands-Bjǫrn; and Þórdís, who was married to Þorgrímr, son of Þorsteinn; their son was Snorri the *goði*.

111. A man was called Dýri, who on the advice of Jarl Rǫgnvaldr went to Iceland from Sunnmœrr. He took Dýrafjord and lived at Hálsar Ridges. His son was Hrafn, who lived at Ketilseyrr Gravel-Bank, the father of Þuríðr, who was married to Vésteinn, son of Vésteinn; their sons were Bergr and Helgi.

112. A man was called Þórðr, son of Víkingr, about whom most people have said that he was a son of King Haraldr Finehair. To him Dýri gave land between Þúfa Mound on Hjallanes Peninsula and Jarðfallsgil Glen, and he lived at Alviðra. He married Þjóðhildr, the sister of Helgi the Skinny. Their son was Þorkell Champion the Rich, who lived there later on. His sons were Þórðr *ǫrvǫnd* and Eyjólfr, the father of Gísli, who married Hallgerðr, the daughter of Vermundr the Thin. Their son was Brandr, the father of Guðmundr the Priest in Hjarðarholt Forest, the father of Priest Magnús. Þorvaldr the White was the name of another son of Þórðr, son of Víkingr. He married Þóra, daughter of Knjúkr. Their son was Þórðr the White or *ǫrvǫnd*, who married Ásdís, daughter of Þormóðr and the mother of Úlfr the Marshal. A daughter of Þórðr *ǫrvǫnd* was Otkatla, who was married to Sturla, son of Þjóðrekr. Their son was Þórðr, who married Hallbera, the daughter of Snorri the *goði*. Ásný was a daughter of Sturla, who was married to Snorri, son of Jǫrundr. Their daughter was Þórdís, the mother of Hǫskuldr the Physician, the father of Margrét, the mother of Abbot Þorfinnr.

113. Ingjaldr, son of Brúni, took Ingjaldssandr Sand-Plain between Hjallanes Peninsula and Ófœra. He was the father of Þorgrímr, the father of Þorbjǫrn Whalebone, the father of Ljótr the Wise, as was written above.

114. Hallvarðr Wind-Gust was in the battle against King Haraldr in Hafrsfjord. He went to Iceland from Sætr, from Hordaland, and took Sugandafjord, 'Wind-Gust-Fjord', and Skálavík Bay.

115. Ǫnundr, son of Víkingr, the brother of Þórðr at Alviðra, took the whole of Ǫnundarfjord and lived at Eyrr Gravel-Bank.

116. Þuríðr Channel-Filler and her son Knucklebone-Steinn went from Hálogaland to Iceland and took Bolungarvík Bay and lived at Vatnsnes Peninsula. She was called 'Channel-Filler' for the reason that during a famine in Hálogaland she brought it about by magic that every channel was full of herring. She also established the Kvíarmið Fishing-Ground in the Ísafjarðardjúp, the 'Deep Sea of the Ísafjord', and for that she took a hornless ewe from every free farmer on Ísafjord. The sons of Knucklebone-Steinn were Ǫgmundr and Egill.

'Þuríðr Channel-Filler and her son Knucklebone-Steinn went from Hálogaland to Iceland and took Bolungarvík Bay and lived at Vatnsnes Peninsula.'
The view across Bolungarvík Bay towards the village of the same name.

117. Helgi was the name of the son of Hrólfr from Gnúpufell Mountain, and on his mother's side he was an Upplander and grew up there. He went to Iceland to visit his relatives. He came into Eyjafjord, and the land was then completely settled there. After that he wanted to go abroad [again], but was driven back into Súgandafjord. He spent the winter with Hallvarðr, and in spring he went to search for a dwelling-place for himself. He found a fjord and there he found a harpoon at the flood-tide mark. He called it Skutilsfjord 'Harpoon-Fjord'. He lived there then. His son was Þorsteinn the Luckless. He went abroad and killed a follower of Jarl Hákon, son of Grjótgarðr, and Eyvindr, the jarl's counsellor, sent him to Vébjǫrn Sygnatrausti. He received him, but

Védís, his sister, advised against it. Therefore Vébjǫrn sold his estate and went to Iceland.

118. Þórólfr Brackish-Taste took part of Skutilsfjord and Skálavík Bay and lived there.

119. Eyvindr Knee went from Agðir to Iceland, with his wife Þuríðr Sleeping Sow. They took Álptafjord and Seyðisfjord and lived there. Their sons were Þorleifr, who has been mentioned above, and Valbrandr, and Bjargey, who was married to Hávarðr the Lame. Their son was Óláfr.

120. Geirr was the name of a famous man in Sogn. He was called Vé-Geirr 'Sanctuary-Geirr', because he was a great sacrificer. He had many children. Sygnakappi 'Champion-of-the-people-of-Sogn' was the oldest of his sons, and Vésteinn and Véþormr, Vémundr and Végestr, Véþorn, and a daughter Védís. These siblings went to Iceland. They had a hard and long voyage. In autumn they took Hlǫðuvík Bay west of Horn. There, Vébjǫrn held a great sacrifice, and said that Jarl Hákon was also making sacrifices that day to do them harm. And while he [Vébjǫrn] was at the sacrifice, his brothers urged him to depart. And they did not heed the sacrifice and put to sea. The same day they wrecked their ship in a storm under big cliffs. They just barely managed to get up there, and Vébjǫrn went ahead. That is now called Sygnakleif 'Cliff of the People of Sogn'. And in winter Atli, a slave of Geirmundr Hell-Skin, took them all in, and he asked them not to pay for their stay; he said that Geirmundr did not lack food. And when Atli met Geirmundr, Geirmundr asked why he was so brazen as to take such men in by his own decision.

Atli replied: 'Because it will be remembered for as long as Iceland is inhabited how great the man must be whose slave dared to do so without his permission.'

Geirmundr replies: 'For these actions of yours you shall receive your freedom and the farm that you have taken care of.'

And Atli then became a great man.

In spring Vébjǫrn took land between Skǫtufjord and Hestfjord, as far as he could go around in a day, and over and above that the land which is called Folafótr. Vébjǫrn was a great warrior, and there is a long saga about him. He gave his sister Védís in marriage to Grímólfr in Unaðsdalr Valley. They came to disagree and Vébjǫrn killed him near Grímólfsvatn 'Grímólfr's Lake'. For that, Vébjǫrn and three other men were killed at the Þingeyrar Assembly on Dýrafjord.

121. Gunnsteinn and Halldórr were the names of the sons of Gunnbjǫrn, after whom the Gunnbjarnarsker 'Gunnbjǫrn's Skerries' are named. Gunnbjǫrn was the son of Úlfr Crow. They took Skǫtufjord and Laugardalr Valley and Ǫgrsvík Bay as far as Mjóvafjord. Bersi was the son of Halldórr, the father of Þormóðr Kolbrún's-Poet. There lived then in Laugardalr Valley Þorbjǫrn, son of Þjóðrekr, who killed Óláfr, the son of Hávarðr the Lame and of Bjargey, daughter of Valbrandr. That led to the saga of the Ísfjord people and the killing of Þorbjǫrn.

About Snæbjǫrn

122. Snæbjǫrn, the son of Eyvindr the Eastman, the brother of Helgi the Skinny, took land between Mjóvafjord and Langadalsá River and lived on Vatsfjord. His son was Hólmsteinn, the father of Snæbjǫrn Boar, who killed Hallbjǫrn, the son of Oddr at Kiðjaberg Cliff near the Hallbjarnarvǫrður Cairns. Before that, he [Hallbjǫrn] had killed his wife Hallgerðr, the daughter of Tongue-Oddr. The mother of Snæbjǫrn Boar was Kjǫlvǫr, and he and Tongue-Oddr were the sons of two sisters. Snæbjǫrn was fostered by Þóroddr on Þingnes Peninsula, and sometimes he was with Tongue-Oddr or his mother. Hallbjǫrn, the son of Oddr from Kiðjaberg Cliff, son of Hallkell, the brother of Ketilbjǫrn the Old, received in marriage Hallgerðr, the daughter of Tongue-Oddr. They spent the first winter with Oddr; Snæbjǫrn Boar was then there. There was little love between the married couple.

Hallbjǫrn prepared his move in spring at the moving-days, and when he was busy with his preparations, Oddr left the house for the hot spring in Reykjaholt Forest. His sheep folds were there. And he did not want to be present when Hallbjǫrn left, because he suspected that Hallgerðr would not want to go with him. Oddr had always made amends between them. When Hallbjǫrn had saddled their horses, he went into the women's chamber. And Hallgerðr sat on the bench and combed her hair; the hair fell all around her and onto the floor. Of all the women of Iceland she was, alongside Hallgerðr Long-Trousers, the one with the most beautiful hair. Hallbjǫrn told her to get up and leave. She sat still and remained silent. Then he took hold of her and [tried to][64] lift her up. Three times this happened. Hallbjǫrn remained standing in front of her and said:

[64] There is no negation in the manuscript. In the text of Hauksbók, it seems as if he succeeded in lifting her up, but Hallbjǫrn's failure is required by the development of the action and the Sturlubók recension confirmes that the absence of a negation is a copying mistake.

> The veil-shrouded goddess of the ale-casks
> makes me play the fool in front of the
> stem of her headgear. It alienates me
> from the oak of the arms.
> I will never gain improvement
> from the bride; sorrow touches me
> in the heart's roof.
> Misfortune makes me pale.

Goddess of the ale-casks = housewife, woman. Stem of her headgear = neck (meaning that the woman turns her back to her husband). Oak of the arms = woman. Heart's roof = chest.

He twisted the hair around his hand and tries to pull her from the bench, but she sat and did not move in response. Then he drew his sword and struck her head off. Then he went out and rode away. They were four[65] men altogether and had two pack-horses. Few people were at home. Immediately [a messenger] was sent to tell Oddr.

Oddr says: 'Tell this to Snæbjǫrn at Kjǫlvararstaðir, but I will not ride after them.'

Snæbjǫrn rode after them with eleven men. And when Hallbjǫrn and his men saw the mounted pursuit, Hallbjǫrn's companions asked him to ride away. But he did not want to. Snæbjǫrn and his men caught up with them at the hills which are now called Hallbjarnarvǫrður 'Hallbjǫrn's Cairns'. Hallbjǫrn and his men went onto the hill and defended themselves from there. There, four[66] of Snæbjǫrn's men fell, and both of Hallbjǫrn's companions. Then Snæbjǫrn hewed one of Hallbjǫrn's feet off at the ankle. Then he hobbled onto the southern height and killed another two men there before he fell. Therefore there are three cairns on one hill and five on the other.

Snæbjǫrn had a ship in the mouth of Grímsá River, and Hrólfr *hinn rauðsenzki* bought a half share. They each had twelve men. Snæbjǫrn was accompanied by Þorkell and Sumarliði, the sons of Þorgeirr the Red, son of Einarr the Stafholt-Dweller. Snæbjǫrn took along Þóroddr from Þingsnes, his relative through fosterage, and his wife; and Hrólfr took along Styrbjǫrn, who spoke this after his dream:

[65] Probably *iiij* is a mistake for *iij*, as later in the story Hallbjǫrn is only accompanied by two men, not by three, which agrees with the Sturlubók recension.

[66] Sturlubók recension: three. This seems to be the correct number, since it agrees with the number of graves given a few sentences later.

I see the deaths
of us both,
most horrid,
northwest in the sea.
Frost and cold,
all kinds of portents;
I know from such
of Snæbjǫrn's killing.

They went to search for the Gunnbjarnarsker skerries and found land. Snæbjǫrn did not want to let [them] explore during the night. Styrbjǫrn went off the ship and found a purse in a burial mound and kept it back. Snæbjǫrn hit him with an axe; then the purse fell down. They built a house, placing it in a snowdrift. Þorkell, the son of Red, found that there was water on a boathook which was sticking out through the window of the house; that was towards the end of winter. Then they dug themselves out. Snæbjǫrn worked on the ship, and Þóroddr and his wife did Snæbjǫrn's share at the house, and Styrbjǫrn and his people did Hrólfr's share; others went hunting. Styrbjǫrn slew Þóroddr and both he and Hrólfr [slew] Snæbjǫrn. The sons of Red and all the others swore oaths to save their lives. They reached Hálogaland and went from there to Iceland and came to Vaðill Ford. Þorkell Rag told this, who had gone earlier than the sons of Red.

Hrólfr built a fort on Strandarheiði Heath. Þorkell Rag sent Sveinungr for Hrólfr's head. First he went to Hermundr at Mýrr Moor, then to Óláfr at Drangar Rock Towers, then to Gestr at Hagi Pasture. He sent him to Hrólfr, his friend. Sveinungr slew Hrólfr and Styrbjǫrn. Then he went to Hagi Pasture. Gestr exchanged his axe for a sword and got him two piebald horses and had a man ride via Vaðill Ford all the way to Kollafjord. He sent Þorbjǫrn the Strong to fetch the horses home. He slew him at Sveinungseyrr Gravel-Bank, because Sveinungr's sword broke below the hilt. Therefore Rag boasted in front of Gestr, on the occasion when their cleverness was being compared, that he had got to Gestr by making him send a man himself for the head of his friend.

123. Óláfr Dye-Head took land from Langadalsá River to Sandeyrará River and lived in Unaðsdalr Valley. He married Þuríðr, daughter of Gunnsteinn. Their son was Grímólfr, who married Védís.

124. Þórólfr Fast-Holding was the name of a famous man in Sogn. He fell out with Jarl Hákon, son of Grjótgarðr, and he went to Iceland. And he took land from Sandeyrará River as far as Gýgjarsporsá, the 'River

of the Ogress's Track', in Hrafnsfjord and lived at Snæfjǫll Mountains. His son was Ófeigr, the father of Otkatla.

125. Ørlygr, the son of Bǫðvarr, [son] of Vígsterkr, he went to Iceland because of the tyranny of King Haraldr Finehair and spent the first winter with Geirmundr Hell-Skin. And in spring Geirmundr gave him a dwelling-place in Aðalvík Bay and the lands that belong to it. Ørlygr married Signý, the daughter [of Óblauðr, and sister] of Hǫgni the White. Their son was Ketill Steam, who married Ýrr, daughter of Geirmundr. Ørlygr took possession of Slétta Plain and Jǫkulsfjord.

126. Hella-Bjǫrn, the son of Herfinnr and Halla, was a great Viking; he was always an enemy of King Haraldr. He came to Bjarnarfjord in Iceland with a ship all covered in shields; since then he has been called Bjǫrn-of-the-Shields. He took land from Straumnes Peninsula as far as Drangar Rocks. He lived in Skjalda-Bjarnarvík 'Shield-Bjǫrn's Bay', and he had another farm on Bjarnarnes 'Bjǫrn's Peninsula'. There one can see the extensive ruins of his house. His son was Þorbjǫrn, the father of Arngerðr, who was married to Þjóðrekr, son of Bjǫrn-of-Slétta. Their sons were Þorbjǫrn and Sturla and Þjóðrekr.

127. Geirólfr was the name of a man who wrecked his ship at Geirólfsgnúpr 'Geirólfr's Overhanging Peak'. On the advice of Bjǫrn, he lived under the overhanging peak after that.

128. Herrøðr hvikatimbr was a noble man. He was killed on the decree of King Haraldr. And his three sons went to Iceland and took land on the Strandir Coastlands. Eyvindarfjord to Eyvindr; Ófeigr, Ófeigsfjord; Ingólfr, Ingólfsfjord. From then on they lived there.

129. Eiríkr String was the name of a man who took land from Ingólfsfjord as far as Veiðilausa and Trékyllisvík Bay. He married Álǫf, the daughter of Ingólfr of Ingólfsfjord. Their son was Flosi, who lived in Vík Bay at the time when some Norwegians wrecked their ship there and built out of the wrecked ship the one which they called Trékylli. On it Flosi went abroad and was driven back into Øxarfjord. From that the *Saga of Bǫðmóðr* was made.

130. Ǫnundr Wooden-Foot [was the name of] a son of Ófeigr *burlufótr*, son of Ívarr Scouring-Rush. Ǫnundr stood against King Haraldr in Hafrsfjord and lost his foot there. After that he went to Iceland and took land from the stepped cliffs of Kleifar as far as Ófœra, Kaldbaksvík Bay, Kolbeinsvík Bay, Byrgisvík Bay, and lived in Kaldbakr until old

age. He was the brother of Guðbjǫrg, the mother of Guðbrandr Ball, the father of Ásta, the mother of King Óláfr the Holy. Ǫnundr had four sons: One was called Grettir; the second Þorgeirr Bottle-Back; the third Ásgeirr Eider-Drake, the father of Kálfr and of Hrefna, who was married to Kjartan, and of Þuríðr, who was married to Þorkell kuggi and later was married to Steinþórr, son of Óláfr Peacock; and the fourth son of Ǫnundr was Þorgrímr Hoary Head, the father of Ásmundr, the father of Grettir the Strong.

131. Bjǫrn was the name of the man who took Bjarnarfjord. He married Ljúfa. Their son was Svanr, who lived at Svanshóll Hill.

132. Steingrímr took the whole of Steingrímsfjord and lived on Trǫllatunga 'Troll Tongue'. His son was Þórir, the father of Halldórr, the father of Þorvaldr Sand-*goði*, the father of Bitterness-Oddi, the father of Steinþórr, the father of Oddr, the father of Rowlock-Snorri, the father of Oddr Monk and Þorlákr[67] and Þórarinn Rogue.

133. Kolli was the name of the man who took Kollafjord and Skriðinsenni Precipice and dwelt under Fell Mountain as long as he lived.

134. A man was called Þorbjǫrn Bitterness, and he was a great Viking and a villain. He went to Iceland with his whole household and took the fjord which is now called Bitra 'Bitterness' and lived there. Somewhat later, Guðlaugr, the brother of Gils Ship-Nosed, wrecked his ship out there on the headland which is now called Guðlaugshǫfði 'Guðlaugr's Headland'. Guðlaugr and his wife and daughter got ashore, but all other people were lost. Then he came to Þorbjǫrn Bitterness, and he murdered both husband and wife, but he took the girl and brought her up. And when Gils Ship-Nosed became aware of this, he set out and took revenge for his brother and killed Þorbjǫrn Bitterness and several other men in addition. Guðlaugsvík 'Guðlaugr's Bay' is named after Guðlaugr.

135. A man was called Bálki, the son of Blæingr, son of Sóti of Sótanes Peninsula. He went to Iceland because of the tyranny of King Haraldr and took the whole of Hrútafjord and lived at each of the two farms called Bálkastaðir, and lastly at Bœr Farm, and died there. His son was Bersi the Godless, who first lived at Bersastaðir on Hrútafjord, and afterwards he took Langavatsdalr Valley, as is written above.

136. Arndís the Rich, the daughter of Steinólfr the Humble, then

[67] Other recensions: Þórólfr.

took land in Hrútafjord outwards from Borðeyrr Gravel-Bank. She lived at Bœr Farm. Her son was Þórðr, who earlier lived on Múli Crag at Saurbœr Farm.

137. Grenjuðr and Þrǫstr, the sons of Hermundr *hǫlknir*, took land on Hrútafjord further in from Borðeyrr Gravel-Bank and lived at the gravel hills of Melar. The son of Þrǫstr was Þorkell at Kerseyrr Gravel-Bank, the father of Guðrún, who was married to Þorbjǫrn *þyna*, the son of Hrómundr the Lame. They lived at Fagrabrekka Slope. Þorleifr Hrómundr's-Fosterling was their son. A son of Hrómundr was called Hásteinn. They all shared one household. Þórir was the name of a son of [Þorkell],[68] son of Þrǫstr. He lived at the gravel hills of Melar. His daughter was called Helga.

At that time, Fraud-Helgi and his brother Jǫrundr came out to Borðeyrr Gravel-Bank. They were Vikings. They all went to the gravel hills of Melar. There were twelve lads coming from the sea. Then Helgi married Helga, daughter of Þórir. Hrómundr and his people lost stud-horses. They ascribed that to Helgi and his people. And Miðfjord-Skeggi summoned them to court to the General Assembly for theft; and Hrómundr and his people were to guard the district and had a good fort at Brekka Slope. The Norwegians prepared their ship. It happened one morning, when a raven came to the skylight at Brekka and cried out loud, that Hrómundr said:

Out at sea I hear the black-tinted
swan of the wound-thorn's
companies cry at daybreak,
meat wakes the bold of mood.
In such a way strife's hawk crowed
earlier, when the cuckoos of Odin's guile
spoke a prophecy, when
fight-nourishers were doomed.

Wound-thorn = sword; sword's companies = warriors; swan of the warriors = raven. The bold of mood = the raven. Strife's hawk = raven. Cuckoo of Odin's guile = raven. Fight-nourisher = warrior.

Þorbjǫrn said:

[68] Manuscript: Þórir. Other minor misreadings in this sentence have also been emended.

Spattered with hail, the seagull
of the slaughter-heap's wave is jubilant,
which comes to the corpses' sea.
Wrath craves morning-venison.
Thus once crowed the corpses' cuckoo
from old *eiðs*-timber, when
the warlords' hawks
wanted the wounds' mead.

Slaughter-heap's wave = blood. Seagull of blood = raven. Corpses' sea = blood. Corpses' cuckoo = raven. The meaning of *eiðs* is unknown; the whole phrase may be a raven kenning. Hawk of the warlords = raven. Mead of the wounds = blood.

At this time the Norwegians get into the fort, because the farmhands had not closed it. The brothers went out. The women said that Hrómundr was too old and Þorleifr too young to go out. He was nineteen[69] years old. He ran out, and Þorleifr had his weapons and said:

Not for me was death, already decreed,
meted out today. We get ready
for the bustle of the valkyrie,
you timber of the rings' flat field!
I am little concerned, though
the colouring-wand of Heðinn's webbing
plays with red shields. Long ago
my lifetime was marked out for me.

Bustle of the valkyrie = battle. Flat field of (painted) rings = shield; timber of the shield = man, warrior. Heðinn's [= warrior's] webbing = mailcoat; colouring-wand of the mailcoat = sword (which, by cutting through armour, colours wounds red).

Six Norwegians fell in the fort, and other men fled; but when Þorbjǫrn tried to lock the fort again, Jǫrundr threw a spear through him. Þorbjǫrn took the spear out of the wound and put it between Jǫrundr's shoulders, so that it came out through the chest, and they both fell to the ground dead. Helgi picked Jǫrundr up and threw him onto his back and ran thus. Hásteinn ran after them, until Helgi threw him (Jǫrundr) off his back.

[69] 'Nineteen' (XIX) in the Hauksbók recension is likely to be a mistake; the other recensions give Þorleifr's age as 'XV', which tallies much better with the statement that he was too young to fight.

Then he turned back. Hrómundr was fallen, and Þorleifr was wounded to death. The women asked for news. Hásteinn spoke:

> Out here on the paving-stones
> the six swords' gods of the wound-stick's
> sweep, whose sacrifice is
> griefless, have suffered death.
> I think that half the law-impeders
> may remain behind.
> I made wounds, edge-inflicted,
> singe those who did not endure.

Wound-stick = sword. The swords' gods of the wound-stick's sweep = the men of the fight = the warriors.

The women asked how many they were. Hásteinn spoke:

> Four of us relatives
> were present there, accused of violence—
> I had no more, at a fight
> of the scabbard's fire—
> and twelve bold bushes of the fight-assembly
> who wanted to make haste
> from Gylfi's horse to meet us.
> We reddened cold weapons.

Fire of the scabbard = sword. Fight-assembly = battle. Bush of the fight-assembly = warrior. Gylfi's horse = the sea-king's horse = ship.

The women asked how many of the Vikings had fallen. Hásteinn spoke:

> Seven attacking-gods of Odin's
> enclosure have hit the earth
> with their noses. Warm blood,
> battle-dew, fell on the field.
> There will not be more fire-timbers
> of Odin's assembly to guide
> the stallion of the sea-king's land
> out of the sea-lord's paths, than came hither.

Attacking-god = man, warrior. Odin's enclosure = shield. Man of the shield = warrior. Battle-dew = blood. Fire = sword. Timber of the sword = warrior. Odin's assembly = battle. The sea-king's land = the sea. Stallion of the sea = ship. The sea-lord's paths = the sea.

Here boasting-trees can see
the sign of a dear day's work
of the noise of the ray of the bow-tongs,
what four have accomplished.
And I thought, swinger
of the fire of the fight's roof, that
we gave the truce-breakers little peace.
The raven tore a bite off a corpse.

Boasting-trees = warriors. The bow-tongs = the 'tongs' that grip and use the bow, i.e. the hand; ray of the hand = sword; noise of the sword = battle. Fight's roof = shield; fire of the shield = sword; swinger of the sword = warrior.

Helgi and his people put out to sea the same day, and all drowned at Helgasker 'Helgi's Skerry' off Skriðinsenni Precipice. Þorleifr recovered and lived at Brekka Slope, but Hásteinn went abroad and fell on the Long Serpent together with King Óláfr, son of Tryggvi.

Here begins the Settlement in the Quarter of the Northland-People

138. Now begins the settlement in the Quarter of the Northland-people.

Eysteinn *meinfretr*, the son of Álfr from Rosta, took Eastern-Hrútafjarðarstrǫnd Coast-Land immediately behind Bálki and lived there for several winters, before he went to Dalr Valley to live and married Þórhildr, the daughter of Þorsteinn the Red. Their sons were Álfr in the Dalir Valleys, Þórðr and Þórólfr Fox and Hrappr.

139. A man was called Þóroddr, who took Hrútafjord and lived at Þóroddsstaðir. His son was Arnórr Downy-Nose, who married Gerðr, the daughter of Bǫðvarr from Bǫðvarshólar Hills. Their sons were Þorbjǫrn, whom Grettir slew, and Þóroddr Poem-Stump, the father of Valgerðr, who was married to Skeggi Short-Handed.

140. Skautaðar-Skeggi was the name of a famous man in Norway. His son was Bjǫrn, who was called Bjǫrn-of-Furs, because he was a Novgorod trader. He went to Iceland and took Miðfjord and Línakradalr Valley. His son was [Miðfjord-Skeggi],[70] a great fighter. He plundered in the East and lay off in Denmark by Zealand. He participated in plundering the burial mound of King Hrólfr Pole, and he took Hrólfr's sword

[70] Omitted from the manuscript.

Skǫfnungr out of it, and the axe of Hjalti, and much other wealth; but he did not get [the sword] Laufi, because Bǫðvarr tried to attack him, but King Hrólfr defended him. Then he went to Iceland and lived at Reykir on Miðfjord. Skeggi's sons were Eiðr and Kollr, the father of Halldórr, the father of Þórdís, who was married to Poet-Helgi, and of Þorkatla. Skeggi's daughters were Hróðný, who was married to Þórðr Yeller, and Þorbjǫrg, who was married to Ásbjǫrn the Rich, son of Hǫrðr. Their daughter was Ingibjǫrg, who was married to Illugi the Black at Gilsbakki Bank.

141. Haraldr Ring was the name of a man of great descent. He came with his ship into Vestrhóp Lagoon and spent the first winter at the place which is called Hringsstaðir 'Ring Steads'. He took the whole Vatsnes Peninsula inland as far as Ambáttará River in the west, everything in as far as Þverá River and there over across as far as Bjargaóss,[71] the 'Estuary of the Cliffs', and everything this side of the cliffs outwards as far as the sea, and lived at Hólar Hills. His son was Þorbrandr, the father of Ásbrandr, the father of Sǫlvi the Magnificent at Ægissíða 'Ægir's Waterside'.

142. A man was called Sóti, who took Vestrhóp Lagoon and lived under Sótafell 'Sóti's Mountain'.

143. Steinarr-of-Hounds was the name of a jarl in England. He married Álǫf, the daughter of Ragnarr Shaggy-Trousers. Their children were Bjǫrn, the father of Auðun Shaft; and Eiríkr, the father of Sigurðr Platters-Baldhead; and Ísgerðr, who was married to Jarl Þórir in Vermaland. Auðun Shaft went to Iceland and took Víðidalr Valley and lived at Auðunarstaðir. Together with him his partner Þorgils Yelling came out [to Iceland], the father of Þórarinn the *goði*. Auðun Shaft was the father of Þóra Moss-Neck, the mother of Úlfhildr, who was married to [Guðbrandr Ball; their daughter was][72] Ásta, the mother of King Óláfr the Holy.

---

empty space for two lines

---

[71] Manuscript: *Braga óss*, which context and the comparison with S show to be a mistake.

[72] Missing from the manuscript, where a space has been left for these words.

The son of Auðun Shaft was Ásgeirr at Ásgeirsá River. He married Jórunn, the daughter of Ingimundr the Old. Their children were Þorvaldr, the father of Dalla, the mother of Bishop Gizurr, and Auðun, the father of Ásgeirr, the father of Auðun, the father of Egill, who married Úlfheiðr, the daughter of Eyjólfr, son of Guðmundr; and their son was Eyjólfr, who was killed at the General Assembly, the father of Ormr, the chaplain of Bishop Þorlákr the Holy. Another son of Auðun Shaft was Eysteinn, the father of Þorsteinn, the father of Helgi, the father of Þórormr, the father of Oddr, the father of Hallbjǫrn, the father of Priest Sighvatr. Ásgeirr's daughter at Ásgeirsá was Þorbjǫrg Pride-of-the-Bench.

144. Ormr was the name of the man who took Ormsdalr 'Ormr's Valley', and lived there. He was the father of Oddr, the father of Þorvaldr, the father of Helgi, the father of Harri, the father of Jóra, the mother of Þórdís, the mother of Tannr, the father of Skapti.

145. Ketill Churl was the name of a famous chieftain in Raumsdalr Valley in Norway. Ketill married Mjǫllda, the daughter of Án Bow-Bender. Their son was called Þorsteinn. At his father's instigation, he killed Jǫkull, the son of Jarl Ingimundr from Gautland and of Vigdís, in the forests towards Upplǫnd. Jǫkull died at his hands. Then Þorsteinn[73] married Þórdís, (Jǫkull's) sister. Their son was Ingimundr the Old. He was brought up in Hefni with Þórir, the father of Grímr and Hrómundr. The seeress Heiðr prophesied to all of them that they would live in the land that then was [still] undiscovered in the sea to the west. And Ingimundr says that he would prevent this. The seeress said that he would not be able to do that. And she stated as a miraculous sign of proof[74] that an amulet would disappear from his purse, and she said that he would find it where he dug holes for his high-seat pillars.

Ingimundr was a great Viking and went raiding in the British Isles. His partner was called Sæmundr, a Hebridean. They came back from their raid at the time when King Haraldr was in battle in Hafrsfjord against Þórir Long-Chin and his men. Ingimundr wanted to help the king, but Sæmundr did not, and there they ended their partnership. After the battle, King Haraldr gave Vigdís, the daughter of Jarl Þórir the Silent, to Ingimundr in marriage. She and Jǫrundr Neck were his [the jarl's] children by a concubine. Ingimundr did not feel at ease anywhere. Therefore King Haraldr encouraged him to seek out his destiny

[73] Missing in manuscript.

[74] The word *jartegn* has connotations of a Christian miraculous sign.

in Iceland. Ingimundr, however, said that he had not intended that. But anyway he sent two Finns after his amulet, travelling to Iceland in the shapes of animals. That [amulet] was a Freyr made of silver.

The Finns came back and had found the amulet and had not been able to get hold of it. They gave him directions to it in a valley between three wooded hills and told him everything about what the land was like, how it was ordered at the place where they were to live. After that Ingimundr went to Iceland, and together with him Jǫrundr Neck, his brother-in-law, and his friends Eyvindr *sørkvir* and Ásmundr the Hvati,[75] and his slaves Friðmundr and Bǫðvarr and Þórir Fox-Beard and Úlfkell. They took the mouth of the Grímsá 'Grímr's River', and they all spent the winter on Hvanneyrr Gravel-Bank with Grímr, Ingimundr's foster-brother; and in spring they went northwards over the heath. They came into the fjord where they found two rams; they called the place there Hrútafjord 'Fjord of the Rams'. Then they went northwards through the district and gave names to many places. He spent the winter in Víðidalr Valley in Ingimundarholt 'Ingimundr's Forest'. From there they saw a

'Ingimundr took the whole Vatnsdalr Valley upwards from Lake Helgavatn and Lake Urðarvatn in the east. He lived at Hof "Temple", and found his amulet when he dug the holes for his high-seat pillars.'
The view across Vatnsdalr Valley from above the farm of Hof.

[75] Perhaps *recte leg.* 'and Hvati', as Hvati occurs as an independent person in the Sturlubók recension (though not elsewhere in the Hauksbók recension).

snow-free mountain in the south-east, and they went there in spring. There Ingimundr recognised the lands towards which he had been pointed. His daughter Þórdís was born in Þórdísarholt 'Þórdís's Forest'.

Ingimundr took the whole Vatnsdalr Valley upwards from Lake Helgavatn and Lake Urðarvatn in the east. He lived at Hof 'Temple', and found his amulet when he dug the holes for his high-seat pillars. Þorsteinn was his son with Vigdís, and Jǫkull and Þórir Buck's Thigh and Hǫgni. A son of Ingimundr with a maidservant was called Smiðr 'Craftsman', and his daughters Jórunn and Þórdís.

146. Jǫrundr Neck took [the land] outwards from Lake Urðarvatn and as far as Mógilslœkr Brook and lived at Grund at the foot of Jǫrundarfell Mountain. His son was Már at Másstaðir. Ásmundr took [the land] outwards from Lake Helgavatn and the Þingeyrar District and lived under the overhanging peak of Gnúpr. Friðmundr took Forsœludalr Valley. Eyvindr *sørkvir* took Blǫndudalr Valley. His sons were Hermundr and Hrómundr the Lame. Ingimundr found a she-bear at the lake, and two bear cubs with her. He called it Húnavatn 'Lake of the Bear Cubs'. After that, Ingimundr went abroad and gave the animal to King Haraldr. Never before had men in Norway seen polar bears. King Haraldr then gave the ship Stígandi to Ingimundr, together with a ship-load of timber, and he sailed to Iceland with two ships, and he was the first man to sail northwestwards around Skagi, and he held his course up into Lake Húnavatn. This place is now called Stígandahróf 'Stígandi's Boatshed', by Þingeyrar. After that Hrafn the Norwegian stayed with Ingimundr and had a good sword and carried that into the temple. Therefore, Ingimundr took it from him. The brothers Hallormr and Þórormr were with Ingimundr. Then Hallormr received his daughter Þórdís in marriage and she brought Kárnsárland as a dowry with her. Their son was Þorgrímr *goði*-of-Kárnsá-River. Þórormr lived in Þórormstunga. Ingimundr lost ten pigs, and they were found the following autumn, and then there were one hundred pigs altogether. The boar was called Beigaðr; he jumped into Lake Svínavatn 'Lake of Pigs', and swam until his trotters fell off. He collapsed and died at Beigaðarhóll 'Beigaðr's Hill'.

147. Hrolleifr the Big and his mother Ljót came out into Borgarfjord. They went northwards around the districts and found no dwelling-place until they came into Skagafjord to Sæmundr. Hrolleifr was the son of Arnaldr, the brother of Sæmundr; therefore he directed them northwards to Hǫfðastrǫnd Coast-Land to Þórðr, and he got [a place] for him in Hrolleifsdalr Valley, and there he lived. Hrolleifr seduced Hróðný, the

daughter of Uni in Unadalr Valley. Oddr, son of Uni, waylaid him and killed his cousin Ljótr, wounding him in the leg, because weapons did not bite his coat. Hrolleifr killed Oddr and two other men, but two got away. For that, Hǫfða-Þórðr[76] had them outlawed from the district as far as waters flowed into Skagafjord. Then Sæmundr sent Hrolleifr to Ingimundr the Old. He settled him at Oddsáss Ridge opposite Hof. He had the fishing in Vatnsdalsá River together with Ingimundr, but he had to go away from the river when the men of Hof came. Yet he did not want to go away before the men of Hof, the sons of Ingimundr. And they fought over the river. Then this was told to Ingimundr, and he was [already] blind at the time, and he had a small boy lead a horse, on which he was sitting, to the river between them. Hrolleifr threw a spear through him. Then they went home. Ingimundr sent the boy to tell Hrolleifr, and he was dead in the high-seat when his sons came home. Hrolleifr told this to his mother. She said that they would then put to the test what would achieve more, the luck of the sons of Ingimundr or her wisdom, and then she told him first to go abroad. Þorsteinn was to pursue Hrolleifr and have a treasure from the inheritance. They did not sit down in their father's high-seat. Ingimundr's sons went north to Sæmundr, and Þorsteinn gave him sixty pieces of silver to send Hrolleifr away. The sons of Ingimundr tracked him from the north over the ridges as far as Vatnsdalr Valley. Þorsteinn sent a farmhand to Áss Ridge to get news. He spoke twelve stanzas he had composed before somebody came to the door. He saw a pile of clothes on the fire, and a red cloth protruded from beneath. Þorsteinn said that Hrolleifr had been there, 'and Ljót must have sacrificed for a long life for him.' They went to Áss, and Þorsteinn wanted to lie in wait over the door, and he could not because of Jǫkull, because he wanted to be there. A man came out and looked around. Then another guided Hrolleifr after himself. Jǫkull reacted to that and knocked over a pile of firewood from above, but nevertheless he managed to throw a stick to his brothers. He went for Hrolleifr, and they both rolled down the slope, and Jǫkull stayed on top. Then Þorsteinn came up, and then they used weapons. At that point, Ljót had come out, and she was walking backwards; she had her head between her feet and her clothes thrown up over her back. Jǫkull struck the head off Hrolleifr and thrust it into Ljót's face. Then she said that she had been too slow: 'now the earth was just about to be turned upside down by my gaze, and you would all have lost your minds.'

[76] Þórðr of Hǫfðastrǫnd.

After that, Þorsteinn chose Hofsland, and Jǫkull kept the sword and lived in Tunga. Þórir had the chieftaincy and lived at Undunfell Mountain and used to fall into a berserk's fury. Hǫgni had the ship Stígandi and was a trader. Smiðr lived at Smiðsstaðir. Þorsteinn married Þuríðr the Priestess, the daughter of Sǫlmundr on Ásbjarnarnes Peninsula. Their sons were Ingólfr the Fair and Guðbrandr. Jǫkull was the son of Bárðr, son of Jǫkull, whom King Óláfr the Holy had killed. Jǫkull the Highwayman said that unlucky killings would long persist in this family.

148. A man was called Eyvindr *auðkúla*. He took Svínadalr Valley and lived at Auðkúlustaðir;[77] and Þorgils Yelling, who came out together with Auðun Shaft, lived at Lake Svínavatn. His sons were Boasting-Ormr and his brothers, who killed Skarpheðinn, son of Véfrøðr, in Vatsskarð.

149. Eyvindr *sørkvir* took Blǫndudalr Valley. His son was Hrómundr the Lame, who killed Hǫgni, son of Ingimundr, on that occasion when Már and the sons of Ingimundr fought about Deildarhjalli Mountain-Ledge. Because of this he was banished from the Quarter of the Northlandmen. His sons were Þorbjǫrn and Hásteinn, who fought with Lowland-Helgi in Hrútafjord. Another son of Eyvindr *sørkvir* was Hermundr, the father of Hildr, who was married to Ávaldr, son of Ingjaldr. Their children were Kolfinna, who was married to Gríss, son of Sæmingr, and Brandr, who killed Galti, son of Óttarr, at the Húnavatn Assembly because of an insult of Hallfreðr's.

150. A man was called Þorbjǫrn *kolka*. He took Kolkumýrar Moors and lived there.

151. A man was called Ævarr, the son of Ketill Thin Slate and of Þuríðr, the daughter of King Haraldr Gold-Beard from Sogn. The sons of Ævarr were Véfrøðr and Karli and Þorbjǫrn Bile and Þórðr Big. Ævarr and his sons other than Véfrøðr went to Iceland from a raiding expedition. He [Véfrøðr] stayed behind raiding. Together with him [Ævarr], his relative Gunnsteinn went out [to Iceland], and Auðólfr and Gautr. Ævarr came with his ship to Blǫnduóss, the 'Estuary of the Blanda'. At that time, the lands west of the Blanda were taken. Ævarr went up along the Blanda to find a land claim for himself and reached the place which is called Móbergsbrekkur Slopes. He set up a high pole and said that he was taking a dwelling-place for his son Véfrøðr there. Then he took the whole Langadalr Valley upwards from there and in like manner there north of

[77] Manuscript: *Raud-*

the ridge. There he distributed lands to his ship's crew. Ævarr lived in Ævarsskarð 'Ævarr's Pass'. Later, Véfrøðr came out [to Iceland] into the estuary of Gǫnguskarðsá River, and he went from the north to his father, and Ævarr did not recognise him. They wrestled so [hard] that all the posts in the houses fell apart before Véfrøðr said who he was. He made his abode at the Móberg Clay Soil Area, as it was allotted to him. And Þorbjǫrn Bíle at Strúgsstaðir 'Bíle Steads', and Gunnsteinn at Gunnsteinsstaðir; Karli at Karlastaðir; Þórðr at Mikilsstaðir 'Big's Steads'; Auðólfr at Auðólfsstaðir. Gautr settled Gautsdalr Valley. He was one-handed. Eyvindr *sørkvir* and his people killed themselves, not wanting to live after the death of Ingimundr the Old. Haukr lived at the place which is called Hauksstaðir. Véfrøðr married Gunnhildr, the daughter of Eiríkr from Goðdalir Valleys, the sister of Duel-Starri. Their sons were Úlfheðinn, whom Fǫstólfr and Þróttólfr killed by Grindalœkr Brook; and Skarpheðinn, whom Boasting-Ormr and his people killed in Vatsskarð; and Húnrøðr, the father of Már, the father of Hafliði.

152. Holti was the name of the man who took Langadalr Valley below Móberg and lived at Holtastaðir. He was the father of Ísrøðr, the father of Ísleifr, the father of Þorvaldr, the father of Þórarinn the Wise. Þorvaldr's daughter was Þórdís, who was married to Halldórr, the son of Snorri the *goði*. Their daughters were Þorkatla, who was married to Guðlaugr, son of Þorfinnr on Straumsfjord; from them the Sturlungar are descended, and the Oddaverjar; the other was Guðrún, who was married to Kjartan, son of Ásgeirr on Vatsfjord. Their son was Þorvaldr, the father . . .

---

empty space for two lines

---

153. Duel-Máni was the name of a man who took Skagastrǫnd Coast-Land, as far west inland as Forsá River, and in the east as far as Mánaþúfa 'Máni's Mound', and lived in Mánavík 'Máni's Bay'. His daughter was married to Þorbrandr in the Dalir Valleys, the father of Máni, the father of Kálfr the Poet.

154. Eilífr the Eagle was the name of a man, the son of Atli, son of Skíði the Old, son of Bárðr in Áll. Eilífr took land from Mánaþúfa as far as Gǫnguskarðsá River and Laxárdalr Valley and lived there. He married Þorlaug, the daughter of Sæmundr at Hlíð Mountainside. Their sons were Sǫlmundr, the father of Guðmundr, the father of Manslaughter-Barði;

another was Atli the Strong, who married Herdís, the daughter of Þórðr from Hǫfði Headland. Their children were Þorlaug, who was married to Guðmundr the Great, and Þórarinn, who married Halla, the daughter of Jǫrundr Neck. Their son was Styrbjǫrn, who married Yngvildr, the daughter of Steinrøðr, son of Heðinn, from Heðinshǫfði Headland. Their daughter was Arndís, who was married to Hamall, son of Þormóðr, son of Þorkell Moon. The son of Eilífr the Eagle was Koðrán at Giljá, the father of Þorvaldr the Far-Traveller, and Þjóðólfr the *goði* at Hof 'Temple', on Skagastrǫnd Coast-Land, and Eysteinn, the father of Þorvaldr Tin-Sapling.

155. Sæmundr the Hebridean was a companion of Ingimundr the Old, as has been written; he brought his ship into the estuary of Gǫnguskarðsá River. Sæmundr took the whole of Sæmundarhlíð Mountainside as far as Vatsskarð above Sæmundarlœkr Brook and lived at Geirmundarstaðir.[78] His son was Geirmundr, who later lived there. Sæmundr's daughter was Reginleif, who was married to Þóroddr Helmet. Their daughter was Hallbera, the mother of Guðmundr the Great, the father of Eyjólfr, the father of Þórey, the mother of Sæmundr the Wise. Arnaldr was the name of another son of Sæmundr's, the father of Rjúpa, who was married to Þorgeirr, the son of Þórðr from Hǫfði Headland. Their son was Halldórr from Hof 'Temple'.

156. Skefill was the name of a man who brought his ship into the estuary of Gǫnguskarðsá River in the same week as Sæmundr. And while Sæmundr was going with fire around his land-claim, Skefill took all the land out beyond Sauðá River. He took it out of Sæmundr's land claim without his permission, and Sæmundr allowed that to stand.

157. A man was called Úlfljótr. He took the whole of Langaholt Forest below Sæmundarlœkr Brook.

158. Þorkell *vingnir*, son of Atli, son of Skíði the Old: he took all the land around Vatsskarð, and Svartárdalr Valley. His son was Armóðr the Squinting, the father of Galti, the father of Þorgeirr, the father of Styrmir, the father of Hallr, the father of Kolfinna.

159. Álfgeirr was the name of the man who took land around Álfgeirsvellir Fields and up as far as Mælifellsá River and lived at Álfgeirsvellir.

[78] *Sic*; other parts of the *Landnámabók* tradition, however, give the place name as *Sæmundarstaðir*.

160. The man was called Þorviðr who took land upwards from Mælifellsá River as far as Gilјá River.

161. Hrosskell was the name of the man who with Eiríkr's advice took the whole Svartárdalr Valley and all the Ýrarfellslǫnd Lands. He took [land] down as far as Gilhagi Pasture and lived at Ýrarfell Mountain. He had the slave who was called Roðrekr. He sent him up beyond Mælifellsdalr Valley in search of land southwards on Kjǫlr. He came to the ravine that runs southwards from Mælifellsdalr Valley and is now called Roðreksgil 'Roðrekr's Ravine'. There he put up a newly barked staff, which they called Land-Prober. After that he turned back.

'Hrosskell . . . had the slave who was called Roðrekr. He sent him up beyond Mælifellsdalr Valley in search of land southwards on Kjǫlr.'
A stretch of the Kjölur road.

162. Vékell the Magician was the name of the man who took land down from Gilá River as far as Mælifellsá River and lived at Mælifell Mountain. He made fun of Roðrekr's journey and a little later went southwards over the mountains in search of land. He came to the mounds which are now called Vékelshaugar 'Vékell's Mounds'. He shot [an arrow] between the mounds. He turned back from there. And when Eiríkr in Goðdalir Valleys learned of that, he sent his slave, who was called Rǫnguðr, southwards onto the mountains. Once more, he went in search of land. He came southwards as far as Blǫndukvíslir, where the river forks, and then went up along the river which flows to the west of Hvinverjadalr Valley and westwards on the lava-field between Reykjavellir Fields

and Kjǫlr; and there he came upon a man's footprints and realised that they came there from the south. He piled up a cairn there at that place which is now called Rangaðarvarða 'Rǫnguðr's Cairn'. From there he went back and Eiríkr gave him his freedom as a reward for his journey. And from then onwards journeys were undertaken over the mountains between the Southlanders and the Northlanders.

163. Eiríkr was the name of a famous man. He went from Norway to Iceland. He was a son of Hróaldr, son of Geirmundr, son of Eiríkr Brisk-Shaggy. Eiríkr took land from Gilá River across the Goðdalir Valleys and down as far as Norðrá River and lived at Hof 'Temple', in the Goðdalir Valleys. He married Þuríðr, the daughter of Þórðr Shaggy, the sister of Helga, who was married to Ketilbjǫrn the Old at Mosfell Mountain. The children of Eiríkr and his wife were Þorkell and Hróaldr, Þorgeirr and Duel-Starri and Gunnhildr. Þorgeirr, son of Eiríkr, married Yngvildr, daughter of Þorgeirr. Their daughter was Rannveig, who was married to Bjarni, son of Iron-Point-Helgi.

164. Crow-Hreiðarr was the name of a man, the son of Ófeigr Wag-Beard, son of Oxen-Þórir. Father and son sailed to Iceland, and when they came within sight of the land, Hreiðarr went to the mast and said that he would not throw his high-seat pillars overboard. He says that it seemed foolish to him to make one's decision according to that. He says that he would rather invoke Thor to guide him towards land, and he says that he would fight for it there, if it should already be taken. And he came into Skagafjord and sailed up onto Borgarsandr Beach until he ran aground. Hávarðr the Heron came to him and invited him to stay with him, and he spent the winter there on Hegranes, the 'Heron's Headland'.

In spring, Hávarðr asked which of his plans he wanted [to put into action]. And he says that he wanted to fight Sæmundr for the lands. But Hávarðr dissuaded him and said that things like that had turned out badly; he asked him to go to visit Eiríkr in Goðdalir, 'and get his advice'. Hreiðarr did so. And when he met Eiríkr, he dissuaded him from this strife and said that it was not wise for men to fight while there was such a small population in the land. He says that he would rather give him the whole tongue of land downwards from Skálamýrr Moor. And he said that Thor had been guiding him there and had turned his prow in that direction when he sailed onto Borgarsandr Beach. Hreiðarr accepted this decision and lived at Steinsstaðir. He chose to die into Mælifell Mountain. His son was Ófeigr Thin-Bearded, the father of Bjǫrn, the father of Tongue-Steinn.

Chapter

165. A man was called Hjálmólfr, who took land down across the slope of Blǫnduhlíð. His son was Þorgrímr *kuggi*, the father of Oddr in Axlarhagi Pasture, the father of Seals-Kálfr; from there come the Axlhegingar.

166. A man was called Ǫnundr the Knowing, who took land upwards from Merkigil Glen, everything on the eastern side of the eastern valley. And when Eiríkr wanted to come there to take land across the valley, everything on the western side, Ǫnundr cast sacrificial lots to find out at what time Eiríkr would be coming to take the land. And Ǫnundr was quicker then and shot a tinder-arrow across the river and in this way sanctified the land in the west for himself and lived between the rivers.

Chapter

167. Kári was the name of the man who took land between Norðrá River and Merkigil Glen and lived in Flatatunga; he was called Tunga-Kári. From him the Silfrstœðingar are descended.

168. Þorbrandr *ørrekr* took the whole slope of Silfrastaðahlíð upwards from Bólstaðará River, and Norðrárdalr Valley in the north, and he lived at Þorbrandsstaðir and had a heatable hall built there so big that all the men who travelled through the valley on that side were to pass through it with their loaded pack-horses, and there was to be food available for all. Ørreksheiðr[79] Heath above Hǫkustaðir is named after him. He was an eminent man and of noble birth.

Chapter

169. Þórðr Dove's-Beak was a freedman of Oxen-Þórir.[80] He brought his ship into Gǫnguskarðáróss Estuary. At that time, the whole western

[79] Manuscript: *Eiriks-*.

[80] This passage provides an interesting instance of the Hauksbók recension confusing similar-sounding names. As the text stands, Þórðr Dove's-Beak acquires a horse which is then, inexplicably, ridden in a race by a man called Þórir. This race, furthermore, creates the place name Dúfunefsskeið 'Dove's-Beak's Stretch of Road'; thus, 'Þórðr Dove's-Beak' apparently has turned into 'Þórir Dove's-Beak'. In the (older) Sturlubók recension, Þórðr Dove's-Beak is called Þórir Dove's-Beak from the start, indicating that the replacement of the name 'Þórir' by 'Þórðr' in its first two occurrences in Hauksbók is a straightforward mistake.

part of the district was settled. At Landbrot Land-Slip he crossed the Jǫkulsá River in a northerly direction and took land between Glóðafeykisá River and Djúpá River and lived at Flugumýrr Moor. At that time, a ship came[81] out [to Iceland] into Kolbeinsáróss Estuary, and it was loaded with livestock, and they lost a foal in the Brimnesskógar Forests, and Þórðr Dove's-Beak bought the chance of finding it and did so. That was the fastest of all horses and was called Fluga: 'Fly'.

'Fluga was lost in a quagmire on Flugumýrr "Fly Swamp".'
The view across the church farm of Flugumýri.

Ǫrn was the name of a man who ranged from one end of the land to the other. He was versed in witchcraft. He waylaid Þórir in Hvinverjadalr Valley, when he was meant to be going southwards over Kjǫlr, and he made a bet with Þórir which of them owned the faster horse, for he had a very good stallion; and each of them staked a hundred pieces of silver. They both rode southwards over Kjǫlr until they came to the stretch of the road which is now called Dúfunefsskeið 'Dove's-Beak's Stretch of Road'; and the difference in speed between the horses was no smaller than that Þórir came back on his second lap to meet Ǫrn in the middle of the course on his first. Ǫrn bore the loss of his money so badly that he did not want to live any longer and went up to the foot of Arnarfell 'Ǫrn's/Eagle's Mountain' and killed himself there, and Fluga

[81] Missing in manuscript.

remained behind there, because she was very exhausted. And when Þórir went home from the Assembly,[82] he found a grey stallion with a remarkable mane by Fluga. She had conceived from him. Eiðfaxi was born to them, who went abroad and killed seven men at Mjǫrs on a single day, and there he himself died. Fluga was lost in a quagmire on Flugumýrr 'Fly Swamp'.

Chapter

170. Kollsveinn the Mighty was the name of a man who took land between the rivers Þverá and Gljúfrá and lived at Kollsveinsstaðir above Þverá River. He held sacrifices at Hofstaðir 'Temple-Steads'.

171. Gunnólfr was the name of a man who took land between the rivers Þverá and Glóðaleykisá and lived at Hvammr 'Grassy Slope'.

About Gormr

172. Gormr was the name of a famous chieftain in Sweden. He married Þóra, the daughter of King Eiríkr of Uppsala. His son was called Þorgils. He married Elín, the daughter of King Burisláfr from Garðar[83] in the east and of Ingibjǫrg, the sister of Dagstyggr, the king of the giants. Their sons were Hergrímr and Herfinnr, who married Halla, the daughter of Heðinn and Arndís, daughter of Heðinn. Gróa was the name of a daughter of Herfinnr and Halla. She was married to Hróarr. Their son was Fraud-Bjǫrn, who took land between the rivers Grjótá and Deildará, before Hjalti and Kolbeinn came out [to Iceland]. He lived at Sleita-Bjarnarstaðir 'Fraud-Bjǫrn's-Steads'. His sons were Ǫrnólfr, who married Þorljót, the daughter of Hjalti, son of Sheath;[84] and Arnbjǫrn, who married Þorlaug, daughter of Þórðr from Hǫfði Headland; and Arnoddr, who married Þórný, the daughter of Sigmundr, son of Þorkell, whom Glúmr killed. Arnfríðr was the name of Fraud-Bjǫrn's daughter, who was married to Circumspect Bǫðvarr, the son of Ǫndóttr. He, Ǫndóttr, came out [to Iceland] into Kolbeinsáróss Estuary and buys land from Fraud-Bjǫrn downwards from Hálsgróf Hollow on

[82] Probably the assembly in Þingvellir, which is in the area one reaches by going southwards over Kjölur.

[83] The kingdom of the Kievan Rus in Ukraine.

[84] Þórðr Sheath (*skálpr*) appears with his full name for the first time only two chapters later, in ch. 174.

the western[85] side and outwards as far as Kolbeinsáróss Estuary, and on the western side downwards from the brook that is located seawards of Nautabú, and inland as far as Gljúfrá River, and he lived in Viðvík Bay.

About Kolbeinn

173. Sigmundr in Vestfold married Ingibjǫrg, the daughter of Rauðr Cradle in Naumudalr Valley, the sister of Þorsteinn Sweeper. Their son was Kolbeinn. He went to Iceland and took land between the rivers Grjótá and Deildará: the valleys Kolbeinsdalr and Hjaltadalr.

About Hjalti

174. Hjalti, son of Þórðr Sheath, came to Iceland and on the advice of Kolbeinn took Hjaltadalr Valley and lived at Hof 'Temple'. His sons were Þorvaldr and Þórðr. That was the most famous funeral banquet in Iceland when they held the funeral banquet for their father. They invited all the chieftains in Iceland, and there were a hundred and twenty invited guests, and all men of worth were seen off with gifts. At that funeral banquet, Oddr Breiðafjord-Man offered the praise-poem he had composed about Hjalti. Before that, Glúmr, son of Geiri, had served a summons to the Þorskafjord Assembly on Oddr; it was about a sheep's milk. Then in spring the sons of Hjalti went from the north in a ship to Steingrímsfjord and went from the north across the heath at the place which is now called Hjaltdœlalaut, the 'Hollow of the Men of Hjalti's Valley'. And when they went to the Assembly, they were fitted out so well that people thought that the gods had come there. About that this has been recited:

> None of the murder-exploring men
> thought anything other,
> iron-timber! than that the
> all-famous gods went there,
> when the sons of hard-grabbing
> Hjalti went to the
> Þorskafjord Assembly with the
> forehead-piece of the forest-fish.

Iron-timber = warrior. Forehead-piece (the 'piece', *tingl*, here being the figurehead of a ship, which usually had the shape of a snake or

[85] Sturlubók: 'eastern'.

dragon) = ornamented helmet; forest-fish = snake; dragon-head-helmet of the snake = terror-inspiring helmet.

From the sons of Hjalti a great family is descended.

About Þórðr

175. A famous man was called Þórðr. He was a son of Bjǫrn Trough-Butter, son of Hróaldr Back, son of Ásleikr, son of Bjǫrn Ironside, son of Ragnarr Shaggy-Trousers. Þórðr went to Iceland and took Hǫfðastrǫnd Coast on Skagafjord between the rivers Unadalsá and Hrolleifsdalsá. Þórðr of Hǫfði Headland married Friðgerðr, the daughter of Þórir *híma* and of Friðgerðr, the daughter of Kjarvalr, the king of the Irish. They had nineteen children. Bjǫrn was a son of theirs who married Þuríðr, the daughter of Refr from Barð, and their children were Arnórr Woman's Nose and Þórdís, the mother of Ormr, the father of Þórdís, the mother of Bótólfr, the father of Þórdís, the mother of Helga, the mother of Guðný, the mother of the sons of Sturla. Þorgeirr was the name of another son of Þórðr. He married Rjúpa, the daughter of Arnaldr, son

'Þorvaldr Hollow-Throat was Þórðr's fourth son. One autumn, he came to Þorvarðsstaðr in Síða, to Smiðkell, and stayed there for a while. Then he went to Surtr's cave and there recited the praise-poem he had composed about the giant in the cave. Then he married Smiðkell's daughter . . .'
The entrance of 'Surtr's Cave' Surtshellir.

of Sæmundr. Their son was Halldór at Hof 'Temple'. Snorri was the third [son]. He married Þorhildr Snow-Grouse, the daughter of Þórðr Yeller. Their son was Þórðr Horse-Head, the father of Stuff-of-a-Man[86] who discovered Vínland the Good, the father of Snorri, the father of Steinunn, the mother of Þorsteinn the Unjust, the father of Guðrún, the mother of Halla, the mother of Flosi, the father of Valgerðr, the mother of Sir Erlendr the Strong.

Þorvaldr Hollow-Throat was Þórðr's fourth son. One autumn, he came to Þorvarðsstaðr in Síða, to Smiðkell, and stayed there for a while. Then he went to Surtr's cave and there recited the praise-poem he had composed about the giant in the cave. Then he married Smiðkell's daughter, and their daughter was Jórunn, the mother of Þorbrandr on Skarfanes Peninsula. Bárðr was Þórðr's fifth son. He married Þórarna, the daughter of Þóroddr Helmet. Their son was Dagr the Poet. Sǫxólfr was Þórðr's sixth son, the seventh Þorgrímr, the eighth Hróarr, the ninth Knǫrr, the tenth Þormóðr the Baldhead, the eleventh Steinn. Þórðr's daughters were Þorlaug, who was married to Arnbjǫrn, son of Lowland-Bjǫrn; their daughter was Guðlaug, who was married to Þorleikr, son of Hǫskuldr; their son was Bolli; Herdís was Þórðr's second daughter, she was married to Atli the Mighty; Þorgríma Ship's-Cheek was the third; Arnbjǫrg the fourth; the sixth[87] Arnleif; the seventh Þuríðr; the eighth Friðgerðr in Hvammr 'Grassy Slope'.

Hrolleifr the Big lived in Hrolleifsdalr Valley, as has already been written. Þórðr expelled him from the north for the killing of Oddr, son of Uni. Then he went into Vatsdalr Valley.

About Friðleifr

176. Friðleifr was the name of a man who stemmed from Gotland on his father's side of the family, and his mother was called Bryngerðr, and she was Flemish. Friðleifr took the whole slope of Sléttahlíð and Friðleifsdalr Valley between the rivers Friðleifsdalsá and Stafá and lived at Holt Forest. His son was Þjóðarr, the father of Ari and of Bryngerðr, the mother of Tongue-Steinn.

[86] Þorfinnr Stuff-of-a-Man.

[87] *Sic.*

About Flóki

177. Flóki, the son of Vilgerðr, daughter of Kári-of-the-Hǫrðar, went to Iceland and took Flókadalr Valley between Flókadalsá River and Reykjarhóll Hill. He lived at Mór 'Moorland'. Flóki married Gróa, the sister of Þórðr from Hǫfði Headland. Their son was Oddleifr Staff, who lived at Stafshóll 'Staff's Hill', and quarrelled with the sons of Hjalti. Flóki's daughter was Þjóðgerðr, the mother of Koðrán, the father of Þjóðgerðr, the mother of Koðrán, the father of Kárr in Vatsdalr Valley.

About Þórðr

178. Þórðr Knob was the name of a man from Sweden, the son of a sister of Bjǫrn at Haugr, and another was called Clasp-Helgi. They sailed to Iceland on the same ship and came to Haganes Peninsula. Þórðr took land upwards from Stífla as far as Tunguá River and lived at Knappsstaðir. He married Æsa, the daughter of Ljótólfr the *goði*. Their son was Hafr, who married Þuríðr, the daughter of Þorkell from Guðdalir Valleys. Their son was Þórarinn, the father of Ófeigr. Clasp-Helgi took land in the east upwards from Haganes Peninsula as far as Flókadalsá River below Barð, and up as far as Tunguá River, and lived at Grindill. He married Gróa the Sharp-Sighted. Their children were Þórólfr Figurehead; and the second Árún, who fought with Friðleifr at Stafshóll Hill; and Þorgerðr, who was married to Geirmundr, son of Sæmundr; and Úlfhildr, who was married to Arnórr, son of Skefill in Gǫnguskarð. Their son was Þorgeirr the Grandiloquent, who killed Sacrifice-Már at Móberg Cliff. Þórunn Blue-Cheek was [also] one.[88]

About Bárðr

179. Bárðr the Hebridean took land upwards from Stífla as far as Mjóvadalsá River. His son was Hallr the Man-of-Mjó-Valley, the father of Þuríðr, who was married to Arnórr Woman's-Nose.

Chapter

180. Brúni the White, the son of Hárekr, the jarl of the Uppland-people, he went to Iceland because he wanted to and took land between Mjóvadalsá River and the Úlfsdalir Valleys. He lived at Brúnastaðir. He married Arnóra, the daughter of Þorgeirr the Mad, son of Ljótólfr the

[88] That is, a daughter of Clasp-Helgi.

goði. Their sons were Ketill and Úlfheðinn and Þórðr, from whom the Barðverjar are descended.

About Úlfr

181. Úlfr the Viking and Óláfr Bench went to Iceland on the same ship. Úlfr took Úlfsdalr Valley and lived there. Óláfr Bench was the son of Karl from Bjarkey Island of Hálogaland; he killed Þórir the Black and was outlawed for that. Óláfr took all the valleys in the west and part of Óláfsfjord as far as the point where it meets Þormóðr['s land-claim], [and] lived at Kvíabekkr. His sons were Steinólfr, the father of Bjǫrn; and Grímólfr; and Arnoddr, the father of Vilborg, the mother of Karl the Red.

About Þormóðr

182. Þormóðr the Mighty was the name of a man from Sweden. He killed Gyrðr, the maternal grandfather of Skjálgr at Jaðarr, and for that he was banished from the land by King Bjǫrn at Haugr. He went to Iceland and came with his ship into Siglufjord and sailed inland at Þormóðseyrr 'Þormóðr's Gravel-Bank'; and therefore he named Siglufjord 'Mast's

'Þormóðr the Mighty . . . went to Iceland and came with his ship into Siglufjord and sailed inland at Þormóðseyrr "Þormóðr's Gravel-Bank"; and therefore he named Siglufjord "Mast's Fjord", and Siglunes "Mast's Promontory".'
The harbour of Siglufjörður.

Fjord', and Siglunes 'Mast's Promontory'. He took all of Siglufjord between the Úlfsdalir Valleys and the Hvanndalir Valleys. He lived at Siglunes. He quarrelled over the Hvanndalir with Óláfr Bench and killed seventeen men before they came to terms, and then each of them in turn were to have the valleys every other summer. Þormóðr was the son of Haraldr the Viking, who married Arngerðr, the daughter of Skíði from Skíðadalr Valley. Their sons were Arngeirr the Sharp and Narfi, the father of Þrándr, the father of Narfi of Hrisey Island; and Alrekr, who at Sléttahlíð Mountainside fought against Knǫrr, son of Þórðr.

About Gunnólfr

183. Gunnólfr the Old, the son of Þorbjǫrn the Whistler from Sogn, he killed Végeirr, the father of Vébjǫrn Champion-of-Sogn, and then went to Iceland. He took Óláfsfjord in the east as far as Reykjaá River and outwards as far as Vámúli Crag and lived at Gunnólfsá River. He married Gróa, the daughter of Þorvarðr from Urðir. Their sons were Steinólfr and Þorgrímr.

Chapter

184. Bjǫrn was the name of a famous man in Götaland, the son of Hrólfr from Ár. He married Hlíf, the daughter of Hrólfr, son of Ingjaldr, son of Fróði the king. Starkaðr the Old served both of them as their poet. Their son was called Eyvindr. Bjǫrn had a disagreement about land with Sigfastr,[89] a relative of Sǫlvarr, the king of the people of Götaland. Sigfastr gave his daughter to Jarl Sǫlvarr. He, the jarl, stuck so firmly by Sigfastr that he resorted to violence to hold all of Bjǫrn's lands. Then Bjǫrn handed all his property in Götaland over to his wife Hlíf and to his son Eyvindr, and Bjǫrn transported silver from the east on twelve horses. Then, in the last night before he left the country, he burned Sigfastr in his house together with thirty men. Then he went to Norway. He came to the west in Agðir into Hvínir to chieftain Grímr, son of Kolbjǫrn the Gelder, the brother of Ingjaldr the Faithful, a relative of Arinbjǫrn in the Fjords, and he received him very well. Bjǫrn and his travelling companions spent the winter with Grímr. And one night when spring was drawing to a close, [Bjǫrn became aware][90] that a man was standing over him with a drawn sword and was about to run

[89] Manuscript: Sighvatr.

[90] Missing in the manuscript.

him through with it. He grabbed him with his hands, and this man had taken money from Grímr to kill him; he [Bjǫrn] did not kill the man.

Grímr wanted to betray him for the money. Therefore Bjǫrn went away and to Ǫndóttr Crow, who lived on Hvínisfjord, the son of Erlingr Bag. Ǫndóttr married Signý, daughter of Sighvatr, from Hlíðir Slopes in Vík Bay in the east.[91] In summertime, Bjǫrn went on raiding expeditions to the British Isles, and in wintertime he stayed with Ǫndóttr. Then Hlíf died in Götaland. Bjǫrn then married Helga, Ǫndóttr's sister. Their son was Þróndr the Swift-Sailing. Then Eyvindr came from the east to his father Bjǫrn. He was a son of Hlíf. He took over the warships of his father and the occupation he had had until he got tired of going to war. In Ireland, Eyvindr then married Rafarta, the daughter of King Kjarvalr. In the Hebrides, she gave birth to a boy and gave him into fosterage there. Eyvindr was called 'the Easterner' for the reason that he crossed the sea westwards, coming from the east, from Sweden. Two years later they came back to the isles to visit the boy, and there they saw a boy with beautiful eyes, but there was no meat on him because he was starved. Because of this, they called the boy Helgi the Skinny. He was then fostered in Ireland.

Bjǫrn died at his brother-in-law Ǫndóttr's, and Grímr said that it was for the king to inherit all his property, because he was a foreigner and his sons were in the west beyond the sea. Ǫndóttr protected the money on behalf of his sister's son Þróndr.

Helgi was brought up in Ireland. He married Þórunn Edge, the daughter of Ketill Flat-Nose from the Hebrides and of Yngvildr, the daughter of Ketill Storm of Hringaríki. Then Helgi went to Iceland with his wife and children, Hrólfr and Ingjaldr and Ingunn, who was married to Hámundr Hell-Skin. He too followed Helgi out [to Iceland]. And when Helgi saw land, he asked Thor through an oracle where he should take land, and the oracle pointed him to Eyjafjord and permitted him to hold neither eastwards nor westwards from there. Then, before the fjord opened up, his son Hrólfr asked whether, if Thor pointed him to the polar sea for winter quarters, he would heed that or not.

Helgi took land outwards beyond Hrísey Island and inwards beyond Svarfaðardalr Valley. He spent the first winter at Hámundarstaðir. They had such a harsh winter that it almost came to the point where they lost all the livestock that they had. And in spring Helgi went up onto Sólarfjall Mountain and saw that there was much less snow to

[91] That is, in Norway.

be seen further into the fjord. He carried all he had onto the ship. He came ashore at Galtarhamarr, the 'Boar-Cliff'. There he drove two pigs ashore, the boar that was called Sǫlvi and a sow. Three years later they were found in Sǫlvadalr 'Sǫlvi's Valley', and by then they were seventy pigs altogether. That winter Helgi lived at Bíldsá, and in the summer he explored the whole district and took the whole of Eyjafjord between the peninsulas Siglunes and Reynisnes and made a great fire by the sea at every river-mouth and in this way sanctified the whole fjord between the islands for himself.

The next winter [Helgi moved his dwelling-place][92] to Kristnes 'Christ-Peninsula', and lived there to his dying day. He was very mixed in faith: he believed in Christ, but nevertheless he invoked Thor for seafaring and bold deeds and everything that he thought to be of greatest import. While Helgi moved his farm, Þórunn Edge was delivered of a child on Þórunnarey 'Þórunn's Island', in the branches of Eyjafjarðará River, and there Þorbjǫrg Islands-Sun was born. Then Helgi distributed land among his sons and relatives. To his son Ingjaldr he gave the land from Outer-Þverá River east of Eyjafjarðará River up as far as Arnarhváll Hill. He lived at Upper-Þverá and built a big temple there. He married Salgerðr, the daughter of Steinólfr the Short from Hrísey Island, son of Ǫlvir Children's-Man.

Their son was Eyjólfr, who married Ástríðr, daughter of Vigfúss of Vǫrs, [son of][93] Kári-of-the-Vikings. [Their][94] sons [were][95] Vigfúss and Manslaughters-Glúmr and Þorsteinn. The son of Manslaughters-Glúmr was Vigfúss, the father of Bergr, the father of Steinunn, the mother of Þorsteinn the Unjust. After that, people started to live in Helgi's land claim with his permission.

Chapter

185. A man was called Þorsteinn Sweeper. He married Hildr, the daughter of Þráinn Black-Giant. Þorsteinn went to Iceland and, following Helgi's advice, took Svarfaðardalr Valley. His children were Karl the Red, who lived at Karlsá; and Guðrún, who was married to the Viking Hafþórr. Their children were Klaufi and Gróa, who was married to Gríss

[92] Missing in the manuscript.
[93] Missing in the manuscript.
[94] Missing in the manuscript.
[95] Missing in the manuscript.

gleðill. Atli *illingr* was the name of a man. He killed Hafþórr and put Karl the Red in irons. Then Klaufi came unexpectedly and killed Atli and took Karl out of the irons. Klaufi married Yngvildr Red-Cheek, the daughter of Ásgeirr Red-Fur-Coat and sister of Óláfr Knuckle-Breaker and Þorleifr the Poet. To spite them, he cut open a bag of dye herbs which they had gathered on his land. Then Þorleifr spoke this:

> Bøggvir cut from me
> a hairless bag,
> and from Óláfr
> a strap and a cloak.
> In the same way shall Bøggvir,
> equipped with malice,
> be smitten
> if we live.

About that the *Saga of the People of Svarfaðardalr Valley* was made.

186. Karl was the name of the man who took the Strǫnd Coast from Upsir all the way out to Mígandi.

187. Hámundr Hell-Skin appropriated to himself the whole of Gamlastrǫnd[96] Coast and [the land] between the valleys Svarfaðardalr and Hǫrgárdalr and lived where Helgi had first lived, and which since then has been called 'at Hámundarstaðir'. Hámundr gave those [lands][97] which were beyond Reistará River to his relative Ǫrn, who before had taken Arnarfjord 'Ǫrn's/Eagle's Fjord'. Ǫrn lived at Arnarnes 'Ǫrn's/ Eagle's Peninsula', and Hámundr sold all the lands that lie between the rivers Reistará and Hǫrgárdalsá to Þorvaldr. After him, Þorvaldsdalr is named: 'Þorvaldr's Valley'. That is where he lived.

Then Helgi the Skinny gave the property between Merkigil Glen and Skjálgsdalsá River to Hámundr, and he lived at Espihóll Hill. His son, who lived there, was Þórir, the father of Þorvaldr Hook, the father of Ketill, the father of Einarr, the father of Þorsteinn the Unjust, the father of Guðrún, the mother of Halla, the mother of Flosi, the father of Valgerðr, the mother of Sir Erlendr, the father of Haukr. Þórunn was the name of the daughter of Ǫrn from Arnarnes Peninsula, who was married to Ásgeirr Red-Fur-Coat, the son of the Herjólfr who took Breiðdalr

[96] Probably *recte* read *Galmansstrǫnd* (*vel sim.*) as in H188, as both passages seem to refer to the same stretch of land. Jakob Benediktsson reads *Galmastrǫnd*.

[97] Added in the manuscript by a later (perhaps seventeenth-century) hand.

Valley. Ásgeirr was the brother of Bǫðmóðr *gerpir*, son of Grímólfr of Agðir. The mother of Ásgeirr and his siblings was Hjálmgerðr, the sister of Broddr and Bogi. Narfi was the name of the son of Ǫrn from Arnarnes; he married Úlfheiðr, daughter of Ingjaldr, son of Helgi the Skinny. After him the Narfasker are named: 'Narfi's Skerries'. Their son was Ásbrandr, the father of Narfi-of-Hella.

188. Galmr was the name of the man who took Galmansstrǫnd Coast between the rivers Þorvaldsdalsá and Reistará. His son was Þorvaldr, the father of Ormr, the father of Bjǫrn, the father of Þóroddr, the father of Þórunn, the mother of Dýrfinna, the mother of Þorsteinn the Smith, son of Skeggi. Hámundr[98] gave land to Þorvaldr between the rivers Reistará and Hǫrgá, but before that he had lived in Þorvaldsdalr 'Þorvaldr's Valley'.

189. Geirleifr was the name of the man who took Hǫrgárdalr Valley up as far as Myrká River. He was Hrappr's son and lived in Old Hagi. His son was Bjǫrn the Rich, from whom the men of Auðbrekka Slope are descended.

190. A man was called Þórðr the Tearing. He took Hǫrgárdalr Valley upwards from Myrká River and downwards as far as Drangar Rock Towers on the other side. His son was Ǫrnólfr, who married Yngvildr Everyone's-Sister. Their sons were Þórðr and Þorvarðr on Kristnes and Steingrímr at Kroppr. Þórðr the Tearing gave some of his land-claim to Skólmr, his relative. His son was Þórólfr the Strong who lived at Myrká River.

191. A man was called Þórir Giants-Burster. He was brought up in Ǫmð in Hálogaland. He was banished from the land by Jarl Hákon, son of Grjótgarðr, and therefore he went to Iceland. He took the whole of Øxnadalr Valley and lived at Vatsá River. His son was Steinrøðr the Mighty who managed to help many a man to whom other spirits caused harm. A woman who possessed magical powers and was prone to do harm was called Geirhildr. A man who possessed second sight saw that Steinrøðr caught her unawares, but she changed herself into the shape of a cow-skin full of water. Steinrøðr was a smith and had an iron goad in his hand. About their meeting, this has been spoken:

The roisterer of hammers
makes the ship-hook ring

[98] Manuscript: Helgi (which is inconsistent with the preceding chapter).

on Geirhildr's . . . skin as hard
as he can, and ever harder.
The long iron staff makes a storm
on the woman's side on Hjaltaeyrr,
which is enough for her;
the troll-woman's ribs are swollen.

Roisterer of the hammers = smith.

The daughter of Steinrøðr was Þorljót, who was married to Þorvarðr on Kristnes Peninsula.

192. A man was called Auðólfr. He went from Jaðarr to Iceland and took Hǫrgárdalr Valley as far downwards from Þverá River as Bægisá River, and lived at Southern Bægisá River. He married Þórhildr, the daughter of Helgi the Skinny. Their daughter was Yngvildr, who was married to Þóroddr Helmet, the father of Arnljótr, the father of Halldórr, the father of Einarr, the father of Jórunn, the mother of Hallr, the father of Gizurr, the father of Þorvaldr, the father of Jarl Gizurr.

193. Eysteinn, son of Ráðúlfr, son of Oxen-Þórir, took land below Bægisá River and lived at Lón. His son was Gunnsteinn, who married Hlíf, the daughter of Heðinn from Mjǫla. Their children were Halldóra, who was married to Manslaughters-Glúmr; and Þorgrímr; and Grímr Gravel-Bank-Leg.

194. Eyvindr Cock was the name of a respected man. He had a ship together with Þorgrímr, son of Hlíf. He was a relative of the sons of Ǫndóttr. They gave him land and he lived in Hanatún 'Cock's Enclosure', and was called Enclosure-Cock. The place there is now called Marbœli. He married Þórunn, the daughter of Stórólfr, son of Oxen-Þórir. His son was Snorri, the *goði* of the Hlíð-men.

The Sons of Ǫndóttr

195. Ǫndóttr Crow, who has been mentioned before, became a rich man, and when his brother-in-law Bjǫrn died, the chieftain Grímr said that the king had to own all his property, because he was a foreigner and his sons were in the west beyond the sea: Eyvindr the Easterner and Þróndr the Swift-Sailing. Yet Ǫndóttr managed to hold on to the property on behalf of Þróndr, the son of his sister. And when Þróndr learned of the death of his father, he sailed from the Hebrides—after which sailing he was called 'the Swift-Sailing'—and then received his paternal inheritance and went to Iceland, as will be told later.

Ǫndóttr's farm stood near the sea and there was only a short distance between it and Ingjaldr's farm. Grímr lived a short distance from Ingjaldr. He went to Ǫndóttr one night when he was cutting wood in the forest for the beer-brewing shortly before Christmas and, relying on the king's protection, he slew him, and four men altogether. And the same night Signý carried all of Ǫndóttr's movable property onto a longship and went with both her sons, Ásmundr and Ásgrímr, and all her farmhands to her father Sighvatr, and she sent her sons to Heðinn, who was bound to her through fosterage, in Sóknadalr Valley, for concealment, because she expected that Grímr would search for them. And to the east of Líðandisnes Peninsula he came after them with two ships and he searched her ship and did not find the boys.

Steinarr was the name of the man who accompanied the boys to Heðinn. Grímr went there to search for them. They found Ǫrnólfr, the son of Heðinn, in the forest. He feigned madness and behaved as if he was having a fit because he did not want to talk. Then they found another son of Heðinn, who was called Úlfr, who was looking after his father's livestock. He took half a hundred of silver from Grímr to give news of the boys. He brought the money to his father and told of this, but he did not go to Grímr.

Grímr did not dare to visit Heðinn, as he doubted the loyalty of the boy, and he went home, and the boys stayed in an underground house until autumn came. Then they secretly went away and wanted to get to Sighvatr, their maternal grandfather, and they became confused about which side of them the sea should lie on. There was a hard frost, and they were without shoes. Then they came to a farm.

Ásmundr said: 'Do you know this farm, brother?'

'No,' said Ásgrímr.

And when they arrived, they recognised the bedroom which their father had had built. They thought themselves to have come to the wrong place then and turned towards Ingjaldr the Faithful. It was Christmas Eve then. They did not reveal their identity there. Gyða was the first to recognise them and reminded Ingjaldr of the kindness of Ǫndóttr and his people and asked him to take them in.

They spent this winter there and did not use their own names. And the following summer Grímr gave a banquet for Jarl Auðun, the jarl of King Haraldr. And that night, when he had been busy brewing beer, the sons of Ǫndóttr burned him in the building. Then they took Ingjaldr's boat and rowed away to the island which lies by Hvínir. Before that, they told Gyða and Ingjaldr what had happened in the matter. He told them to leave and never to come into his sight again. They drew their boat ashore and went to a house. They heard a conversation between men in the house who were saying that they had been travelling with Jarl Auðun during the night. When they had heard that, they went to the boat and rowed to the mainland.

They saw where the jarl's longship lay, with a canopy pitched over it. They went to the shelter which they had been told that the jarl was sleeping in; and his men were on the ship, and two men were keeping watch over the jarl. Ásmundr gripped them both and held them. Ásgrímr went to the jarl and put the point of his spear against the jarl's chest and asked him to pay him the weregild for his father. Then the jarl handed over three golden rings and a velvet cloak, and Ásgrímr gave him a name and called him Auðun Nanny-Goat. The sons of Ǫndóttr ran to the boat and rowed out along the fjord and into the maelstrom that was in the fjord, and there they spread the cloak out on the sea, because they saw that the jarl's men were rowing after them and they would not get away.

The jarl's men found the cloak and believed that they had drowned, and the sons of Ǫndóttr went northwards around Stim to Súrnadalr Valley to Eiríkr Keen-on-Beer, a landed man.[99] There lived Hallsteinn Horse, another landed man. They exchanged Yule drinks and Eiríkr hosted them first and did so well, but Hallsteinn struck Eiríkr with a drinking horn when they were at his place. And when Eiríkr had gone home and Hallsteinn was sitting [at home] afterwards, Ásgrímr entered alone and gave Hallsteinn a serious wound and then ran out and to the forest, and they after him.

Ásgrímr dived into the river and swam through the frost, and Hallsteinn's farmhands wounded him severely with missiles. He managed to reach an old woman in the forest. She slaughtered her calf and laid the calf's intestines next to Ásgrímr. Thus it seemed to those who came in as if his bowels were lying there and he was dead. They went home, and the old woman secretly nursed him back to health in an underground room.

That summer Ásmundr went to Iceland, thinking his brother Ásgrímr dead. Helgi the Skinny then gave him land to settle at Kræklingahlíð Mountainside. At that time, Bǫðólfr from Hvínir went out [to Iceland] with him. His sons were Skeggi, and Þórir Wedge-Mountain. Later Bǫðólfr married Þorbjǫrg Islands-Sun. Their daughter was Þorgerðr, who was married to Ásmundr, son of Ǫndóttr.

[99] That is, a man holding land from the king.

Hallsteinn died of his wounds that same spring. Eiríkr Keen-on-Beer then gave Ásgrímr a thirty-oared longship, and he went raiding with it and kept to that occupation for some summers. King Haraldr sent out Þorgeirr, the son of Grímr's sister, to get Ásgrímr's head, and supplied him with two warships. He did not find him. Then he went to Iceland and intended to kill Ásmundr, and he came to Eyrar Islands and spent the winter in Hvinverjadalr Valley. The following summer, Ásgrímr came out to Eyrar Islands and had a half-share in a ship together with Þórir Wedge-Mountain, and there were twenty-four men on it. They had a falling-out, and Ásgrímr bought out his half of the ship. Þórir rode north with half the crew and came to Hvinverjadalr Valley and told about Ásgrímr's movements and then rode home.

Half a month later, Ásgrímr rode from the ship and was a guest of Þróndr the Swift-Sailing in Þróndarholt Forest. He offered him winter quarters and said to him that because of Þorgeirr it would not be safe to ride north. Ásgrímr went north anyway, together with eleven men, and they had twelve laden horses and bags on top. The day they rode over Kjǫlr, he told them to ride in chainmail and to wear hooded cloaks on top and to say, in case Þorgeirr and his men found them, that it was Þórir Wedge-Mountain who was travelling there, and that Ásgrímr had gone north. They spent two nights at Þorgeirr's, because he thought them to be Þórir and his men. He had over thirty men. He rode to the road with them, and when he came home, he went to sleep and dreamed that a woman came to him and told him who had been with him as guests. Then they rode after Ásgrímr. Ásgrímr and his men waited on the mound Southern Vékelshaugr, and there his brother Ásmundr came to meet him with forty men. He made peace with Þorgeirr and his men. Not many years later, Ásgrímr went abroad and married Geirríðr, daughter of Eiríkr Keen-on-Beer. Their son was Elliði-Grímr. They went then to Iceland and Helgi the Skinny gave Ásgrímr a land-claim on the slope of Kræklingahlíð, and the brothers and their people had the whole slope, and it was called Kræklingahlíð 'Slope of the Kræklingar, the Crowlings', for the reason that they were the sons of Ǫndóttr Crow.[100] Ásmundr lived at Southern Glerá, and Ásgrímr at Northern [Glerá]. Ásgrímr's son

[100] The toponym *Kræklingahlíð* is here explained with reference to Ǫndóttr's nickname 'Crow' (*kráka*): 'Slope of the Crowlings'. In Modern Icelandic, however, *kræklingur* is the designation of the edible blue mussel (*Mytilus edulis*), perhaps suggesting that the place name should rather be interpreted as 'Slope of Mussels'.

was Elliði-Grímr, the father of Ásgrímr, the father of Sigfúss, the father of Þorgerðr, the mother of Grímr, the father of Svertingr, the father of Vigdís, the mother of Hvamm-Sturla.

196. Helgi the Skinny gave his relative Hámundr land between Merkigil Glen and Skjálgsdalsá River, and he lived at Southern Espihóll Hill. His son was Þórir, who lived there. He married Þórdís, daughter of Kaðall. Their sons were Þórarinn at Northern Espihóll Hill and Þorvaldr Hook at Grund and Þorgrímr at Mǫðrufell Mountain and Vigdís.

197. Helgi gave his daughter Þóra in marriage to Gunnarr, the son of Úlfljótr, who brought the laws out [to Iceland], and [he gave him] land upwards from Skjálgsdalsá River as far as Háls Ridge. He lived in Djúpadalr Valley. Their children were Þorsteinn and Steinólfr and Yngvildr.

198. Helgi gave Auðun the Rotten, the son of Þórólfr Butter, son of Þorsteinn Snow-Ice, son of Grímr *kambann*, his daughter Helga and land upwards from Háls Ridge as far as Villingadalr Valley. He lived at Saurbœr Farm. Their children were Einarr, the father of Eyjólfr, the father of Guðmundr the Great; and Vigdís, the mother of Halli the White, the father of Ormr, the father of Gellir, the father of Ormr, the father of Halli, the father of Þorgeirr, the father of Þorvarðr and of Ari, the father of Bishop Guðmundr. Hámundr Hell-Skin married Helga, daughter of Helgi, after the death of her sister Ingunn, and their daughter was Yngvildr Everyone's-Sister, who was married to Ǫrnólfr.

199. To his son Hrólfr, Helgi gave all the lands east of Eyjafjarðará River upwards from Hváll Hill, and he lived at Gnúpufell Mountain and there built a big temple. He married Þórarna, the daughter of Þrándr Thin-Legged. Their children were Hafliði the Open-Handed and Valþjófr, Víðarr and Grani, Bǫðvarr and Ingjaldr, Eyvindr, Guðlaug,[101] who was married to Þorkell the Black. Valþjófr was the father of Helgi, the father of Þórir, the father of Arnórr, the father of Þuríðr, the mother of Þórdís, the mother of Vigdís, the mother of Hvamm-Sturla.

200. Helgi gave his daughter Hlíf in marriage to Þorgeirr, the son of Þórðr Beam, and land outwards from Þverá River as far as Varðgjá Chasm. They lived at Fiskilœkr Brook. Their children were Þórðr and Helga.

201. Skagi, son of Skopti, was the name of a famous man at Mœrr. He got into an argument with Eysteinn Rattler and therefore went to

[101] Manuscript: *-lavgr* (the masculine form of the name).

Iceland. On the advice of Helgi, he took the Northern Eyjafjarðarstrǫnd Coast outwards from Varðgjá Chasm as far as Fnjóskadalsá River and lived in Sigluvík Bay. His son was Þorbjǫrn, the father of Heðinn the Mild, who had Svalbarð built sixteen winters before Christianity. He married Ragnheiðr, the daughter of Eyjólfr, son of Valgerðr.

202. A man was called Þórir Flap, the son of Ketill Seal, son of Ǫrnólfr, son of Bjǫrnólfr, son of Grímr Woolly-Cheeks. Ketill Seal married Jórunn, the daughter of Þorgnýr, a law-man of Sweden. Ketill Seal was a great Viking. He went to Hjaltland with Turf-Einarr, and when he prepared himself for the voyage to Iceland, a man from his crew was called Gautr, and when they were waiting to put to sea, Vikings came at them and wanted to rob them, but Gautr clubbed their forecastle-man to death with the tiller at the helm. With that, the Vikings turned away. From then on he was called Helm-Gautr. Þórir and his men went to Iceland and came to Skjálfandafljótsóss Estuary. Þórir took Kaldakinn between the Skuggabjǫrg Cliffs and Ljósavatsskarð. He did not like it there and went away. Then he spoke this:

Here lies—driver of ships!—
Kaldakinn of old,
and unscathed am I going
away together with Helm-Gautr.

Driver of ships = seafarer.

Then he took the whole of Hnjóskadalr Valley as far as Ódeila and lived at Lundr 'Grove'; he sacrificed in the grove. Ormr Bag's-Back was a son of [Þórir] Flap [and] the father of Hlenni the Old, and Þorkell the Black in Hleiðrargarðr [was also a son of Þórir]. He married Guðlaug, daughter of Hrólfr. Their son was Ǫngull the Black; and Hrafn, the father of Þórðr at Stokkahlaða; and Guðríðr, who was married to Þorgeirr the *goði* at Lake Ljósavatn.

203. Þengill the Swift-Sailing went from Hálogaland to Iceland. On the advice of Helgi he took land outwards from Hnjóská River as far as Grenivíkr Bay and lived at Hǫfði Headland. His sons were Vermundr, the father of Ásólfr at Hǫfði Headland, and Hallsteinn, who spoke this when he came back ashore, when he learned of the death of his father:

The headland droops,
Þengill is dead!

The slopes smile
at Hallsteinn.

204. Þormóðr was the name of the man who took Grenivík Bay and Hvallátr 'Whale Breeding Place', and the whole Strǫnd Coast-Land outwards as far as Þorgeirsfjord. His son was Snǫrtr, from whom the Snertlingar are descended.

205. Þorgeirr was the name of the man who took Þorgeirsfjord and Hvalvatsfjord.

206. Loðinn Angle was the name of a man. He was brought up in Ǫngull 'Angle', in Hálogaland. He went to Iceland because of the tyranny of Jarl Hákon, son of Grjótgarðr. In Ǫngull, King Sigarr had lived at Steig, and there is Signýjarbruðr 'Signý's Well', and Hagbarðshólmr 'Hagbarðr's Holm'. He took Flateyjardalr Valley upwards as far as the Gunnsteinar 'Gunn-Boulders', and made sacrifices to them.[102] There lies Ódeila between his and Þórir Flap's land-claims. Ásbjǫrn *dettiáss* was the son of Eyvindr, the father of Finnbogi the Mighty.

207. Bárðr, the son of Bjǫrn-of-Heyjangr, came with his ship into Skjálfandafljótsóss Estuary and took the whole of Bárðardalr Valley upwards from Kálfborgará River and Eyjardalsá River and lived for a while at Lundarbrekka Slope. Then he noticed that the winds coming from the interior of the land were better than the winds coming from the sea, and he expected there would be higher-quality land south of the heath. He sent his sons south one March. They then found rough horsetail and other vegetation. And the following spring Bárðr made a little sledge for every animal that was able to walk, and made it pull its own fodder and a part of the movable property. He went on Bárðargata, 'Bárðr's Road', across Vánarskarð Pass and then took Fljótshverfi and lived at Gnúpar Peaks. He was called Bárðr-of-Gnúpar. His son was Sigmundr, the father of Þorsteinn, who married Æsa, the daughter of Hrólfr Redbeard. Their daughter was Þórunn, who was married to Þorkell *leifr*, and their son was Þorgeirr at Lake Ljósavatn. Another son of

[102] According to the Sturlubók recension, Ǫngull died during the crossing to Iceland. The taking of Flateyjardalr valley and the sacrifices at the Gunn-Boulders are there ascribed to his son Eyvindr. The difference seems to have been caused by Haukr (or one of his sources) accidentally skipping a line while inserting some additional material about Ǫngull in Hálogaland not found in Sturlubók.

Bárðr's was Þorsteinn, the father of Þórir, who was at Fitjar with King Hákon and cut a hole in a cowskin and used it as armour. Because of that he was called Leather Neck. He married Fjǫrleif,[103] daughter of Eyvindr. Their sons were Hávarðr in Fellsmúli Crag and Herjólfr at Lake Mývatn and Ketill in Húsavík Bay and Vémundr Fringed-Quilt, who married Halldóra, the daughter of Þorkell the Black; and Áskell and Háls, who lived at Helgastaðir.

208. Þorfiðr Moon, the son of Áskell the Charmer, he took land below Eyjardalsá River as far as Landamót and across Ljósavatsskarð and lived at Øxará River . . .[104]

His son was Þorkell *leifr* the Tall, the father of Þorgeirr the *goði*. First, Þorgeirr married Guðríðr, the daughter of Þorkell the Black. Their sons were Þorkell Fish and Hǫskuldr, Tjǫrvi and Kolgrímr, Þorsteinn and Þorvarðr; and Sigríðr. Later, he married Salgerðr, the daughter of Arngeirr the Easterner. He also married Þorkatla, daughter of Kollr-of-the-Valleys. His sons with these women were Þorgrímr, Óttarr, Þorgils. These were born out of wedlock: Þorgrímr and Finni the Dream-interpreter. His mother was called Lekný, a foreigner.

209. Heðinn and Hǫskuldr, the sons of Þorsteinn Giant, took land above Tunga. Heðinn lived at Heðinshǫfði Headland and married Guðrún. Their daughter was Arnríðr, who was married to Ketill, son of Fjǫrleif; and Guðrún was their daughter who was married to Hrólfr at Gnúpufell Mountain. Hǫskuldr took all the lands east of Laxá River and lived in Skǫrð. After him, Hǫskuldsvatn is named, 'Hǫskuldr's Lake', because he drowned in it. In their land-claim lies Húsavík Bay, where Garðarr had winter quarters. Hǫskuldr's son was Hróaldr, who married Ægileifa, the daughter of Hrólfr, son of Helgi the Skinny.

210. The foster-brothers Vestmaðr and Úlfr went to Iceland on one ship and took the whole of Reykjardalr Valley west of Laxá River, upwards as far as Vestmannsvatn, 'Vestmaðr's Lake'. Vestmaðr married Guðlaug. Úlfr lived below Skrattafell Mountain. His son was Geirólfr, who married Vigdís, daughter of Konáll, after Þorgrímr; their son was Hallr.

[103] Manuscript: Freyleif (against which reading cf. chapter 209).

[104] Here Hauksbók appears to have skipped one sentence, which in Sturlubók reads, 'Þórir, the son of Grímr Grey-Coat's-Mull (*gráfeldarmúli*) of Rogaland, took [land] across Ljósavatsskarð.'

'Heðinn and Hǫskuldr, the sons of Þorsteinn Giant, took land above Tunga .... In their land-claim lies Húsavík Bay, where Garðarr had winter quarters.' *The town of Húsavík seen from Húsavík Bay.*

211. A man was called Þorsteinn Headland. He was a chieftain in Hǫrðaland. His sons were Eyvindr and Ketill the Hǫrðalander. Eyvindr went to Iceland and took Reykjadalr Valley upwards from Lake Vestmannsvatn and lived at Helgastaðir, and his burial mound is there. His son was Áskell, who received his death-blow by the Eyjafjarðará River opposite Kroppr, on that occasion when Steingrímr wanted to take revenge for a blow with a sheep's head. Áskell was married to Grenjaðr's daughter. Their son was Manslaughters-Skúta. Fjǫrleif was the name of a daughter of Eyvindr, who was married to Þórir Leather Neck. Náttfari, who had sailed out [to Iceland] with Garðarr, appropriated Reykjardalr Valley to himself earlier and had made his sign on the trees, but Eyvindr drove him away. His brother Ketill lived at Einarsstaðir. His son was Konáll, who was married to Oddný, daughter of Einarr, the sister of Eyjólfr, son of Valgerðr. Their son was Einarr. Another son of Konáll's was Þórðr; he was the father of Sokki at Breiðamýrr Moor, the father of Konáll.

212. A man was called Grenjaðr, son of Hrappr, the brother of Geirleifr. He took Þegjandadalr Valley and Hraunaheiði Heath, Þorgerðarfell Mountain and Laxárdalr Valley in its lower part. He lived at Grenjaðarstaðir. He was married to Þorgerðr, the daughter of Helgi Horse. Their son was Þorgils Disaster-Point, the father of Qnundr, the father of Hallbera, the mother of Þorgerðr, the mother of Abbot Hallr and of Hallbera, who was married to Hreinn, son of Styrmir.

213. A man was called Bǫðólfr, the son of Grímr, son of Grímólfr of Agðir, the brother of Bǫðmóðr. He married Þórunn, the daughter of Þórólfr the Wise; their son was Skeggi. They went to Iceland and wrecked their ship on Tjǫrnes Peninsula and spent the first winter at Bǫðólfsskytja Nook. He took the whole of Tjǫrnes Peninsula between Tunguá River and Óss Estuary. Later, Bǫðólfr married Þorbjǫrg Islands-Sun, the daughter of Helgi. Their daughter was Þorgerðr, who was married to Ásmundr, son of Ǫndóttr. Their son was Þorleifr, the father of Þuríðr, who was married to Ljótr-of-the-Fields.

214. Skeggi, son of Bǫðólfr, took Kelduhverfi up as far as Keldunes Peninsula and lived at Miklagarðr Yard. He married Helga, the daughter of Þorgeirr at Fiskilœkr Brook. Their son was Þórir, a great trader. He had a trading ship built in Sogn; Bishop Sigurðr the Rich blessed it, who was with King Óláfr, son of Tryggvi, and baptised Þórir. From that trading ship come the ship's prows which stood in front of the door at Miklagarðr Yard for a long time afterwards, very useful for predicting the weather, well into the time of of Bishop Brandr. Þórir's son was Ormr. He was murdered by Grettir, son of Ásmundr. Grettir composed this about Þórir:

I do not at all ride to a meeting
with the shield's caring-poles;
alone I go away; a hard task
has been determined for this man.
I do not want to meet
the wise conquerors of Odin's timber.
I search for an opportunity for myself;
I will not seem mad to you.

The shield's caring-poles = warriors. Odin's timber = shield; conquerors of the shield = warriors.

I withdraw from where
Þórir's very large hosts travel.
It is not convenient for me
to disappear in their uproar.
We shun a meeting with famous men.
My path lies to the forest.
I have to keep Heimdall's sword
safe. Thus we save [our] lives.

Heimdallr's sword = head.

Þórir's son was called Án, the father of Ǫrn, the father of Ingibjǫrg, the mother of Skúmr, the father of Abbot Þorkell.

215. A man was called Máni. He was brought up in Ǫmð in Hálogaland. He went to Iceland and was wrecked on the Tjǫrnes Peninsula and lived at Máná River for a few winters. Then Bǫðólfr drove him away from there, and he then took [land] below Kálfborgará River, between Fljót Water and Rauðaskriða, and lived at Mánafell Mountain. His son was Ketill, who married Valdís, daughter of Þorbrandr, who bought the Rauðaskriðulǫnd Lands from Máni. His daughter was Dalla, the sister of Þorgeirr, son of Galti. She was married to Þorvaldr, son of Hjalti.

216. Ljótr Unwashed was the name of the man who took Kelduhverfi upwards from Keldunes Peninsula. His son was Gríss, the father of Galti in Áss.

217. Ǫnundr also took Kelduhverfi upwards from Keldunes Peninsula and lived at Áss Ridge. He was the son of Blæingr, son of Sóti, the brother of Bálki on Hrútafjord. Ǫnundr's daughter was Þorbjǫrg, who was married to Hallgils, son of Þorbrandr, from Rauðaskriða Land-Slip.

218. Þorsteinn, the son of Sigmundr, son of Stooping-Bárðr, lived first at Lake Mývatn. His son was Þorgrímr, the father of Arnórr at Reykjahlíð Mountainside, who married Þorkatla, the daughter of Bǫðvarr, son of Hrólfr from Gnúpufell Mountain. Their son was Bǫðvarr.

219. Þorkell the Tall came young to Iceland and lived first at Lake Grœnavatn, which branches off from Lake Mývatn. His son was Sigmundr, who married Vigdís, the daughter of Þórir of Espihóll Hill. He was killed by Glúmr on the field Vitazgjafi. Þorkell's daughter was Arndís, who was married to Vígfúss, the brother of Manslaughters-Glúmr. Þorkell got a son in his old age; he was called Dagr,[105] who married Yngvildr, the daughter of Hallr at Síða, whose previous husband was Eyjólfr the Lame.

220. Geiri was the name of the man who first lived to the south of Lake Mývatn at Geirastaðir. His sons were Glúmr the Poet, and Þorkell. Geiri and his sons fought against Þorgeirr Cut-Cheek and felled his son Þorsteinn. For that killing they were banished from the north from the district. Geiri spent the winter at Geirastaðir by Lake Húnavatn. Then

[105] Here Haukr seems to have skipped over a few words. Instead of stating that Dagr was the husband of Yngvildr, the Sturlubók recension reads: '. . . Dagr. He was the father of Þórarinn, who was married to Yngvildr . . . '

they went to Breiðafjord and lived at Geirastaðir on the Króksfjord. Glúmr married Ingunn, the daughter of Þórólfr, son of Véleifr. Their children were Þórðr, who married Guðrún, daughter of Ósvífr; and Þorgerðr, who was married to Þórarinn, son of Ingjaldr; their son was Helga's-Steinarr.

221. Jarl Turf-Einarr got a daughter in his youth; she was called Þórdís. Jarl Rǫgnvaldr brought her up and married her to Þorgeirr Blunderhead. Their son was Einarr. He went to Orkney to visit his relatives. They did not want to accept him as a relative. Then he went to Iceland with the two brothers Vestmaðr and Vémundr. They sailed north of the land and westwards around Slétta Plain into the fjord. They placed an axe on the peak of Reistargnúpr and therefore gave it the name Øxarfjord 'Fjord of the Axe'. They set up an eagle in the west and called the place Arnarþúfa 'Eagle's Mound'. And in a third place they set up a cross. They call that place Krossáss 'Cross Ridge'. Thus they consecrated the whole of Øxarfjord for themselves. Einarr's children were Eyjólfr, whom Galti, son of Gríss, killed; and Ljót, the mother of Hrói the Scorched, who took revenge for Eyjólfr and killed Galti. The sons of Glíru-Halli, Brandr and Bergr, who fell in Bǫðvarsdalr Valley, were the sons of Ljótr's daughter.

222. Reistr was the name of a man, the son of Ketill-of-Bjarney Island and of Hildr, the sister of Ketill Thistle; [Reistr was] the father of Arnsteinn the *goði*. He took land between the overhanging mountains Reistargnúpr and Rauðagnúpr and lived in Leirhǫfn Harbour.

223. Arngeirr was the name of the man who took the whole of Slétta Plain between Hávararlón Lagoon and Sveinungsvík Bay. His children were Þorgils and Oddr and Þuríðr, who was married to Steinólfr in Þjórsárdalr Valley. In his youth, Oddr was dull, always sitting by the fireside, and was called Coal-Biter. Then a polar bear killed them both, Arngeirr and Þorgils. Oddr went to search for them, and the bear was just sucking the blood out of them. Oddr killed the bear and brought it home and ate it whole, and said that he took revenge for his father when he killed the bear and for his brother when he ate it. Afterwards, Oddr was bad and difficult to deal with. He had such great powers of shape-shifting that one evening he left his home in Hraunhǫfn Harbour and the following morning reached Þjórsárdalr Valley[106] to come to the rescue of his sister Þuríðr, when the people of Þjórsárdalr Valley wanted to stone her for witchcraft and sorcery.

[106] On the opposite side of Iceland.

'Oddr . . . had such great powers of shape-shifting that one evening he left his home in Hraunhǫfn Harbour and the following morning reached Þjórsárdalr Valley to come to the rescue of his sister Þuríðr, when the people of Þjórsárdalr Valley wanted to stone her for witchcraft and sorcery.'
The lighthouse of Hraunhafnartangi, 'Hraunhöfn-spit-of-land', at dusk.

224. Sveinungr and Kolli took the bays which are called after them: Sveinungsvík, 'Sveinungr's Bay', and Kollavík, 'Kolli's Bay'.

225. A bad and difficult man was called Ketill Thistle. He took the Þistilsfjord 'Thistle Fjord', between the peninsulas Hundsnes and Sauðanes. His son was Sigmundr, who took land on Snjófjallsnes Peninsula. He was the father of Einarr of Laugarbrekka Slope.

Here begins the Settlement in the Quarter of the Eastfjordmen

Now here begins the settlement in the Quarter of the Eastfjordmen, and people say that this quarter was the first in Iceland to be fully settled.

226. A man was called Gunnólfr *kroppa*, the son of the chieftain Þórir the Hawk-Nosed. He took Gunnólfsvík Bay and Gunnólfsfell Mountain and the whole Langanes Peninsula beyond Helkunduheiðr Heath and lived in Fagravík Bay. His son was Skúli Dearth.

227. Finni was the name of the man who took the Finnafjord. His son was Þórarinn, the father of Sigurðr, the father of Glíru-Halli.

228. Hróðgeirr the White, son of Hrappr, took Sandvík Bay north of Digranes Peninsula, everything as far as the Miðfjord, and lived at

Skeggjastaðir. His daughter was Ingibjǫrg, who was married to Þorsteinn the White. Alrekr was Hróðgeirr's brother, who came out [to Iceland] together with him. He was the father of Ljótólfr the *goði* in Svarfaðardalr Valley.

229. Eyvindr *vápni* and Refr the Red, the sons of Þorsteinn *þjokkubein*, went to Iceland out of Trondheim, from Strind, because they had a disagreement with King Haraldr, and each of them had his own ship. Refr was driven back and King Haraldr had him killed, but Eyvindr came into the Vápnafjord and took the whole fjord from Vestradalsá River onwards and lived in Inner Krossavík Bay. His son was Þorbjǫrn.

230. Steinbjǫrn Short-Horn was the name of the son of Refr the Red. He went to Iceland and came into the Vápnafjord. Eyvindr, his father's brother, gave him all the land between Vápnafjarðará River and Vestradalsá River. He lived at Hof. His sons were Þormóðr Yard's-Gaze, who lived in Sunnudalr Valley; another one was Refr at Refsstaðir; the third Egill at Egilsstaðir, the father of Þórarinn and Þrǫstr and Hallbjǫrn and Hallfríðr, who was married to Þorkell, son of Geitir.

231. Hróaldr *bjóla* was the foster-brother of Eyvindr *vápni*. He took land to the west of Vestradalsá River, half the valley and the whole Selárdalr Valley outwards [as far as][107] Digranes. He lived at Torfastaðir. His son was Ísrøðr, the father of Gunnhildr, who was married to Ásólfr on Hǫfði Headland.

232. A man was called Ǫlvir the White, the son of Ǫlvir, son of Oxen-Þórir. He was a landed man and lived in the Álmdalir Valleys. He got into an argument with Jarl Hákon, son of Grjótgarðr. He went to Yrjar and died there, but his son Þorsteinn the White went to Iceland and came with his ship into the Vápnafjord after the settlement. He bought land from Vápni[108] and lived at Tóptavǫllr Field for several winters, beyond Síreksstaðr, before he got hold of the Hofslǫnd Lands by demanding repayment of his interest-money from Steinbjǫrn Short-Horn; but he had nothing to pay with except for the land. Thenceforth, Þorsteinn lived there for sixty winters and was wise. He married Ingibjǫrg, the daughter of Hróðgeirr the White. Their children were Þorgils and Þórðr, Ǫnundr and Þorbjǫrg and Þóra. Þorgils married Ásvǫr, the daughter of Þórir, son of Porridge-Atli. Their son was Spike-Helgi,

[107] Missing in the manuscript.
[108] Eyvindr *vápni* (above, ch. 229).

'Steinbjǫrn Short-Horn was the name of the son of Refr the Red. He went to Iceland and came into the Vápnafjord. Eyvindr, his father's brother, gave him all the land between Vápnafjarðará River and Vestradalsá River. He lived at Hof.' *The river flowing past Hof.*

who earlier married Halla, daughter of Lýtingr, son of Arnbjǫrn. Their son was Manslaughters-Bjarni. He married Rannveig, the daughter of Eiríkr in the Goðdalir Valleys. Their son was Shaggy-Broddi, and their daughter Yngvildr, who was married to Þorsteinn, son of Hallr. Shaggy-Broddi married Guðrún, the daughter of Einarr *sælendingr* and of Halldóra, daughter of Einarr. Their children were Þórir and Bjarni House-Long. Þórir married Steinunn, the daughter of Þorgrímr the Tall. Their daughter was Guðrún, who was married to Flosi, the son of Kolbeinn. Their son was Bjarni, the father of Bjarni, who married Halla, daughter of Jǫrundr. Their children were Flosi the Priest and Torfi the Priest and Einarr Bride and Guðrún, who was married to Þórðr, son of Sturla; and Guðrún, who was married to Einarr, son of Bergþórr; and Helga, the mother of Sigríðr, daughter of Sighvatr. Flosi the Priest married Ragnhildr, the daughter of Bǫrkr at Baugsstaðir. Their children were Bjarni and Einarr; Halla, the mother of Sir Kristófórus; and Þórdís, the mother of Lady Ingigerðr, the mother of Lady Guðrún and of Hallbera. Valgerðr was Flosi's daughter, the mother of Sir Erlendr the Strong, the father of Haukr and Valgerðr.

233. Þorsteinn the Charmer and Lýtingr went to Iceland. Lýtingr took the whole of the Eastern Vápnafjarðarstrǫnd Coast-Land, Bǫðvarsdalr Valley and Fagradalr Valley, and lived in Krossavík Bay and dwelled

here for not many winters. From him the Vápnfirðingar are descended. Geitir was Lýtingr's son, the father of Þorkell.

234. Þorfiðr was the name of the man who was the first to live at Skeggjastaðir, on the advice of Þórðr Straw. His son was Þorsteinn the Fair, who killed Einarr, the son of Þórir, son of Porridge-Atli; and his two brothers, Þorkell and Heðinn, who killed Þorgils, the father of Spike-Helgi.

235. Þorsteinn the Charmer took the whole of Hlíð Mountainside inland from the Ósfjǫll Mountains and upwards as far as the Hvamsá[109] River, and lived at Forsvǫllr Field. His son was Þorvaldr, the father of Þorgeirr, the father of Hallgeirr, the father of Hrappr at Forsvǫllr Field.

236. Hákon was the name of the man who took the whole of Jǫkulsdalr Valley west of the Jǫkulsá River and above Teigará River and lived at Hákonarstaðir. His daughter was Þorbjǫrg, whom the sons of Brynjólfr the Old, Gunnbjǫrn and Hallgrímr, married. Teigr 'Strip of Meadow' lay untaken between Þorsteinn the Charmer and Hákon. They transferred it to the temple. It is now called Hofsteigr 'the Temple's Strip of Meadow'.

237. Skjǫldólfr, son of Vémundr, the brother of Kári-of-Berðla, took Jǫkulsdalr Valley east of the Jǫkulsá River and upwards from Knefilsdalsá River and lived at Skjǫldólfsstaðir. His children were Þorsteinn, who married Fastný, daughter of Brynjólfr the Old; and Sigríðr, who was married to Ǫzurr, son of Brynjólfr. Their son was Bersi, after whom Bersastaðir is named.

238. Þórðr Cross-Stick, the son of Þórólfr *hálmi*, the brother of Helgi *bunhauss*, he took all the Tungulǫnd Lands between Jǫkulsá River and Lagarfljót Water beyond Rangá River. His son was Þórólfr *hálmi*, who married Guðríðr, daughter of Brynjólfr the Old. Their son was Þórðr Cross-Stick, the father of Þóroddr, the father of Brandr, the father of Steinunn, the mother of Rannveig, the mother of Sæhildr, who was married to Gizurr.

239. Ǫzurr Brisket took land between the rivers Ormsá and Rangá. He married Guðný, daughter of Brynjólfr. Their son was Ásmundr, the father of Mǫrðr.

[109] *Recte leg.* Hvanná.

'Porridge-Atli took the eastern shore of Lagarfljót Water, the whole area between Giljá River and the Vallanes Peninsula west of Uxalœkr Brook.'
The southern tip of Lagarfljót Water seen from its eastern shore.

240. Ketill and Porridge-Atli, the sons of Þórir He-Partridge, went from Veradalr Valley to Iceland and took land in Fljótsdalr Valley before Brynjólfr came out [to Iceland], both Lagarfljótsstrandir Coast-Lands, Ketill to the west of the *fljót*-Water between the rivers Hengiforsá and Ormsá. Ketill went abroad and stayed with Véþormr, the son of Vémundr the Old. Then he bought from Véþormr Arneiðr, the daughter of Jarl Ásbjǫrn Blaze-of-the-Skerries, whom Véþormr's son Holmfastr had taken during a raid on that occasion when Grímr, the son of Véþormr's sister, and his people killed Jarl Ásbjǫrn on the Hebrides. Ketill Noise bought Arneiðr for twice the price that Véþormr had first placed on her. But before she and Ketill went to Iceland, Arneiðr found a large amount of silver under the roots of a tree and hid it from Ketill so that he would marry her. They went out [to Iceland] and lived at Arneiðarstaðir. Their son was Þiðrandi, the father of Ketill in Njarðvík Bay. Porridge-Atli took the eastern shore of Lagarfljót Water, the whole area between Giljá River and the Vallanes Peninsula west of Uxalœkr Brook. His sons were Þorbjǫrn and Þórir, who married Ásvǫr, daughter of Brynjólfr.

241. Þorgeirr, son of Vestarr, was the name of a man. He had three sons, and one was Brynjólfr the Old, another Ævarr the Old, the third

Herjólfr. They all went to Iceland, and each of them was on his own ship. Brynjólfr came with his ship into the Eskifjord and took land above the mountain, the whole Fljótsdalr Valley above Hengiforsá River in the west and above Gilsá River in the east, and the whole Skriðudalr Valley, and thus the Vellir Fields outwards as far as the Eyvindará River, and he took a large piece of the land-claim of Uni, son of Garðarr, and lived there with his relatives by both blood and marriage. He had ten children, and then he married Helga, whom his brother Herjólfr had had, and they had three children. Their son was Ǫzurr, the father of Bersi, the father of Órœkja, the father of Holmsteinn, the father of Helga, the mother of Holmsteinn, the father of Hallgerðr, the mother of Þorbjǫrg, who was married to Loptr, son of the bishop.

'Brynjólfr came with his ship into Eskifjord and took land above the mountain . . .'
The village of Eskifjörður in its eponymous fjord.

242. A man was called Ævarr the Old, the brother of Brynjólfr, he came out [to Iceland] into the Reyðarfjord and went up across the mountains. To him Brynjólfr gave the whole of Skriðudalr Valley above Gilsá River. He lived at Arnaldsstaðir.

243. Ásrøðr was the name of the man who married Ásvǫr, daughter of Herjólfr, the daughter of Brynjólfr's brother and his step-daughter. She brought all the lands between the rivers Gilsá and Eyvindará as her dowry with her. They lived at Ketilsstaðir. Their son was Þorvaldr Hollow-Throat, the father of Þorbergr, the father of Hafljótr, the father of Þórhaddr Hollow. Hollow-Throat's daughter was Þórunn, who was

married to Þorbjǫrn, son of Porridge-Atli; another one was Ástríðr, the mother of Ásbjǫrn Shaggy-Head, the father of Þórarinn on Seyðarfjord, the father of Ásbjǫrn, the father of Kolskeggr the Wise and of Ingileif, the mother of Hallr, the father of Finnr the Law-Speaker.

244. A man was called Hrafnkell, son of Hrafn. He came out [to Iceland] late in the time of the settlements. He spent the first winter in Breiðdalr Valley, and in spring he crossed the mountains. He rested in Skriðudalr Valley and fell asleep. Then he dreamed that a man came to him and told him to get up and go away as fast as possible. He woke up and went away, and when he had gone only a short distance, the whole mountain fell down, and a boar and a bull that he owned were buried. Then he took Hrafnkelsdalr Valley and lived at Steinrøðarstaðir. His son was Ásbjǫrn, the father of Helgi; and Þórir, the father of Hrafnkell the *goði*, the father of Steinbjǫrn.

About Uni the Dane

245. Uni the Dane, or the Unborn, the son of Garðarr who discovered Iceland, went to Iceland on the advice of King Haraldr Finehair and intended to subjugate the land to himself, and from then on the king had promised to make him his jarl. Uni took land at the place which is now called Unaóss Estuary and built houses there. He appropriated land to himself south of Lagarfljót Water, the whole district as far as Unalœkr Brook; but when the local inhabitants realised his intentions, they started to be angry with him and did not want to sell him livestock or dwellings and he was not able to hold his ground there. Uni went away and came into the Southern Álptafjord. He did not manage to settle down there. Then he went east with eleven men and at the beginning of the winter he came to Leiðólfr the Champion in Skógahverfi. He took them in.

Uni loved Þórunn, the daughter of Leiðólfr, and in spring she was with child. Then Uni tried to run away with his men, but Leiðólfr rode after him, and they met by Flangastaðir and fought, because Uni did not want to go back with Leiðólfr. There several of Uni's men fell, and afterwards he went against his will, because Leiðólfr wanted him to get married and to settle down there and to be his heir. Somewhat later Uni ran away when Leiðólfr was not at home, but Leiðólfr rode after him when he learned of it, and they met by Kálfagrafir. He was then so angry that he killed Uni and all his companions.

Uni's and Þórunn's son was Hróarr the *goði* of Tunga. He was Leiðólfr's heir and was the greatest warrior. He married the sister of

Gunnarr from Hlíðarendi. Their son was Hámundr the Lame, the greatest fighter. Tjǫrvi the Mocker and Gunnarr were the sons of Hróarr's sister. Tjǫrvi asked for the hand of Ástríðr Woman-Wisdom-Slope, daughter of Móðólfr, but her brothers, Ketill and Hrólfr, denied him the woman, and they gave her to Þórir, son of Ketill. Then Tjǫrvi drew their likeness on the wall of the privy, and every evening, when Hróarr and his people went to the privy, he spat into the face of the likeness of Þórir and kissed her likeness, until Hróarr scraped it off. After that, Tjǫrvi carved them onto the hilt of his knife and spoke this:

Earlier, we have painted
the young bride of destiny
there on the wall, as well as Þórir.
That was placed with banter.
Now I have carved
the goddess of the ale-cask
on my hilt. I spoke much . . . with
the fair goddess of the maelstrom-acorn.

Goddess of the ale-cask = woman (who dispenses drink). Goddess of the maelstrom-acorn = goddess of the amber bead = woman (who wears jewellery).

This led to the slaying of Hróarr and his sister's sons.

246. Þorkell Full-Wise was the name of the man who took the whole of Njarðvík Bay and lived there. His daughter was Þórhildr, who was married to Ævarr the Old, and their daughter was Yngvildr, the mother of Ketill in Njarðvík, son of Þiðrandi.

247. Vetrliði was the name of a man, the son of Arnbjǫrn, son of Óláfr Long-Neck, [the brother of Lýtingr][110] and Þorsteinn Charmer and Þorbjǫrn in Arnarholt Forest. Óláfr Long-Neck was the son of Bjǫrn Whale-Side. Vetrliði took Borgarfjord and lived there.

248. Þórir Bowline was the name of the man who took Breiðavík Bay and lived there. His sons were Gunnsteinn and Sveinungr. Now Kolskeggr has previously told about the settlement.[111]

[110] Missing in the manuscript.

[111] Haukr also refers elsewhere to Kolskeggr 'the Wise' as one of the sources he used in composing his recension of the *Book of Settlements*; see the introduction and ch. 354.

249. Þorsteinn Horse-Fly took Húsavík Bay first and lived there. His son was Án, from whom the Húsvíkingar are descended.

250. A man was called Loðmundr the Old, and another Bjólfr, his foster-brother. They went to Iceland from Vǫrs from Þulunes. Loðmundr had great magical powers. He threw his high-seat pillars overboard into the sea and said that they should settle at the place where it would wash them ashore. And the foster-brothers took the East Fjords, and Loðmundr took the Loðmundarfjord and lived there for three winters. Then he got word that his high-seat pillars were on land to the south. After that he carried what he owned onto a ship. And when the sail was hoisted, he lay down and ordered that no man should pronounce his name. And when he had lain there for a little while, there was a great noise, and a great avalanche fell onto the farm that Loðmundr had had.

After that he sat up and said: 'It is my curse that henceforth the ship that sails out here shall never come [back] from the sea safe and sound.'

He held southwards past Horn and westwards past Hjǫrleifshǫfði Headland and went ashore a bit further to the west. He took land where the pillars had come ashore and between Hafrsá River and Fúlalœkr Brook; that is now the Jǫkulsá River on Sólheimasandr Sand-Plain. He lived at Loðmundarhvammr 'Loðmundr's Grassy Slope'. That is now called Sólheimar.

Þrasi lived there in Skógar and there was ill-feeling in his and Loðmundr's relationship as neighbours. One morning, Þrasi saw a sudden great flood coming from above. And these waters he diverted by means of his witchcraft eastwards past Sólheimar. A slave of Loðmundr's saw it and said that the sea was flooding over the land from the north. Loðmundr was then blind and spoke to the slave:

'Bring me in a ladle a little of what you consider to be the sea.'

He did so.

Loðmundr said: 'It does not seem to me that this is the sea. Follow me to the water and stick the point of my staff into the water.'

He did so. There was a ring in the staff. Loðmundr held onto the staff and bit into the ring. Next, all the waters flowed westwards past Skógar. Then each of them diverted the waters away from himself, until they met at some ravine and agreed that the river should flow to the sea at the place where the distance was shortest. In this flood, the Sólheimasandr Sand-Plain was created. There is the place where the Quarters [of Iceland] meet, and Jǫkulsá River in the middle of the sand-plain. Loðmundr's son was Sumarliði, the father of Þorsteinn Flattery-Mouth, the father

'In this flood, the Sólheimasandr Sand-Plain was created. There is the place where the Quarters [of Iceland] meet, and Jǫkulsá River in the middle of the sand-plain.' *The sand-plain of Sólheimasandur.*

of Þóra, the mother of Steinn, son of Brandakr, the father of Þóra, who was married to Skapti the Law-Speaker.

251. Bjólfr, Loðmundr's foster-brother, took the whole of Seyðisfjord and lived there his whole life. He gave his daughter Helga to Án the Mighty, and as her dowry she brought the whole lower shore of Seyðisfjord as far as Vestdalsá River. And Bjólfr's son was called Ísólfr, from whom the Seyðfirðingar are descended.

252. Eyvindr was the name of a man who came out [to Iceland] together with Brynjólfr and moved his dwelling place into Mjóvafjord and lived there. His son was Hrafn, who sold the Mjóvafjarðarland Land to Þorkell Veil, who lived there from then on. From him the Veil-Family is descended.

253. Egill the Red was the name of the man who took Norðrfjord and lived out on Nes Peninsula. His son was Óláfr, from whom the Nesmenn are descended, the 'Men of the Peninsula'.

254. Freysteinn the Fair was the name of the man who took Sandvík Bay and Barðsnes Peninsula and Hellisfjord and Viðfjord.

'Bjólfr, Loðmundr's foster-brother, took the whole of Seyðisfjord and lived there his whole life.' *Fjord and village of Seyðisfjörður seen from the south-west.*

About Þórir

255. Þórir the Tall, and Krumr was the name of another: they went from Vǫrs to Iceland, and where they arrived and took land, Þórir took Krossavík Bay and [the land] between Gerpir and Reyðarfjord. From him the Krossvíkingar are descended. And Krumr took land on Hafranes Peninsula and everything as far as Þernunes Peninsula and all the outer land, both Skrúðr and other outlying islands and three parcels of land opposite Þernunes Peninsula. From him the Krymlingar are descended.

About Ævarr

256. Ævarr was first in Reyðarfjord before he travelled up across the mountains; and Brynjólfr in Eskifjord before he moved upwards to settle Fljótsdalr Valley, as has been written earlier.

About Sæmundr

257. Sæmundr was the name of the man who took the whole of Fáskrúðsfjord and lived there. His son was Ǫlmóðr, from whom the Ǫlmœðlingar are descended.

Chapter

258. Þórhaddr the Old was a temple-priest in Trøndelag, inland at Mærin. He wanted to go to Iceland and before [going] dismantled the temple and took the earth and the pillars of the temple with him. And he came into Stǫðvarfjord and laid the holiness of Mærin on the whole fjord and did not allow anyone to destroy anything there, except for domestic livestock. He lived there his whole life. From him the Stǫðfirðingar are descended.

259. Hjalti was the name of the man who took the Kleifarlǫnd Lands and the whole Breiðdalr Valley. His son was Kolgrímr, from whom many men are descended.

260. Herjólfr was the name of the man who took all the land outwards as far as the Hvalsnesskriður Land-Slips. His son was Eyvindr *vápni*, from whom theVæpnlingar are descended.

261. Herjólfr, Brynjólfr's brother, took the Heydalalǫnd Lands below Tinnudalsá River and outwards as far as Ormsá River. His son was Ǫzurr, from whom the Breiðdœlir are descended.

262. Skjǫldólfr was the name of the man who took the whole of Streiti beyond the overhanging peak of Gnúpr, inwards on the other side as far as Óss Estuary and as far as Skjǫldólfsnes Peninsula by Fagradalsá River in Breiðdalr Valley. His son was Háleygr, who lived there later on. From him the Háleygja Family is descended.

About Þjóðrekr

263. Þjóðrekr was the name of a man. First he took the whole Breiðdalr Valley, but he ran away from there because of Brynjólfr and [retreated] down into Berufjord and took there all the more northern coast-land of Berufjord and [land] in the south and Búlandsnes Peninsula and inland as far as the Rauðaskriður Land-Slips on the other side, and lived for three winters at the place which is now called Skáli 'Hall'. Then Bjǫrn the Tall bought lands from him, and from him the Berufirðingar are descended.

Chapter

264. Bjǫrn Singed-Horn was the name of the man who took the Northern Álptafjord inland from the Rauðaskriður Land-Slips and Sviðinhornadalr 'Singed-Horn's Valley'.

265. A relative of Bǫðvarr the White was called Þorsteinn Pipe-Leg, and he went to Iceland with him. He took [land] beyond Leiruvágr Bay as far as the Hvalsnesskriður Land-Slips. His son was Kollr the Grey, the father of Þorsteinn, the father of Þorgrímr in Borgarhǫfn, the father of Steinunn, who was married to Bishop Gizurr.

266. Bǫðvarr the White, the son of Þorleifr Middle, son of Bǫðvarr Snow-Thunder, son of Þorleifr Whale-Guts, son of Án, son of Ǫrn Edge, son of King Þórir, son of Bǫðvarr-of-the-Pigs, son of King Kaun, son of Sǫlvi, son of King Hrólfr from Berg, son of the giant Svási from the north from Dofrar—King Hrólfr married Góa, after whom the month Gói is named;[112] she was the sister of Górr and Nórr, after whom Nóregr 'Norway' is named—and his relative Firebrand-Ǫnundr went from Vǫrs to Iceland and came into the Southern Álptafjord. Bǫðvarr took [land] inland from Leiruvágr Bay—all the valleys that lie there—and outwards in the other direction as far as Múli Crag, and lived at Hof 'Temple'. There he erected a large temple (*hof*). Bǫðvarr's son was Þorsteinn, who married Þórdís, the daughter of Ǫzurr Wedge-Shaped Ice-Pool, son of Hrollaugr. Their son was Hallr-of-Síða, who married Jóreiðr, daughter of Þiðrandi, and from there a great family is descended. Their son was Þorsteinn, the father of Ámundi, the father of Guðrún, the mother of Þórdís, the mother of Helga, the mother of Guðný, the mother of the sons of Sturla.

267. Firebrand-Ǫnundr took land north of Múli Crag: Kamsdalr Valley and Melrakkanes Peninsula and inland as far as Hamarsá River, and many men are descended from him

Chapter

268. Þórðr Shaggy took all the lands in Lón north of Jǫkulsá River, between it and Lónsheiðr Heath, and lived in Bær for ten winters. And when he got word of his high-seat pillars in Leiruvágr Bay below the heath, then he sold his lands to the law-speaker Úlfljótr, who came out there into Lón, the son of Þóra, the daughter of Ketill Kári-of-the-Hǫrðar, son of Áslákr Bifra-Kári, son of Án, son of Ǫrn Edge. Þórðr lived for several winters in Lón from the time he got news of his high-seat pillars, but when Úlfljótr was sixty years of age he went to Norway and was there for three winters. There, he and Þorleifr the Wise, his mother's brother,

[112] One of the winter months, from mid-February to mid-March.

'Bǫðvarr the White . . . and his relative Firebrand-Ǫnundr went from Vǫrs to Iceland and came into the Southern Álptafjord. Bǫðvarr took [land] inland from Leiruvágr Bay—all the valleys that lie there—and outwards in the other direction as far as Múli Crag, and lived at Hof "Temple". There he erected a large temple (hof).' *The farm of Hof in Hofsdalur Valley on Álftafjörður.*

established the laws which have since been called Úlfljótr's Laws. And when he came out [to Iceland], the General Assembly was established and people have since had a single law here in the land.

It was the beginning of the pagan laws that men should not have a ship with a figurehead on the sea, and if they had, then they should take the figurehead off before coming within sight of land and should not sail towards the shore with gaping heads or grinning mouths so that the land-spirits would take fright at it.

A ring of two ounces or more should lie on the altar in every main temple. Every *goði* should wear this ring on his arm for all those law-assemblies which he himself should hold, and before that [he should] redden it in the bloodiness of the blood of an ox which he had sacrificed there himself. Every man who had to perform legal business in court there should first swear an oath on that ring and name two or more witnesses to support him.

'I name witnesses in this matter,' he should say, 'that I swear an oath on the ring, a law-oath. Thus help me Freyr and Njǫrðr and the almighty God, that I shall in this way prosecute this cause or defend or bear witness or give verdicts or judgements as I know them to be most right and most true and in greatest accordance with the laws, and perform all legitimate pleadings which fall to me as long as I am at this assembly.'

Then the country was divided into quarters, and there were to be three assemblies in a quarter and three main temples in every assembly district. There were men elected to take care of the temples, with regard to intellect and righteousness. They were to pronounce judgements at the assembly and preside over the law-suits. Therefore they were called *guðar* 'priests'. Every man was to give a tax to the temple, as they do now for the church tithe.

About Þorsteinn

269. Þorsteinn Leg, the son of Bjǫrn Blue-Tooth, went from the Hebrides to Iceland and took all the lands north of Horn as far as Jǫkulsá River in Lón and lived in Bǫðvarsholt Forest for three winters. Then he sold the land and went back to the Hebrides.

Chapter

270. Jarl Rǫgnvaldr in Mœrr, the son of Eysteinn Rattle, son of Ívarr the jarl of the Upplendingar, son of Hálfdan the Old: Rǫgnvaldr married Ragnhildr, the daughter of Hrólfr *nefja*. Their son was Ívarr, who fell in the Hebrides [when he was there] with King Haraldr Finehair. Another was Walk-Hrólfr, who conquered Normandy. From him the jarls of Rouen and the kings of England are descended. The third was Jarl Þórir the Silent, who married Álǫf Improvement-of-the-Season, the daughter of King Haraldr Finehair. And their daughter was Bergljót, the mother of Jarl Hákon the Great.

Rǫgnvaldr had three sons out of wedlock. One was called Hrollaugr, a second Einarr, the third Hallaðr, the one who stepped down from the jarldom of Orkney. And when Jarl Rǫgnvaldr got word of that, he called his sons together and asked which of them would go to Orkney then. And Þórir asked him to prepare his journey. The jarl said that he should succeed to the rule there after his father. Then Hrólfr stepped forward and declared that he was willing to undertake the trip. Rǫgnvaldr said that he was well suited by virtue of his strength and prowess; but he said that he thought that there was too much overbearing in his character to make it possible for him to rule over a kingdom immediately. Then Hrollaugr stepped forward and asked if he wanted him to go. Rǫgnvaldr said that he would not become a jarl.

'You do not have the temperament for war. Your path will lead you to Iceland, and there you will become prominent and blessed with great offspring in that country. But your fate does not lie here.'

Then Einarr stepped forward and said: 'Let me go to Orkney, and I will promise you that which will seem best to you: that I will never come back, nor will you catch sight of me again.'

The jarl said: 'It seems good to me that you go away, but I expect little from you, since all your mother's family is slave-born.'

After that, Einarr went to the west and brought Orkney under his rule, as it says in his saga. Hrollaugr went to King Haraldr and was with him for a while, since after that father and son were never of the same mind again.

Then, following the advice of King Haraldr, he went to Iceland and had his wife and sons with him. He came to the east at Horn and there he threw his high-seat pillars overboard, and they were washed ashore in Hornafjord. Yet he was driven away and westwards along the land. He then got a hard voyage and had little water. They took land in the west in Leiruvágr Bay in the Nesjar Peninsulas, and there he spent the first winter. Then he got word of his pillars and went to the east. He spent the second winter at the foot of Ingólfsfell Mountain. Then he went eastwards into Hornafjord and took land west of Horn as far as the Kvíá River and lived first at the foot of the Skarðsbrekka Slope on Hornafjord and then at Breiðabólstaðr in Fellshverfi. He was a great chieftain and he maintained friendly relations with King Haraldr, and the king sent him a sword and an ale-horn and a gold ring which weighed five ounces. That sword was then owned by Kollr, the son of Hallr at Síða. Hrollaugr was the father of Ǫzurr Wedge-Shaped Ice-Pool, who married Gró, the daughter of Þórðr *illugi*. Their daughter was Þórdís, the mother of Hallr at Síða. Another son of Hrollaugr was Hróaldr, the father of Óttarr Whale-Calm, the father of Guðlaug, the mother of Þorgerðr, the mother of Járngerðr, the mother of Valgerðr, the mother of Bǫðvarr, the father of Guðný, the mother of the sons of Sturla.

Ǫnundr was Hrollaugr's third son. Hallr at Síða married Jóreiðr, daughter of Þiðrandi. Their son was Þorsteinn, the father of Magnús, the father of Einarr, the father of Bishop Magnús. Another son of Hallr was Egill, the father of Þorgerðr, the mother of Bishop Jón the Holy. Þorvarðr, son of Hallr, was the father of Þórdís, the mother of Jórunn, the mother of Hallr the Priest, the father of Gizurr, the father of Bishop Magnús and Þorvaldr, the father of Jarl Gizurr. Yngvildr, daughter of Hallr, was the mother of Þórey, the mother of Priest Sæmundr the Wise.

Þorsteinn, son of Hallr, was the father of Guðríðr, the mother of Jóreiðr, the mother of Priest Ari the Wise. Þorgerðr, daughter of Hallr, was the mother of Yngvildr, the mother of Ljótr, as has been written earlier.

'Hrollaugr . . . came to the east at Horn and there he threw his high-seat pillars overboard . . .' *Farm ruins below the mountains of Horn.*

About Ketill

271. Ketill was the name of the man to whom Hrollaugr sold the Hornarfjarðarstrǫnd Coast-Land from Horn in the west onwards and eastwards as far as Hamrar Rocks. He lived at Meðalfell Mountain. From him the Hornfirðingar are descended.

Chapter

272. Auðun the Red bought land from Hrollaugr from the west from Hamrar Rocks and westwards on the other side as far as Viðborðr. He lived at Hofsfell 'Temple-Mountain', and erected a large temple (*hof*) there. From him the Hofsfellingar are descended.

273. Úlfr the Man-of-Vǫrs bought land from Hrollaugr southwards from the Heinabergsár Rivers as far as Heggsgerðismúli Crag and was the first man to live at Skálafell Mountain. From him the Vǫrsar are descended. Later, Úlfr moved his farm to Pappýli and lived at

Breiðabólstaðr, and his burial mound is there, and Þorgeirr's mound likewise. Þorgeirr was the son of Úlfr-of-the-Vǫrsar, who lived at Hof, 'Temple', in Pappýli.

Chapter

274. Þorsteinn the Squinting bought land from Hrollaugr, everything from Viðborðr southwards across Mýrar Moors as far as Heinabergsá River. His son was Vestmarr, from whom the Mýrar-men are descended.

275. Þórðr *illugi*, the son of Eyvindr Oaken-Hook, son of Helgi, son of Helgi, son of Bjǫrn the Ungartered, he wrecked his ship on Breiðársandr beach. To him Hrollaugr gave land between the rivers Jǫkulsá and Kvíá. He lived at the foot of Fell Mountain by Breiðá River. His sons were Ǫrn the Strong, who fought against Þórdís Jarl's-Daughter, the sister of Hrollaugr; and Eyvindr the Smith. His daughters were Gróa, who was married to Ǫzurr; and Þórdís, the mother of Þorbjǫrg, the mother of Þórdís, the mother of Þórðr *illugi*, who killed Manslaughters-Skúta.

276. A man was called Ásbjǫrn, the son of Bjǫrn-of-Heyjangr. He died on the sea between Iceland and Norway when he wanted to go out [to Iceland]. But his wife Þorgerðr and their sons went out [to Iceland]. But it was said that a woman must not take land more widely than she would be able to lead a two-year-old heifer around during a spring-length day between sunrise and sunset, a half-grown(?) cow and well-behaved. Therefore Þorgerðr led her heifer away from Tóptafell Mountain, not far from Kvíá River, southwards and into Kiðjaleit by Jǫkulsfell Mountain in the west. In this way, Þorgerðr took land around the whole of Ingólfshǫfðahverfi between the rivers Kvíá and Jǫkulsá and lived at Sandfell Mountain. Her son was Ǫzurr in Bakkarholt Forest, and the older one Véþormr, the father of Þuríðr the Temple-Priestess. Ǫzurr was the father of Þórðr Freyr's-*goði*. Álfheiðr was the mother of Þórðr Freyr's-*goði* and of Þuríðr Temple-Priestess.

Chapter

277. Another son of Bjǫrn-of-Heyjangr was called Helgi. He went to Iceland and on the advice of Þorgerðr from Sandfell Mountain lived at Rauðalœkr Brook. His son was Hildir, from whom the Rauðlœkingar are descended.

Chapter

278. Bjǫrn-of-Heyjangr's third son was called Bárðr, who first took Bárðardalr Valley towards the north, but then he went southwards on Bárðargata 'Bárðr's Road', across Vánarskarð Pass and took the whole of Fljótshverfi and lived at Gnúpar Peaks. He was called Bárðr-of-Gnúpar. His sons were Þorsteinn and Sigmundr, Egill and Nefsteinn, Þorbjǫrn *krumr*, Hjǫrr and Þorgrímr and Bjǫrn, the father of Geiri at Lundar Groves, the father of Þorkell the Physician, the father of Geiri, the father of Canon Þorkell, the friend of Bishop Þorlákr the Holy, who founded the religious house at Þykkvabœr Farm.

Chapter

279. Eyvindr *karpi* took land between Almannafljót Water and Geirlandsá River and lived at Fors west of Móðólfsgnúpr Peak. His sons were Móðólfr the Smith, the father of Hrólfr and Ketill and Ástríðr Woman-Wisdom-Slope; another was Ǫnundr, the father of Þraslaug, the mother of Tyrfingr. Before Almannafljót Water flooded it was called Raptalœkr Brook.

About Ketill

280. Ketill the Foolish, the son of Jórunn Woman-Wisdom's-Slope, the daughter of Ketill Flat-Nose, went to Iceland from the Hebrides and was a good Christian. He took land between the rivers Geirlandsá and Fjaðrá above Nýkomi. Ketill lived at Kirkjubœr Farm. Before, Irish monks had settled there, and pagan men could not live there. Ketill's son was Ásbjǫrn, the father of Þorsteinn, the father of Surtr, the father of Sighvatr the Law-Speaker, the father of Fleinn,[113] the father of Guðrún, the mother of Narfi and of Loðmundr, son of Skeggi.

Chapter

281. Bǫðmóðr was the name of the man who took land between Drífandi and Fjarðará River and upwards as far as Bǫðmóðshraun Lava-field and lived in Bǫðmóðstunga. His son was Óleifr, after whom Óleifsborg is named. He lived at Holt Forest. His son was Vestarr, the father of Helgi, the father of Gróa, who was married to Glœðir.

[113] Or: Kolbeinn.

About Eysteinn

282. Eysteinn the Fat went from Sunnmœrr to Iceland. He took land east of Geirlandsá River as far as the point where his land met with that of Ketill the Foolish and lived in Geirland. His son was Þorsteinn from Keldugnúpr Peak.

283. Eysteinn, the son of Hrani, son of Hildir Difficulty, went to Iceland from Norway. He bought lands from Eysteinn the Fat, those which he had taken, and said that they were lands-in-between. He lived at Skarð. His children were Hildir and Þorljót, who was married to Þorsteinn at Keldugnúpr Peak. Hildir wanted to move his residence to Kirkjubœr Farm after [the death of] Ketill the Foolish and thought that a pagan man would be able to live there, but when he came near the fence of the home-field, he suddenly dropped dead. He lies there in Hildishaugr 'Hildir's Mound'.

'Hildir wanted to move his residence to Kirkjubœr Farm after [the death of] Ketill the Foolish and thought that a pagan man would be able to live there, but when he came near the fence of the home-field, he suddenly dropped dead. He lies there in Hildishaugr "Hildir's Mound".'
The rock formation today shown as 'Hildir's Mound'.

About Molda-Gnúpr

284. A man was called Hrólfr the Hewer. He lived in Norðmœrr; his farm was called Moldatún. His sons were Vémundr and Molda-Gnúpr, great warriors and blacksmiths. Vémundr spoke this:

I alone
brought death
to eleven.
Blow more![114]

Gnúpr went to Iceland because of manslaughters and took land west of Kúðafljót Water as far as Eyjar[á River], the whole of the Álptaver Fishing-Ground. A large lake lay there then and a hunting-ground for swans on it. Gnúpr was a powerful man and sold land to those men that came out [to Iceland] later, and it was densely settled there before the lava flowed from above. Then all fled westwards to Hǫfðabrekka Slope and built booths on Tjaldavǫllr 'Tent-Field', but Vémundr the Smith, the son of Sigmundr Disgrace, who owned the land there, did not allow them residence there.

Then they went to Hrossagarðr Yard and spent the winter there. There two sons of Molda-Gnúpr and he himself fell, and his son Bjǫrn took revenge for him and them. Bjǫrn went to Grindavík Bay and settled down there. Bjǫrn had almost no livestock. He dreamed that a being from the mountain came to him and offered to enter into companionship with him, and he said yes. Then a little later a he-goat came to his goats. Therefore he was called He-Goat-Bjǫrn. He became both powerful and very wealthy. A woman who possessed second sight saw that all the land-spirits were following He-Goat-Bjǫrn when he went to the assembly, as well as his brothers Þorsteinn and Þórðr when they were fishing. He-Goat-Bjǫrn married Jórunn, the step-daughter of his brother Gnúpr. From Molda-Gnúpr many great men in Iceland are descended, both bishops and law-speakers.

About Vilbaldr

285. Vilbaldr was the name of a man, the brother of Áskell-of-the-Thread-Hook. They were the sons of Dofnak. He came from Ireland

[114] The 'blowing' refers to Vémundr's bellows, as according to the Sturlubók recension he spoke this stanza while working in his smithy.

and had the ship which was called Kúði. He came into Kúðafljótsóss Estuary. [He][115] took all the Tungulǫnd Lands between the rivers Skaptá and Hólmsá and lived in Búland. His children were Bjólan, the father of Þorsteinn; and Ǫlvir Mouth; and Bjollok, who was married to Áslákr.

Chapter

286. A man was called Leiðólfr, the Champion. He took land east of Skaptá River as far as Drífandi and lived at Á east of Skaptá River outwards from Skál, and he had another farm at Leiðólfsstaðir at the foot of Leiðólfsfell Mountain, and there was a large number of settlements there then. He was the father of Þórunn, the mother of Hróarr the *goði* of Tunga. Hróarr married Arngunnr, the daughter of Hámundr, the sister of Gunnarr at Hlíðarendi. Vébrandr was the name of a son of Hróarr and a maidservant. Hróarr married Þórunn Eyebrow, the daughter of Brynjólfr in Hvammr 'Grassy Slope' in Mýdalr Valley. Their son was called Þorfiðr.

At first Hróarr lived at Ásar Ridges. Then he took the Lómagnúpslǫnd Lands from Eysteinn, the son of Þorsteinn Sparrow and of Auðr, daughter of Eyvindr, the sister of Móðólfr and Brandi. Þraslaug was the daughter of Þorsteinn Sparrow, who was married to Þórðr Freyr's-*goði*. Ǫnundr Pocket-Back, a relative of Þorsteinn's children, challenged Hróarr to a duel at the Skaftafell Assembly, and he fell at Hróarr's feet. Þorsteinn the Upplander married Þórunn Eyebrow and took her abroad. Hróarr also went abroad. Then he killed in a duel the berserk Þrǫstr, who tried to rape his wife Sigríðr, but he and Þorsteinn reached a settlement.

Chapter

287. A man was called Ísólfr. He came out [to Iceland] late in the time of the settlement and demanded lands or a duel from Vilbaldr; and Vilbaldr did not want to fight and moved away from Búland. He then had land between Hólmsá River and Kúðafljót Water, and Ísólfr moved then to Búland and had land between Kúðafljót Water and Skaptá River. His son was Hrani at Hranastaðir, and a daughter Bjǫrg, who was married to Ǫnundr, the son of Eyvindr *karpi*. Their daughter was Þraslaug, who was married to Þórarinn, the son of Ǫlvir on Hǫfði Headland.

288. Hrafn Haven-Key was a great Viking. He went to Iceland and took land between the rivers Hólmsá and Eyjará and lived at Dynskógar

[115] Instead of *hann*, the manuscript has *land*, which is clearly a mistake.

Forests. He foresaw a volcanic eruption and moved his farm then to Lágey Island. His son was Áslákr the Aur-*goði*. From there the Lágeyingar are descended.

289. A man was called Eysteinn, the son of Þorsteinn Man-of-the-Rock-Pillars. He went to Iceland from Hálogaland and wrecked his ship and himself was maimed in the mast and rigging. He bought Fagradalr Valley, but an old woman was washed off the ship in Kerlingarfjord, the 'Fjord of the Old Woman'. The Hǫfðársandr Sand-Plain is there now.

290. Ǫlvir, the son of Eysteinn, took land east of Grímsá River. Since Hjǫrleifr had been killed, no man had dared to take [land] there because of the land-spirits. Ǫlvir lived at Hǫfði Headland. His son was Þórarinn at Hǫfði, a half-brother—with the same mother—of Halldórr, son of Ǫrnólfr, whom Mǫrðr *órækja* killed under Hamrar Rocks, and of Arnórr, whom Flosi and Kolbeinn, the sons of Þórðr Freyr's-*goði*, killed at the Skaptafell Assembly.

291. Sigmundr *kleykir*, the son of Ǫnundr *bíldr*, took land between the rivers Grímsá and Kerlingará, which flowed there to the west of Hǫfði Headland. From Sigmundr three bishops are descended: Þorlákr the Holy and Páll and Brandr.

292. Bjǫrn was the name of a rich man and a great dandy. He went to Iceland from Valdres and took land between the rivers Kerlingará and Hafrsá and lived at the rowan-tree grove of Reynir. He quarrelled with Loðmundr the Old. From Bjǫrn-in-Reynir the Holy Bishop Þorlákr is descended.

293. Loðmundr the Old took land between Hafrsá River and Fúlalœkr Brook, as has been written earlier. What is now Jǫkulsá River on the Sólheimasandr Sand-Plain, which separates the Quarters of the country, was then called Fúlalœkr Brook. Loðmundr had a great number of children. His son was called Váli, the father of Sigmundr, who married Oddlaug, the daughter of Eyvindr the Orcadian. Another son of Loðmundr was called Sumarliði, the father of Þorsteinn Flattery-Mouth in Mǫrk, the father of Þóra, the mother of Steinn, the father of Þóra, the mother of Surtr the White, Skapti's stepson; he was a son of Sumarliði. Skapti the Law-Speaker married Þóra after Sumarliði. Vémundr was the name of Loðmundr's third son, the father of Þorkatla, who was married to Þorsteinn Cudgel. Their daughter was Arnkatla, the mother of

Hrói and Þórdís, who was married to Steinn, Brandakr's [son].[116] Their daughter was Þóra. Ari was the name of Loðmundr's fourth son; and Hróaldr; and Ófeigr was the name of an illegitimate son of Loðmundr. He married Þraslaug, daughter of Eyvindr. From him a large number of men is descended.

Here begins the Settlement in the Quarter of the Southland-People, and it tells how much Land each shall take

294. Here begins the settlement in the Quarter of the Southland-people, where the quality of the land is the best in the whole of Iceland and where the most famous men have settled, both clerics and laymen. In Iceland, the East Fjords were settled first, and [the area] between Hornafjord and Reykjanes Peninsula was last to be fully settled. There weather and surf directed the landing of men because of the unsheltered and harbourless coast. Some of those who came out [to Iceland] first settled next to the mountains and observed the quality of the land from the fact that the livestock were eager to go from the sea to the mountains. To those men who came out [to Iceland] later, it seemed that the ones who came earlier had taken land too widely; and on that question King Haraldr Finehair then stipulated that nobody should take [land] more widely than he would be able to carry fire over in a day together with his ship's crew. Men should kindle the fire when the sun was in the east; they were to make other smoking fires so that each could be seen from the next, and those fires which had been made when the sun was in the east should burn until night. Then they should walk until the sun was in the west and should there make other fires.

295. Þórólfr, the son of Herjólfr Breaker-of-Horns, and his brother Óláfr were kings in Upplǫnd. With them was Fleinn the Poet, son of Hjǫrr, who was brought up in the north in Mœrr on that island not far from Borgundr which is called Jǫsureið; his father lived there. Fleinn went to Denmark to visit King Eysteinn, and there he received much honour for his poetry so that the king gave him his daughter. Þrasi was the son of Þórólfr. He went from Hǫrðaland to Iceland and took land between the rivers Jǫkulsá and Kaldaklofsá and lived at Bjallabrekka Slope; the place there is now called Þrasastaðir, not far east of the waterfall, and Þrasi's tomb is west of the Forsá, the 'Waterfall-River', quite near the river at Drangshlíð Mountainside below the overhanging peak,

[116] The patronymic has been truncated in the manuscript, but cf. ch. 250 above.

and a landslide has fallen onto it. Geirmundr was the son of Þrasi, the father of Þorbjǫrn, the father of Brandr, the father of Skeggi, the father of Bolli at Skógar Forests, the father of Skeggi, the father of Hildr, who was married to Njáll, son of Sigmundr, at Skógar; their son was Skeggi, the father of Eyjólfr, the father of Brandr, who is now living at Skógar.

296. Hrafn the Stay-at-Home was the name of an eminent man, the son of Valgarðr, son of Vémundr Word-Plane, son of Þórólfr Creeks'-Nosed, son of Hrœrekr Throwing-Ring, son of Haraldr Battle-Tooth, the king of the Danes. He went to Iceland from Trøndelag and took [land] between the rivers Kaldaklofsá and Lambafellsá; he lived at Raufarfell Mountain. His children were Helgi Blue-Dry-Log and Freygerðr and Jǫrundr the *goði*, the father of Svartr, the father of Loðmundr, the father of Sigfúss, the father of Sæmundr the Wise, the father of Loptr, who married Þóra, the daughter of King Magnús Bare-Legged. Their sons were Jón, the father of Sæmundr and Bishop Páll and Sigurðr, the father of Jón in Áss, the father of Salgerðr, the mother of Steinunn.

About Ásgeirr Pincers

297. Ásgeirr Pincers was the name of a man, the son of Óleifr the White, son of Skæringr, son of Þórólfr; his mother was Þórhildr, the daughter of Þorsteinn Raider-of-Tombs. Ásgeirr went to Iceland and took land between the rivers Seljalandsá and Lambafellsá and lived at the place which is now called *at Auðnar* 'at the Wastelands'. His son was Jǫrundr and Þorkell, the father of Ǫgmundr, the father of Bishop Jón the Holy. Ásgeirr's daughter was Helga, the mother of Þórunn, the mother of Halla, the mother of Bishop Þorlákr the Holy. Ásgeirr forsook pagan sacrifices of his own free will.

298. Þorgeirr the Hordalander, the son of Bárðr Cup-of-Whey-Water, went from Viggja in Trøndelag to Iceland. He bought land from Ásgeirr Pincers between the rivers Lambafellsá and Írá and lived at Holt Forest. Five winters later he married Ásgerðr, the daughter of Askr *hinn ómálgi*, and their sons were Þorgrímr the Great and Þórir-of-the-Copses, the father of Þorleifr Raven and Notch-Geirr.

299. Ófeigr was the name of a famous man in Raumsdalr Valley. He fell out with King Haraldr and therefore went to Iceland. He married Ásgerðr, the daughter of Askr *hinn ómálgi*; but when he was ready for [moving to] Iceland, King Haraldr sent men to him and had him killed, and Ásgerðr went out [to Iceland] with their children, and with her

was her illegitimate brother, who was called Þórólfr. Ásgerðr took land between Seljalandsmúli Crag and Markarfljót Water and the whole of Langanes Peninsula upwards as far as Jǫlðusteinn Stone, and lived in the north on Katanes Peninsula. The children of Ófeigr and Ásgerðr were Þorgeirr *gollnir* and Þorsteinn Bottle-Beard, Þorbjǫrn the Quiet and Álǫf Ship-Shield, who was married to Þorbergr Grain-Hill. Their children were Eysteinn and Hafþóra, who was married to Eiðr, son of Skeggi. Þorgerðr was a daughter of Ófeigr who was married to Fiðr, son of Otkell.

300. Þórólfr, the brother of Ásgerðr, on her advice took land west of Fljót Water between the two Deildará Rivers and lived at Þórólfsfell Mountain. With him Þorgeir *gollnir* was brought up, the son of Ásgerðr, who lived there from then on. He was the father of Njáll, who together with eight men was burned in his house at Bergþórshváll.

301. Ásbjǫrn, son of Reyrketill, and his brother Steinfiðr took land above Krossá River and east of Fljót Water. Steinfiðr lived at Steinfinnsstaðir, and no men are descended from him. Ásbjǫrn dedicated his land-claim to Thor and called it Þórsmǫrk 'Thor's Forest'. His son

'Ásbjǫrn, son of Reyrketill, and his brother Steinfiðr took land above Krossá River and east of Fljót Water . . . Ásbjǫrn dedicated his land-claim to Thor and called it Þórsmǫrk "Thor's Forest".'
Þórsmörk and the river Krossá flowing through the valley.

was Ketill the Rich, who married Þorgerðr, daughter of Gollnir.[117] Their children were Helgi and Ásgerðr.

302. Herjólfr, the son of Bárðr, son of Bárekr, the brother of Hallgrímr *sviðbálki*, first settled on the Vestmannaeyjar Islands and lived in Herjólfsdalr Valley inside Ægisdyrr, the 'Door of the Sea Giant', where now the lava-field has burned. His son was Ormr the Rich, who lived at Ormsstaðir down by Hamarr Rock, where now everything is molten, and he alone owned all the islands. They lie off Eyjasandr Sand-Plain, and before there was a fishing-harbour there and no men's winter-quarters. Ormr married Þorgerðr, the daughter of Oddr Cold-Mouth. Their daughter was Halldóra, who was married to Eilífr, son of Brandr-of-the-Fields.

'Herjólfr, the son of Bárðr, son of Bárekr, the brother of Hallgrímr *sviðbálki*, first settled on the Vestmannaeyjar Islands and lived in Herjólfsdalr Valley inside Ægisdyrr, the "Door of the Sea Giant", where now the lava-field has burned.' *The view of Heimaey, the main island of the Westman Islands, from Helgafell Mountain.*

About Ketill Salmon

303. Ketill Salmon was the name of a famous man in Naumudalr Valley, the son of Þorkell, the jarl of the people of Naumudalr, and of Hrafnhildr, the daughter of Ketill Salmon from Hrafnista, son of Hallbjǫrn Half Troll. Ketill lived in Naumudalr Valley when King Haraldr Finehair sent Hallvarðr Hard-Traveller and Sigtryggr Swift-Traveller to Þórólfr, son of Kveld-Úlfr, a relative of Ketill's. Then Ketill assembled a host and wanted to help Þórólfr, but King Haraldr went on

[117] Þorgeirr *gollnir*. In the Sturlubók recension, his daughter is called Þuríðr.

the inland road over Eldueið and got himself a ship in Naumudalr Valley and thus went northwards into Álǫst on Sandnes Peninsula, and there he killed Þórólfr, son of Kveld-Úlfr, and then he went southwards along the coast; and he met then many men who wanted to come to Þórólfr's help, and the king then chased them away. A little later Ketill Salmon went northwards into Torgar and burned in their houses Hárekr and Hrœrekr, the sons of Hildiríðr, who had defamed Þórólfr with deadly slander.

After that Ketill went to Iceland, together with his wife Ingunn and their sons. He came with his ship into the Rangáróss Estuary and spent the first winter at the house-ruins of Hrafntóptir. Ketill took all the lands between Þjórsá River and Markarfljót Water. There within Ketill's land-claim, many noble men then took [land]. He appropriated the land between Rangá River and Hróarslœkr Brook especially for himself, everything below Lake Reyðarvatn, and lived at Hof 'Temple'. When Ketill had brought most of his things to Hof, his wife Ingunn gave birth and there delivered Hrafn, who later became law-speaker. Therefore the place is now called 'by Hrafntóptir' ('by Hrafn's House-Walls').[118]

Salmon also had all the lands east of Eastern Rangá River [and][119] Vatsfell Mountain in his possession, as far as the brook which flows beyond Breiðabólstaðr, and above Þverá River everything except Dufþaksholt Forest and Mýrr Moor. That he gave to the man who was called Dufþakr. He had great shape-shifting powers. Helgi was the name of another son of Salmon's. He married Valdís, daughter of Jólgeirr. Their daughter was Helga, who was married to Oddbjǫrn the Ship-Wright. After him Oddbjarnarleiði is named, 'Oddbjǫrn's Tomb'. The children of Oddbjǫrn and Helga were Hróaldr, Kolbeinn and Kolfinna and Ásvǫr. Stórólfr was Salmon's third son. His children were Ormr the Strong and Otkell and Hrafnhildr, who was married to Gunnarr, son of Baugr. Their son was Hámundr, the father of Gunnarr at Hlíðarendi.

Salmon's fourth son was called Vestarr. He married Móeiðr. Their children were Ásmundr Beardless; Ásbjǫrn and Aldís, the mother of Brandr-of-the-Fields; and Ásvǫr, the mother of Helgi the Black. One was called Æsa. Herjólfr was the name of Salmon's fifth son, the father

[118] In its specific Icelandic sense, *tópt* designates the unroofed rectangular walls of a building; thus, the place name seems to designate the site of an abandoned farm as a site of communal memory, with *tóptir* denoting 'house ruins'. (In this sense the word is used, for instance, in ch. 126 above: 'There one can see the large ruins of his house [*skálatóptir*].')

[119] Missing in the manuscript.

of Sumarliði, the father of Vetrliði the Poet. They lived at Sumarliðabœr Farm; the place is now called 'under Brekka' ('under the Slope'). Vetrliði was killed for defamation by Þangbrandr the Priest and Guðleifr, son of Ari, of Reykjarhólar. Sveinbjǫrn[120] the *goði* was the son of Hrafn, son of Salmon, who married Unnr, the daughter of Sigmundr. Their son was Arngrímr.[121]

304. Sighvatr the Red was the name of a noble man in Hálogaland. He married Rannveig, the daughter of Eyvindr Lamb, the father of a sister of Eyvindr the Plagiariser-of-Poets. Her mother was Ingibjǫrg, daughter of Hávarr, son of Grjótgarðr Háleygja-Jarl. Sighvatr went to Iceland and on the advice of [Ketill] Salmon took land in his land-claim west of Markarfljót Water, Einhyrningsmǫrk Forest above Deildará River, and lived in Bólstaðr. His son was Sigmundr, the father of Mǫrðr Fiddle, who in his day was the greatest chieftain in Rangárvellir Fields; and any assembly he did not come to was called an 'assembly without point'. Sigmundr fell at the Sandhólar-ferry; his burial mound is there east of Þjórsá River. Rannveig as well was a daughter of Sigmundr's, who was married to Hámundr, son of Gunnarr. Their son was Gunnarr at Hlíðarendi. Sighvatr's son was Bárekr, the father of Þórðr, the father of Steini.

305. Jǫrundr the *goði*, the son of Hrafn the Stay-at-Home, settled west of Fljót Water at the place which is now called 'at Svertingsstaðir'. There he built a great temple. A small piece of land lay unclaimed between Krossá River and Jǫldusteinn; Jǫrundr went around this land with fire and transferred it to the temple. Jǫrundr married Þuríðr, the daughter of Þorbjǫrn-the-Man-from-Gaul, and their wedding was at Skarfanes Peninsula with Flosi, who owned all the lands between the rivers Þjórsá and Engá. Their children were Úlfr the Aur-*goði* and Þórunn, who was married to Vigfúss at Hlíð Mountainside; and Valgarðr at Hof 'Temple'. His mother was Þorlaug, the daughter of Hrafn, son of [Ketill] Salmon; he married Unnr, the daughter of Mǫrðr Fiddle, after Hrútr on Kambsnes Peninsula.

[120] Sturlubók recension: Sæbjǫrn.

[121] Sturlubók recension: Arngeirr.

About Þorkell Bound-Foot

306. On the advice of [Ketill] Salmon, Þorkell Bound-Foot took land around Þríhyrningr, the 'Triple Peak', and lived there at the foot of the mountain. He had great shape-shifting powers. His children were Bǫrkr Blue-Tooth's-Beard, the father of Starkaðr under Þríhyrningr; and Þórunn,[122] who was married to Ormr the Strong; and Dagrún, the mother of Bersi.

About Baugr and his sons

307. Baugr was the name of a man, a foster-brother of [Ketill] Salmon. [He][123] went to Iceland and spent the first winter in Baugsstaðir and the second with Salmon. Baugr was the son of Rauðr, son of Kjallakr, son of Kjarvalr, King of the Irish. On the advice of Salmon, he took the whole of Fljótshlíð Mountainside down across Breiðabólstaðr as far as the point where his land met that of Salmon, and he lived at Hlíðarendi 'Slope's End'. His sons were Gunnarr and Eyvindr and Steinn the Valiant, and Hildr was a daughter, who was married to Ǫrn in Væligerði.

Steinn the Valiant and Sigmundr, the son of Sighvatr the Red, went abroad from Eyrar Gravel-Banks and came to the Sandhólar-ferry all at the same time, Sigmundr and his travelling-companions and Steinn, and each of them wanted to be the first to cross the river. Sigmundr and his men challenged Steinn's farm-hands and drove them from the ship. Then Steinn appeared on the scene and gave Sigmundr a death-blow. For this killing the sons of Baugr were all banished from Hlíð Mountainside. Gunnarr went to Gunnarsholt Forest and Eyvindr to the foot of the Fjǫll Mountains eastwards into Eyvindarhólar Hills, and Steinn outwards to Snjallshǫfði 'the Valiant's Headland'. Þorgerðr, Sigmundr's daughter, was displeased that the killer of her father went to that place and she egged on Ǫnundr Axe, a free farmer of his, to take revenge for Sigmundr. Ǫnundr went with thirty men to Snjallshǫfði Headland and there set fire to the houses. Steinn the Valiant came out and gave himself up. They led him onto the headland and killed him there. The charge for this killing was brought in by his brother Gunnarr. He married Hrafnhildr, daughter of Stórólfr, the sister of Ormr the Strong. Hámundr was their son. Ǫnundr was outlawed for the killing of Steinn the Valiant. He spent two winters with many people around him.

[122] Sturlubók recension: Þórný.

[123] Missing in the manuscript.

Ǫrn in Væligerði, a relative of Gunnarr's, kept an eye on Ǫnundr. After Christmas during the third winter, Gunnarr went with thirty men to Ǫnundr, following Ǫrn's instruction. Ǫnundr [was coming][124] from a game together with twelve men, [heading] towards his horses. They met in Orrostudalr, the 'Valley of the Battle'. There Ǫnundr fell together with four men, and one of Gunnarr's. Gunnarr was wearing a blue cloak. He rode uphill across Holt Forest towards Þjórsá River, and not far from the river he fell from horseback and was dead of his wounds. And when Ǫnundr's sons grew up, Sigmundr *kleykir* and Eilífr the Rich, they went to see their relative Mǫrðr Fiddle about the prosecution of the killing. Mǫrðr said that that was complicated, concerning an outlawed man. They said that they were most opposed to Ǫrn, who lived nearest to them. Mǫrðr propounded that they should get a case of outlawry against Ǫrn and in this way get him out of the district. Ǫnundr's sons undertook a lawsuit about grazing rights against Ǫrn; and it was the agreement that Ǫrn should be slain by the sons of Ǫnundr as an outlaw having forfeited his immunity everywhere except in Væligerði[125] and within bowshot of the sanctuary of his own estate. The sons of Ǫnundr always surrounded him, but he took good care of himself. Then once it happened, when Ǫrn was driving cattle from his land, that they came after him and killed him. And people thought that he had fallen as an outlaw having forfeited immunity.[126] Þorleifr Spark, Ǫrn's brother, paid Þormóðr, son of Þjóstarr, to return Ǫrn to the status of a man under the protection of the law. Þormóðr had then come out to Eyrar Gravel-Banks. He then shot such a long shot from his bow that Ǫrn's death was within the bowshot which determined the range of the sanctuary. Then Hámundr, son of Gunnarr, and Þorleifr brought a charge forward for the killing of Ǫrn, but Mǫrðr supported the brothers. They did not pay a fine, but were to be banished from the district of Flói. Then Mǫrðr asked for the hand of Þorkatla, daughter of Ketilbjǫrn, on behalf of Eilífr, and as her dowry she brought the Hofðalǫnd[127] Lands with her, and Eilífr lived there; and Sigmundr married Arngunnr, the daughter of Þorsteinn Man-of-the-Rock-Pillars. Then Mǫrðr married his sister Rannveig to Hámundr, son of Gunnarr, and he then went to live at Hlíðarendi, and their sons were Gunnarr at

[124] Missing in the manuscript.

[125] Manuscript: Velugerdi.

[126] That is, unprotected by the law, having been beyond bowshot range from his house.

[127] Manuscript: Hæda lannd.

Hlíðarendi and Hjǫrtr and Helgi and Hafr and Ormr Corner-of-the-Forest, who fell on the Long Serpent together with King Óláfr.

308. Hildir and Hallgeirr and Ljót, their sister, were Irish. They went to Iceland and took land between Fljót Water and Rangá River, the whole Eyjasveit district up as far as Þverá River. Hildir lived on Hildisey Island. He was the father of Móciðr at Móciðarhváll Hill. Hallgeirr lived on Hallgeirsey Island. His daughter was Mábil, who was married to Helgi, son of [Ketill] Salmon. And Ljót lived at Ljótarstaðir.

309. Dufþakr in Dufþaksholt Forest was a freedman of the brothers. He had great shape-shifting powers, and so did Stórólfr, son of [Ketill] Salmon. He lived then at Hváll Hill. They got into an argument about the grazing. One night, a man with second sight saw that a great bear came from Hváll Hill and a bull from Dufþaksholt Forest, and they met at Stórólfsvǫllr Field and, angry, set upon each other, and the bear was stronger. In the morning there was a valley left behind where they had met, as if the earth had been turned over, and that is now called Ǫldugróf 'Wave Pit'. They were both injured and lay in bed.

310. The brothers Eilífr and Bjǫrn went from Sogn to Iceland. Eilífr took Little Oddi up as far as Lake Reyðarvatn and as far as Víkingslœkr Brook. He married Helga, the daughter of Ǫnundr *bíldr*. Their son was Eilífr the Young, who married Oddný, the daughter of Oddr the Thin. Their daughter was Þuríðr, who was married to Þorgeirr in Oddi. Their daughter was Helga.

311. Bjǫrn lived in Svínhagi Pasture and took land up along Rangá River. His children were Þorsteinn, the father of Grímr Baldhead-of-the-Forests; and Hallveig, the mother of Þórunn, the mother of Guðrún, the mother of Sæmundr, the father of Bishop Brandr.

312. A man was called Kollr, the son of Óttarr Ball. He took land east of Lake Reyðarvatn and Stotalœkr Brook from Trǫllaskógr 'Forest of the Trolls', as far as the point where his land met that of Þorsteinn Tent-Pitcher, and he lived in Sandgil Glen. His son was Egill, who lay in ambush for Gunnarr, son of Hámundr, by Knafahólar Hills and fell there himself together with two Norwegians and his farmhand Ari; and Hjǫrtr, Gunnarr's brother, out of his company. Gunnarr's sons were Grani and Hámundr. Gunnarr fought with Otkell from Kirkjubœr Farm by a yard at Hof 'Temple', and there fell Otkell and Skammkell. Geir the *goði* and Gizurr the White and Ásgrímr, son of Ship-Grímr, and Stǫrkuðr

from the foot of the triple-peaked mountain of Þríhyrningr, the son of Bárðr Blue-Beard,[128] son of Þorkell Bound-Foot, who married Þuríðr, daughter of Egill, from Sandgil Glen—they went during the season of the *leið*-Assembly[129] and came during the night with thirty men to Hlíðarendi, and Gunnarr was there with one grown man. Two men out of Geirr's company fell, and sixteen were wounded, before Gunarr fell.

313. A man was called Hrólfr Redbeard. He took all the Hólmslǫnd Lands between the rivers Fiská and Rangá and lived at Fors 'Waterfall'. His children were Þorsteinn Rednosed, who lived there later on; and Þóra, the mother of Þorkell Moon; and Ása, the mother of Þórný, the mother of Þorgeirr at Lake Ljósavatn; and Helga, the mother of Oddr from Mjósyndi. Oddr's daughter was Ásbjǫrg, who was married to Þorsteinn the *goði*, the father of Bjǫrn the Wise, the father of Skeggi, the father of Markús the Law-Speaker.

Þorsteinn Rednosed was a great sacrificer. He sacrificed to the waterfall (*fors*), and people were to bring all the leftover food to the waterfall. He also had great foreknowledge of the future. Þorsteinn had his sheep counted out of the public fold: twenty hundreds—and then the whole fold ran away from there. And the reason that the herd of sheep was so big was that he foresaw in autumn which ones were doomed to death, and had all these slaughtered. And in the last autumn of his life, he said in the public sheep fold:

'Now slaughter those sheep you want. Now I am doomed to die, or else the whole herd of sheep, unless it be both.'

And in the night in which Þorsteinn died, something drove the whole herd of sheep out into the waterfall, and they perished there. Helga was the name of his daughter, who was married to Helgi Roe, son of Kjallakr.

314. Úlfr Wolf was the name of a powerful chieftain in Norway in Telemark. He lived at Fíflavellir Fields in Tinnsdalr Valley. His son was Ásgrímr, the father of Þorsteinn and Þorlaug. Þorkatla was the name of their mother, who was called 'Buckle'. King Haraldr Finehair sent his relative Þórormr from Þruma from Agðir to collect taxes from Ásgrímr, as the king ordered him, but he did not pay, because he had a little earlier sent the king a horse from Gotland and much silver, and he said that should be a gift and not tribute, because he had never paid taxes before. The king sent the money back and did not want to accept it. Þorkatla,

[128] In ch. 306 above, his name is given as 'Bǫrkr Blue-Tooth's-Beard'.

[129] This assembly was held shortly after midsummer.

Ásgrímr's wife, gave birth to a male child. Ásgrímr ordered that it should be exposed. The slave that was to dig a grave for it sharpened the hoe, and the boy was laid down on the floor. Then it was heard by them all how the boy spoke this:

> May he leave the boy to his mother,
> I am cold on the floor.
> Where would the boy be even more fittingly
> than with his father's eagles?
> There is no reason to sharpen the iron,
> nor to diminish the turf.
> Let be the ugly work!
> I shall yet live with men.

Then the boy was sprinkled with water and called Þorsteinn. And when Þórormr came a second time to collect taxes, Ásgrímr summoned an assembly and asked the farmers whether they wanted to pay the king such taxes as were demanded. They asked him to answer for them and yet did not want to pay. The assembly was by a forest, and then, when he was least on his guard, a slave of Þórormr's jumped forward at Ásgrímr and killed him; the farmers killed him immediately. Þorsteinn was then on a raiding expedition, and when he got word of the killing of his father, he sold his lands for silver and made himself ready to go to Iceland from Grenmarr, east of Líðandisnes Peninsula; and before he went, Þorsteinn burned Þórormr in his house in Þruma and took revenge for his father. His brother was called Þorgeirr. He was ten winters old when Þórormr had their father killed.

He went to Iceland with Þorsteinn and Þórunn, their mother's sister, and took Þórunnarhálsar Ridges and lived there after that. Þorsteinn came into Rangáróss Estuary and on the advice of Flosi took land above Víkingslœkr Brook and outwards as far as the point where his land met that of Bjǫrn-of-Svínhagi Pasture, and he lived in Eastern Skarð. In his time a ship came into Rangáróss Estuary, on which there was a great disease, and nobody wanted to [take][130] them[131] in; but Þorsteinn sought them out and made them a tent-booth at the place which is now called Tjaldastaðir 'Tents-Steads',[132] and he himself tended them there as

[130] Missing in the manuscript.

[131] That is, the crew.

[132] The manuscript has *Tialldar staðir*, which is not a grammatically correct form if a derivation of the name from *tjald* 'tent' is intended, as clearly suggested

long as they lived; but they all died. From then onwards, he was called Þorsteinn Tent-Pitcher. And the one of them who lived longest hid gold and silver and buried it deep so that nobody has found it since.

Þorsteinn was first married to Þuríðr, daughter of Gunnarr, son of Hámundr. Their children were Gunnarr, Þórhallr, Jósteinn, Jórunn. Later, Þorsteinn married Þuríðr, the daughter of Sigfúss at Hlíð Mountainside; their children were Skeggi and Þorkatla, Rannveig and Arnóra. And Þorgeirr, Þorsteinn's brother, bought Oddaland from Hrafn, son of [Ketill] Salmon, both Strandir Coast-Lands and Varmadalr Valley, and the whole tongue of land between Hróarslœkr Brook and Rangá River. He lived first in Oddi 'Tongue of Land', and married Þuríðr, the daughter of Eilífr the Young; their daughter was Helga, who was married to Svartr, son of Úlfr; their son was Loðmundr in Oddi, the father of Sigfúss the Priest, the father of Sæmundr the Wise.

315. A man was called Flosi, the son of Þorbjǫrn-the-Man-from-Gaul. He killed three stewards of King Haraldr Finehair and after that went to Iceland. He took land east of Rangá River, the whole Eastern Rangárvellir Fields. His daughter was Ásný, the mother of Þuríðr, who was married to Brandr-of-the-Fields. The son of Brandr-of-the-Fields was Flosi, the father of Kolbeinn, the father of Guðrún, who was married to Sæmundr the Wise. Flosi married Guðrún, daughter of Þórir, son of Shaggy-Broddi. Their sons were Kolbeinn, who has been mentioned earlier, and Bjarni, the father of Bjarni, the father of Flosi, the father of Valgerðr, the mother of Sir Erlendr, the father of Haukr. Because of that Loðmundr the Old, the son of Flosi's sister, went to Gaular to sacrifice, because Flosi had no peace in Norway. Flosi the Norwegian married Þórdís the Tall, the daughter of Þórunn the Rich, daughter of Ketill the One-Handed. Their daughter was Ásný, who was married to Þorgeirr.

316. A man was called Ketill the One-Handed, the son of Auðun Thin-Hair. He took the Outer Rangárvellir Fields above Lœkjarbotnar and east of Þjórsá River and lived at Á River. He married Ásleif, daughter of Þorgils. Their son was Auðun, the father of Brynjólfr, the father of Bergþórr, the father of Þorlákr, the father of Þórhallr, the father of Bishop Þorlákr the Holy.

---

by the story. However, it is not particularly uncommon in later (twentieth-century) place-storytelling for an internal final -r, like that in Tjalda[r]staðir to be either inserted or omitted ungrammatically: in spoken language, unless enunciated very carefully, an -r in this position appears to be almost inaudible.

317. Ketill Salmon-Trout, a cousin of Ketill the One-Handed, took the outer land along Þjórsá River and lived on the Outer Vellir Fields. His son was Helgi Roe, who married Helga, the daughter of Þorsteinn Rednosed. Their son was Oddr the Thin, the father of Ásgerðr, who was married to Þorsteinn the *goði*, and of Oddný, who was married to Eilífr the Young.

318. Ormr the Rich, the son of Úlfr the Sharp, took land along Rangá River on the advice of Ketill the One-Handed and lived in Húsagarðr Yard, and after him his son Áskell, and his son built the first farm on Vellir Fields. From him the Vallverjar are descended.

About Þorsteinn

319. Þorsteinn *launan* was the name of a man from Norway, a great trader. It was prophesied to him that he would die in that land which was not yet settled then. Þorsteinn went to Iceland in his old age, together with his son Þorgils. They took the upper part of the Þjórsárholt Forest and settled in Lunansholt Forest, and there Þorsteinn is buried in a mound. Þorgils's daughter was Ásleif, who was married to Ketill the One-Handed. Their sons were Auðun, who has been mentioned earlier, and Eilífr, the father of Þorgeirr, the father of Skeggi, the father of Hjalti in Þjórsárdalr Valley. He was the father of Jórunn, the mother of Guðrún, the mother of Einarr, the father of Bishop Magnús. Gunnsteinn Killer-of-Berserks, the son of Bǫlverkr Pole-of-Hidden-Pegs, killed two berserks, and earlier the second one of them had killed Grjótgarðr the Háleygja-Jarl in Sǫlvi inland from Agðanes. Gunnsteinn was then, on his ship northwards in Hefni, shot from the forest with a Finnish arrow. Gunnsteinn's son was Þorgeirr, who married Þórunn the Rich, the daughter of Ketill the One-Handed. Their daughter was Þórdís the Great.

320. The brothers Ráðormr and Jólgeirr came from the British Isles across the sea to Iceland. They took land between the rivers Þjórsá and Rangá. Ráðormr appropriated land east of Rauðalœkr Brook to himself and lived in Vétleifsholt Forest. His daughter was Arnbjǫrg, who was married to Svertingr, son of Hjǫrleifr. Their children were Grímr the Law-Speaker and Jórunn. Later, Arnbjǫrg was married to Gnúpr, son of Molda-Gnúpr, and their children were Hallsteinn at Hjalli Mountain Ledge and Rannveig, the mother of Skapti the Law-Speaker, and Geirný, the mother of Poet-Hrafn. Jólgeirr appropriated land beyond Rauðalœkr Brook and as far as Steinslœkr Brook to himself. He lived at Jólgeirsstaðir.

321. Áskell[133] *hnokkan*, the son of Dufþakr, son of Dufníall, son of Kjarvalr, king of the Irish, he took land between Steinslœkr Brook and Þjórsá River and lived at Áskelshǫfði Headland. His son was Ásmundr, the father of Ásgautr, the father of Skeggi, the father of Þorvaldr, the father of Þorlaug, the mother of Þorgerðr, the mother of Bishop Jón the Holy.

322. Þorkell Digger, the foster-brother of Ráðormr, appropriated all the land between the rivers Rangá and Þjórsá to himself and lived in Háfr. He married Þórunn the Orcadian. Their daughter was Þórdís, the mother of Skeggi, the father of Þorvaldr at Áss Ridge. From there his relative Hjalti and his eleven companions took riding-horses to the General Assembly, on that occasion when he had come out [to Iceland] with Christianity, and no one else dared [to support him], because of the bullying of Rúnólfr, son of Úlfr, who had Hjalti outlawed for blasphemy.

Now the men are written of who have received and taken land in the land-claim of Ketill Salmon.

323. Loptr, the son of Ormr, son of Fróði, went to Iceland from Gaular at a young age and took land beyond Þjórsá River and upwards as far as Skúfslœkr Brook, and Eastern Breiðamýrr Moor upwards as far as Súluholt Forest, and lived at Gaulverjabœr Farm, and [so did] his mother Oddný, the daughter of Þorbjǫrn-the-Man-from-Gaul. Loptr went abroad every third summer for his own and his uncle Flosi's sake, in order to sacrifice at the temple which Þorbjǫrn, his mother's father, had maintained there in Gaular. Þorbjǫrn was a powerful chieftain in Norway in Fjalafylki. He was a son of Ormarr. He married Hildr, daughter of Úlfarr and of Þórunn Snow Grouse-of-Grœningr. Vémundr the Old, the son of Víkingr Devil-of-Skáney-Island, a relative of Bjǫrn the Ungartered, was a powerful chieftain. His son was Fróði, the father of Ormr, the father of Loptr the Old; from him many great men are descended: Þorlákr the Holy and Bishop Brandr and Bishop Páll.

324. Þorviðr, the son of Úlfarr, the brother of Hildr, went to Iceland from Vǫrs, and his relative Loptr gave him land on Breiðamýrr Moor, and he lived at Vǫrsabœr Farm. His children were Hrafn and Hallveig, who was married to Ǫzurr the White; their son was Þorgrímr the Bearded.

[133] Manuscript: Ásgeirr (but cf. chapter 285).

325. A man was called Þórarinn, the son of Þorkell from Alviðra, son of Hallbjǫrn Champion-of-the-Hǫrðar. He came with his ship into Þjórsáróss Estuary and had a young bull's head on the stem of his ship, and the river there is named after that.[134] Þórarinn took land above Skúfslœkr Brook as far as Rauðá River along Þjórsá River. His daughter was Heimlaug, whom Loptr got to have at the age of sixty.

326. A king in Sogn was called Haraldr Gold-Beard. He married Sǫlvǫr, the daughter of Jarl Hundólfr, the sister of Jarl Atli the Thin. Their daughters were Þóra, who was married to Hálfdan the Black, King of the Upplendingar; and Þuríðr, who was married to Ketill Thin Slate. Haraldr the Young was the son of Hálfdan and Þóra; to him Haraldr Gold-Beard gave his name and kingdom. King Haraldr was the first of them to die, and then Þóra, and Haraldr the Young last. Then the kingdom fell to King Hálfdan, and he put Jarl Atli the Thin in charge of it. Then King Hálfdan married Ragnhildr, the daughter of Sigurðr Stag, and their son was Haraldr Finehair.

At the time when King Haraldr came to power in Norway and married into the family of Jarl Hákon, son of Grjótgarðr, he put the county of Sogn into the hands of Jarl Hákon, his relative by marriage, when the king went eastwards to Vík Bay. But Jarl Atli did not want to let go of the rule before meeting King Haraldr. The jarls pressed this case with zeal and levied an army. They met in Fjalir in Stafanessvágr Bay and fought. There Jarl Hákon fell, and Atli was wounded and was brought to Atley Island and there died of his wounds. And after that his son Hásteinn held power until King Haraldr and Jarl Sigurðr levied an army against him. Then Hásteinn escaped and undertook the voyage to Iceland. He married Þóra, daughter of Ǫlvir; their sons were Ǫlvir and Atli.

On the sea, Hásteinn threw the partition-beams [of his hall] overboard in accordance with the old custom. They came to the Stálfjara Foreshore off Stokkseyri Gravel-Bank, but Hásteinn came into Hásteinssund Strait east of Stokkseyri and was wrecked there. He took land between the rivers Rauðá and Ǫlfusá, upwards as far as Fyllarlœkr Brook, and the whole of Breiðamýrr Moor up at Holt Forest. He lived at Stokkseyrr Gravel-Bank, and his son Atli after him, before he moved to Traðarholt Forest. Another son of Hásteinn was called Ǫlvir. He lived at Stjǫrnusteinar Stones. He died without children, but Atli took over the whole inheritance after him. A freedman of Ǫlvir was Brattr, who lived

[134] Þjórsá: 'river (*á*) of the young bull (*þjórr*)'.

in Brattsholt Forest, and Leiðólfr at Leiðólfsstaðir. Atli was the father of Þórðr the Languid, the father of Þorgils Scar-Legg's-Stepson, the father of Grímr Tinkler, the father of Ingjaldr, the father of Grímr, the father of Bǫrkr and Einarr, the father of Hallkatla, who was married to Hrafn, son of Sveinbjǫrn; their daughter was Steinunn, the mother of Sir Hrafn; and Herdís, the mother of Áli, the father of Steinunn, who was married to Haukr, son of Erlendr. Bǫrkr, son of Grímr, was the father of Ragnhildr, who was married to Flosi, son of Bjarni; their children were Einarr and Bjarni and Valgerðr, the mother of Sir Erlendr, the father of Haukr. Þórdís was a second daughter of Flosi, the mother of Lady Ingigerðr, the mother of Lady Guðrún and Abbess Hallbera. Halla as well was a daughter of Flosi, the mother of Sir Kristófórus.

327. Hallsteinn was the name of a man, a relative of Hásteinn, who went from Sogn to Iceland. Hásteinn gave him the outer part of Eyrarbakki Bank. He lived on Framnes Peninsula. His son was Þorsteinn, the father of Arngrímr, who was killed while digging up dry logs. His son was Þorbjǫrn on Framnes Peninsula.

328. Þórir, the son of chieftain Ási, son of Ingjaldr, son of Hróaldr, went to Iceland and took the whole of Kallnesingahreppr upwards from Fyllarlœkr Brook and lived at Selfors Waterfall. His son was Tyrfingr, the father of Þorbjǫrn the Priest and Hámundr the Priest in Goðdalir Valleys.

329. Hróðgeirr the Wise and his brother Oddgeirr, whom Finnr the Rich and Harbour-Ormr bought out of their land-claim, they took Hraungerðinga-hreppr, and Oddgeirr lived at Oddgeirshólar Hills. His son was Þorsteinn Oxen-Spike, the father of Hróðgeirr, the father of Ǫgurr in Kambakista. And a daughter of Hróðgeirr the Wise was Gunnvǫr, who was married to Kolgrímr the Old. From there are the Kvistlingar [descended].

330. Ǫnundr *bíldr*, who was mentioned earlier, took land east of Hróarslœkr Brook, as has been mentioned earlier.

331. A man was called Ǫzurr the White, the son of Þorleifr from Sogn. Ǫzurr committed manslaughter within a sacred precinct in Upplǫnd when he was on the bride's journey together with Sigurðr *hrísi*. For that he was chased out of the land to Iceland and first took all the Holtalǫnd Lands between Þjórsá River and Hraunslœkr Brook. He was seventeen years old when he committed the manslaughter. He married Hallveig, the daughter of Þorviðr. Their son was Þorgrímr the Bearded, the father of Ǫzurr, the father of Þorbjǫrn, the father of Þórarinn, the father of

Grímr, son of Tófa. Ǫzurr lived in Kampaholt Forest. His freedman was Bǫðvarr, who lived in Bǫðvarstóptir by Víðiskógr Forest. To him Ǫzurr gave a share in the forest, and reserved it for himself in case he[135] should die without children. Ǫrn from Vælugerði, who has been mentioned earlier, summoned Bǫðvarr to court for sheep stealing. Therefore Bǫðvarr made over his wealth to Atli, son of Hásteinn, and he, acting against Ǫrn, brought the case down.[136]

Ǫzurr died when Þorgrímr was young. Then Hrafn, son of Þorviðr, received the custody of Þorgrímr's property. After Bǫðvarr's death, Hrafn laid claim to Víðiskógr Forest and banished Atli from it, but Atli thought that he owned it. Atli and three companions went for wood. Leiðólfr was travelling with him. A shepherd told this to Hrafn, and he rode after them with ten men. They met in Orrostudalr, the 'Valley of the Battle', and fought there. There four of Hrafn's farmhands fell and he himself was gravely wounded. One farmhand of Atli's fell and he himself was wounded with lethal wounds and rode home. Ǫnundr *bíldr* separated them. Þórðr the Languid, the son of Atli, was fifteen winters old when Hrafn rode to a ship in Einarshǫfn Harbour. He rode home during the night and was in a blue cloak. Þórðr waylaid him by Haugavað Ford not far from Traðarholt Forest and killed him there with a spear. Hrafn's burial mound is there east of the road, and west of it is Hásteinn's burial mound and Ǫlvir's mound and Atli's mound. The killings cancelled each other out.

Þórðr became famous for that. He then married Þórunn, the daughter of Ásgeirr Devil-of-the-Norwegians, who killed a Norwegian ship's crew in Grímsáróss Estuary for a robbery that he had suffered in Norway. Þórðr was twenty-two winters old when he bought a ship in Knarrarsund 'Merchantman's Sound', and wanted to claim his inheritance. Then he hid a large amount of money. Therefore Þórunn did not want to go away and took up her abode in Traðarholt Forest. At that time, Þorgils, Þórðr's son, was two winters old. Þórðr's ship was lost, and she did not get news of it. One winter later, Þorgrímr Scar-Leg came to marry Þórunn. He was the son of Þormóðr and of Þuríðr, daughter of Ketilbjǫrn. He married Þórunn, and their son was Hæringr.

332. A man was called Óláfr-with-Meeting-Eyebrows. He went to Iceland from Lófót. He took the whole of Skeið between Þjórsá River

[135] That is, Bǫðvarr.

[136] Sentence emended (dittography error in the manuscript).

and Sandlœkr Brook. He had great shape-shifting powers. Óláfr lived at Óláfsvellir Fields. He lies in Brúnahaugr 'Mound of the Brows'[137] at the foot of Vǫrðufell 'Mountain of the Cairn'. Óláfr married Áshildr, and their sons were Helgi the Trustworthy and Þórir Snowfall, the father of Þorkell Gold-Curls, the father of Ormr, the father of Helga, the mother of Oddr, son of Hallvarðr. Vaði was Óláfr's third son, the father of Gerðr.

Since Óláfr was dead, Þorgrímr Scar-Leg took an interest in Áshildr, but Helgi the Trustworthy objected to it. He waylaid Þorgrímr by the crossroads below Áshildarmýrr Moor. Helgi asked him to desist from his visits. Þorgrímr said that he did not have a child's heart. They fought and Þorgrímr fell. Áshildr asked where Helgi had been. He spoke a stanza:

> I was where Scar-Leg fell
> to the ground;(?) the friend of the household
> advanced in battle, and the glorious
> sword-tongues sang loud.
> I gave to Odin Þormóðr's
> mighty, courageous heir.
> To the lord of the gallows we gave
> Odin's sacrifice, and a corpse to the raven.

Friend of the household = Helgi, who is speaking the stanza. Sword-tongues = blades. Lord of the gallows = Odin. Odin's sacrifice = the dead warrior.

Áshildr said that he had dealt himself his own death-blow. Helgi took a passage in a ship in Einarshǫfn Harbour. Hæringr, the son of Þorgrímr, was then sixteen winters old. He rode to Hǫfði Headland to find Teitr. Teitr and his men rode fifteen strong to prevent Helgi from going. They and Helgi met in Merkrhraun Lava-field up from Mǫrk Forest by Helgahváll 'Helgi's Hill'. Helgi and his companions were three altogether. There fell Helgi and a man on his side and one of Teitr's. These killings cancelled each other out. Helgi's son was Sigurðr the Man-from-Land and Skefill the Man-from-Haukadalr, the father of Helgi the Worthy,

[137] The term *brún* used here can refer both literally to 'eyebrows' and metaphorically to the 'brow' of a mountain or a similar topographical feature, raising the question whether the mound might have been named from its topographical location, its unusual name then prompting the invention of a matching settler figure. Here it may also be significant that the site is located under a mountain named *Vǫrðufell*, 'mountain of the *varða*', a *varða* being a cairn erected primarily as a visual topographical marker rather than a burial monument.

who fought against Sigurðr, the son of Ljótr Fish-Back, at the General Assembly on Øxarárhólmi Island. About that, Helgi composed this:

> Bandaged is my right hand,
> goddess of the snake's ground!
> I got a wound from the god of the wave's fire;
> I do not tell a lie with that.

Snake's ground = dragon's ground = the substance on which the dragon is lying = gold; goddess of gold = woman. The wave's fire = gold; god of the gold = man.

Hrafn was Skefill's second son, the father of Grímr, the father of Ásgeirr, the father of Helgi.

333. Þrándr the Swift-Sailing, son of Bjǫrn, the brother of Eyvindr the Norwegian, who has been mentioned earlier, was in Hafrsfjord against King Haraldr and was then banished from the land to Iceland late in the time of the settlement. He took land between the rivers Þjórsá and Laxá and upwards as far as Kaflá River and as far as Sandlœkr Brook. He lived in Þrándarholt Forest. His daughter was Helga, who was married to Þormóðr *skapti*.

334. A famous man in Norway was called Ǫlvir Children's-Man. He was a great Viking. He did not allow children to be picked up with the points of spears, as was then the custom of Vikings; because of that he was called 'Children's-Man'. His sons were Steinólfr, the father of Una, who was married to Þorbjǫrn Man-of-Salmon; and Einarr, the father of Ófeigr Frowner and Óleifr Broad, the father of Þormóðr *skapti*. Steinmóðr was Ǫlvir's third son, the father of Konáll, the father of Aldís *hin barreyska*, who was married to Óláfr *feilan*. Konáll's son was Steinmóðr, the father of Halldóra, who was married to Eilífr, son of Ketill the One-Handed.

The two relatives Ófeigr Frowner and Þormóðr *skapti* went to Iceland and spent the first winter with their relative Þorbjǫrn Man-of-Salmon. And in spring he gave them Gnúpverjahreppr: to Ófeigr the outer part between the rivers Þverá and Kálfá, and [he][138] lived at Ófeigsstaðir near Steinholt Forest; and to Þormóðr he gave the eastern part, and he lived at Skaptaholt Forest. Þormóðr's daughters were Þórvǫr, the mother of Þóroddr the *goði*, the father of Skapti; and Þórvé, the mother

[138] Missing in the manuscript.

of Þorsteinn the *goði*, the father of Bjarni the Wise. Ófeigr fell fighting against Þorbjǫrn Jarls'-Champion in Grettisgeil Glen near Hæll. Ófeigr's daughter was Aldís, the mother of Brandr-of-the-Fields.

335. Þorbjǫrn Man-of-Salmon took the whole of Þjórsárdalr Valley and the whole of Gnúpverjahreppr down as far as Kálfá River and lived the first winter at Miðhús House. He had three winter-quarters before he came to Hagi Pasture; there he lived until his dying day. His sons were Otkell in Þjórsárdalr Valley and Þorgils, the father of Otkatla and of Þorkell *trandill*, the father of Gaukr in Stǫng. Otkatla was the mother of Þorkatla, the mother of Þorvaldr, the father of Dalla, the mother of Bishop Gizurr.

Brynjólfr and Már, sons of Naddoddr and of Jórunn, the daughter of Ǫlvir Children's-Man, came to Iceland early during the settlement of the land. They took Hrunamannahreppr as the streams split it this way. Brynjólfr lived at Berghylr Depth. His sons were Þorleifr, the father of Brǫndólfr, the father of Þorkell Baldhead-of-the-Scots, the father of Þórarinn, the father of Hallr in Haukadalr Valley and of Þorlákr, the father of Rúnólfr, the father of Bishop Þorlákr.[139] Már lived at Másstaðir. His son was Beinir, the father of Kolgríma, the mother of Skeggi, the father of Hjalti.

336. A man from Norway was called Þorbjǫrn Jarls'-Champion. He went from Orkney to Iceland. From Már, son of Naddoddr, he bought land in Hrunamannahreppr, everything below Selslœkr Brook between it and Laxá River. He lived in Hólar Hills. His sons were Sǫlmundr, the father of Kári-of-the-Burning; and Þormóðr, the father of Finna, who was married to Þórormr on Karlafjord. Their daughter was Álfgerðr, the mother of Gestr, the father of Valgerðr, the mother of Þorleifr the Harsh.

337. Þorbrandr, son of Þorbjǫrn the Brave, and his son Ásbrandr came to Iceland late in the time of the settlement and Ketilbjǫrn directed them towards a land-claim above the height which runs on by Stakksá River and as far as Kaldakvísl River-Fork, and they lived in Haukadalr Valley. They thought that was too little land, as Western Tunga was then [already] settled. Then they extended their land-claim and took the upper part of Hrunamannahreppr in a straight line from Múli Crag into Ingjaldsgnúpr Peak area above Gylðarhagi Pasture. Ásbrandr's children were Vébrandr and Arngerðr. Vébrandr was the father of Oddlaug, who was married to Svertingr, son of Rúnólfr.

[139] *Sic.*

About Ketilbjǫrn the Old

338. A famous man in Naumudalr Valley was called Ketilbjǫrn. He was the son of Ketill and Æsa, the daughter of Jarl Hákon, son of Grjótgarðr. He married Helga, the daughter of Þórðr Shaggy. Ketilbjǫrn went to Iceland when the land was widely settled by the sea. He had the ship which was called Elliði. He came into Elliðaáróss, the 'Estuary of Elliði's River', below the heath. He spent the first winter with his relative Þórðr Shaggy. And in spring he went up across the heath to search for good land for himself. They had night-quarters and made a hut for themselves at the place which is now called Skálabrekka 'Slope of the Hut', in Bláskógar Woods. And when they went away from there, they came to the river which they called Øxará 'River of the Axe', because they lost their axe there in it. They took a break under the mountain height which they called Reyðarmúli 'Trout's Crag'; there the river-trout which they took out of the river were left behind after them.

Ketilbjǫrn took the whole of Grímsnes upwards from Hǫskuldslœkr Brook, and the whole of Laugardalr Valley, and the whole of Byskupstunga 'Bishop's Tongue of Land',[140] upwards as far as Stakksá River, and lived at Mosfell Mountain. Their children were Teitr and Þormóðr, Þorleifr and Ketill, Þorkatla and Oddleif, Þorgerðr, Þuríðr. And an illegitimate son of Ketilbjǫrn's was Skæringr. Ketilbjǫrn was so rich in movable property that he told his sons to forge the cross-beam in the temple, which they were having built, out of silver. They did not want to do that. Then he transported the silver up onto the mountain, on two oxen and [with the help of] his slave Haki and his maidservant Bót. They hid the money in such a way that is has not been found since. He killed Haki in Hakaskarð 'Haki's Hollow', and Bót in Bótarskarð 'Bót's Hollow'.

Teitr married Álǫf, the daughter of Bǫðvarr of Vǫrs, son of Kári-of-the-Vikings. Their son was Gizurr the White, the father of Bishop Ísleifr, the father of Bishop Gizurr. A second son of Teitr's was Ketilbjǫrn, the father of Kollr, the father of Þorkell, the father of Kollr, the Bishop of the Víkverjar. Many great men are descended from Ketilbjǫrn.

339. Eyfrøðr the Old took the eastern tongue of land between Kaldakvísl River-Fork and Hvítá River and lived in Tunga 'Tongue of Land'. Together with him Dry-Log-Oddr came out [to Iceland], who lived at Drumb-Oddsstaðir 'Dry-Log-Oddr's-Steads'.

[140] Mosfell lies opposite the episcopal see of Skálholt, separated from it by the river Brúará.

340. A man was called Ásgeirr, son of Úlfr. To him Ketilbjǫrn gave his daughter Þorgerðr. She brought all the Hlíðarlǫnd Lands above Hagagarðr Yard with her as her dowry. He lived at the slope of Outer Hlíð. Their son was Geirr the *goði* and Þorgeirr, the father of Bárðr at Mosfell Mountain.

341. Eilífr the Rich, the son of Ǫnundr *bíldr*, married Þorkatla, daughter of Ketilbjǫrn, and she brought the Hǫfðalǫnd Lands with her as her dowry. There they lived. Their son was Þórir, the father of Þórarinn the Happy.

342. Véþormr, the son of Vémundr the Old, was a powerful chieftain. He took to flight from King Haraldr, [going] eastwards to Jamtaland, and there he cleared forests for a settlement. His son was called Hólmfastr, and the son of his sister was called Grímr. They went on a raiding expedition to the British Isles, and in the Hebrides they killed Jarl Ásbjǫrn Blaze-of-the-Skerries, and there they took his wife Álǫf as plunder, and his daughter Arneiðr, and Hólmfastr got her by lot, and his father received her and let her be a maidservant. Grímr got Álǫf, the daughter of Þórðr *vaggagði*, who had been married to the jarl. Grímr went to Iceland and took the whole of Grímsnes upwards as far as Lake Svínavatn and lived at Ǫndurðunes Peninsula for four winters, and then at Búrfell Mountain. His son was Þorgils, who married Æsa, the sister of Gestr, son of Oddleifr. Their sons were Þórarinn at Búrfell Mountain and Jǫrundr at Miðengi Meadow.

About Hallkell

343. Hallkell, a brother of Ketilbjǫrn by the same mother, he went to Iceland and spent the first winter with Ketilbjǫrn. Ketilbjǫrn offered to give him land. It seemed to him the behaviour of a little man to accept land from him, and he demanded lands from Grímr, or else a duel. At the foot of Hallkelshólar Hills, Grímr fought a duel with Hallkell and fell there. And Hallkell then lived at Hólar Hills. His sons were Otkell, who killed Gunnarr, son of Hámundr; and Oðr at Kiðjaberg Cliff, the father of Hallbjǫrn, who was killed at Hallbjarnarvǫrður 'Hallbjǫrn's Cairns'; and Hallkell, the father of Hallvarðr, the father of Þorsteinn, whom Einarr the Shetlander killed. The son of Hallkell, son of Oddr, was Bjarni, the father of Hallr, the father of Ormr, the father of Bárðr, the father of Valgerðr, the mother of Halldóra, who was married to Bishop Magnús, son of Gizurr. Now the settlement of Ingólfr has been reached.

About Þorgrímr bíldr

344. Þorgrímr *bíldr*, a brother of Ǫnundr *bíldr* who had the same mother as he, was the son of Úlfr from Hóll Hill. He took all the lands above Þverá River and settled at Bíldsfjall Mountain.

About Steinrøðr

345. Steinrøðr, son of Melpatrekr, a noble man of Ireland, he was a freedman of Þorgrímr *bíldr*. He married Þorgrímr's daughter and was the most promising of all men. He took all the Vatslǫnd Lands and lived at Steinrøðsstaðir. His son was Þormóðr, the father of Kárr, the father of Þormóðr, the father of Brandr, the father of Þórir, the father of Brandr at Þingvǫllr Assembly Field.

About Hrolleifr

346. Hrolleifr, son of Einarr, son of Ǫlvir Children's-Man, came into Leiruvágr Bay at a time when everything by the sea was [already] settled. He took land as far as the point where his lands met those of Steinrøðr, everything beyond Øxará River, which flows around Þingvǫllr Assembly Field, and lived for several winters at Heiðabœr Farm. Then he challenged Eyvindr in Kvíguvágar Bays to a duel or a sale of land; and Eyvindr chose that they rather make a deal about the lands. Eyvindr then lived at Heiðabœr Farm for several winters and then went from Rosmhvalanes Peninsula to Bœjarsker Skerry; but Hrolleifr lived then in Kvíguvágar Bays and is buried there in a mound. His son was Svertingr, the father of Grímr the Law-Speaker at Mosfell Mountain.

347. Ormr the Old, the son of Jarl Eyvindr, son of Arnmóðr Jarl[141] the Stingy. Ormr took land between the rivers Varmá and Þverá, everything around Ingólfsfell Mountain, and lived in Hvammr 'Grassy Slope'. He married Þórunn, the daughter of Ketill the Kjǫlr-Traveller, the one who clubbed the *finngálkn*-chimaera to death; she was the great-aunt of Grímr the Hálogalander. Their son was Ormr the Old, the father of Darri, the father of Ǫrn. He was also against King Haraldr in Hafrsfjord.

348. Álfr the Man-from-Agðir ran from King Haraldr Finehair from Agðir in Norway. He went to Iceland and came with his ship into the

[141] The deviant word order reflects an omission in the manuscript; *recte* the passage should probably read 'son of Jarl Arnmóðr, son of Jarl Nereiðr the Stingy'.

estuary that is named after him and is called Álfsóss 'Álfr's Estuary'. He took all the lands beyond Varmá River and lived at Gnúpar Peaks. Þorgrímr, son of Grímólfr, the son of his brother, came out [to Iceland] together with him, the one who became his heir, because Álfr did not have a child. Þorgrímr's son was Eyvindr, the father of Þóroddr the *goði*, the father of Skapti. Ǫzurr as well was a son of Eyvindr, who married Bera, the daughter of Egill, son of Baldhead-Grímr. Þorgrímr's mother was Kormlǫð, the daughter of Kjarvall, King of the Irish. The daughter of Þóroddr the *goði* was Helga, the mother of Grímr Tinkler, the father of Ingjaldr, the father of Grímr, the father of Bǫrkr, the father of Ragnhildr, the mother of Valgerðr, the mother of Sir Erlendr, the father of Haukr.

About Þórir Autumn-Darkness

349. Þórir Autumn-Darkness took Selvágr Bay and Krýsuvík Bay, and his son Heggr lived at Vágr Bay, and his second son Bǫðmóðr was the father of Þórarinn, the father of Súgandi, the father of Þorvarðr, the father of Þórhildr, the mother of Sigurðr, son of Þorgrímr. The sons of Molda-Gnúpr settled Grindavík Bay, as was written earlier.

350. Steinunnr the Old, a kinswoman of Ingólfr's, went to Iceland and spent the first winter with him. He offered to give to her the whole of Rosmhvalanes Peninsula beyond Hvassahraun lava-field, but she [gave][142] an English spotted frock with a hood [in return][143] and wanted to call it a purchase; that seemed to her better protection from a reversal. Steinunnr had been married to Herlaugr, the brother of Baldhead-Grímr. Their sons were Njáll and Arnórr.

351. A relative and foster-relative of Steinunnr was called Eyvindr. She gave land to him between Kvíguvágabjǫrg Cliffs and Hvassahraun Lava-field. His son was Erlingr, the father of Þórarinn, the father of Sighvatr, the father of Þórarna, the mother of Þorbjǫrn, son of Arnþjófr in Krýsuvík Bay, and of Álǫf, the mother of Finnr the Law-Speaker and of Freygerðr, the mother of Loptr, the father of Guðlaugr the Smith.

352. Herjólfr, who has been mentioned earlier, was a relative of Ingólfr's and his foster-brother. Therefore Ingólfr gave him land between Reykjanes Peninsula and Vágr Bay. His son was Bárðr, the father of Herjólfr, the one who went to Greenland and came into the sea-fens. On

[142] Missing in the manuscript.
[143] Missing in the manuscript.

his ship there was a man from the Hebrides. He composed the *Praise-Poem of the Sea-Fens*. Here is its beginning:

All listen to our toast of the dark
mountain hall of Dvalinn.

Dvalinn = a dwarf; hall of the dwarf in the dark mountains = his abode, as dwarfs are living in rocks and cliffs; the toast drunk in the dwarf's hall = the mead of poetry = poetry. Thus, the two verses mean: 'All listen to my poem.'

About Ásbjǫrn

353. A man was called Ásbjǫrn, son of Ǫzurr, son of Ingólfr's brother. He took land between Hraunholtslœkr Brook and Hvassahraun Lava-field, the whole of Álptanes Peninsula, and lived at Skúlastaðir. His son was Egill, the father of Ǫzurr, the father of Þórarinn, the father of Óláfr, the father of Sveinbjǫrn, the father of Ásmundr, the father of Sveinbjǫrn, the father of Styrkárr, the father of He-Goat-Bjǫrn, the father of Þorsteinn and Gizurr on Seltjarnarnes Peninsula.

About the Distribution of the Land

354. Now a perusal has been made of the land-takings that there have been in Iceland, according to what wise men have written, first Ari the Priest the Learned, son of Þorgils, and Kolskeggr the Wise. And this book [I],[144] Haukr, son of Erlendr, have written, on the basis of the book which Sir Sturla the Law-Speaker had written, the most learned man, and on the basis of the second book, which Styrmir the Learned had written. And I took from each of the two that which explained more; and a great part was what they both said in agreement with each other. And therefore it is not surprising if this *Book of Settlements* is longer than any other.

And these settlers are the noblest that have been in the Quarter of the Southland-People: Hrafn the Stay-at-Home; Ketill Salmon; Sighvatr the Red; Hásteinn, son of Atli; Ketilbjǫrn the Old; Helgi *bjóla*; Ingólfr; Ørlygr the Old; Kolgrímr the Old; Bjǫrn Gold-Bearer; Ǫnundr Broad-Beard. And in the Quarter of the Eastfjordmen: Þorsteinn the White; Brynjólfr the Old; Porridge-Atli and Ketill, sons of Þiðrandi; Hrafnkell the *goði*; Bǫðvarr the White; Hrollaugr, son of Jarl Rǫgnvaldr; Ǫzurr,

[144] Later addition in the margin of the manuscript.

son of Ásbjǫrn, son of Bjǫrn-of-Heyjangr, from whom the Freysgyðlingar are descended; Ketill the Foolish; Leiðólfr the Champion. And in the Quarter of the Northland-People: Auðun Shaft; Ingimundr the Old; Ævarr; Sæmundr; Eiríkr in Guðdalir Valleys; Þórðr-of-Hǫfði; Helgi the Skinny; Eyvindr, son of Þorsteinn; Hámundr Hell-Skin. And in the Quarter of the Westfjordmen: Hrosskell; Baldhead-Grímr; Seal-Þórir; Bjǫrn the Easterner; Þórólfr Beard-of-Mostr; Auðr the Deep-Minded; Geirmundr Hell-Skin; Úlfr the Squint-Eyed; Þórðr, son of Víkingr.

355. Learned men say that the land became fully settled within sixty winters, so that it has not become more densely settled since. At that time, many of the settlers and their sons were still alive. And when the land had been settled for sixty winters, the following chieftains were the greatest in Iceland. In the Quarter of the Southland-People: Mǫrðr Fiddle; Jǫrundr the *goði*; Geirr the *goði*; Þorsteinn, son of Ingólfr; Oddr-of-Tunga. And in the Quarter of the Westfjordmen: Egill, son of Baldhead-Grímr; Þorgrímr, son of Kjallakr; Þórðr Yeller. And in the north: Skeggi-of-the-Miðfjord; Þorsteinn, son of Ingimundr;[145] the Guðdœlir; the sons of Hjalti; Eyjólfr, son of Valgerðr; Áskell the *goði*. And in the Quarter of the Eastfjordmen: Þorsteinn the White; Hrafnkell the *goði*; Þorsteinn, the father of Hallr-of-Síða; Þórðr Freyr's-*goði*. Hrafn, son of [Ketill] Salmon, at that time held the office of the law-speaker.

356. Wise men say that the following settlers had been baptised: Helgi the Skinny; Ørlygr the Old; Helgi *bjóla*; Jǫrundr the Christian; Auðr the Deep-Minded; Ketill the Foolish. And they had for the most part come from the British Isles. Some kept Christianity well to their dying day; but that was not handed on widely over the generations, because the sons of those few built temples and sacrificed; and the land was all pagan for nearly one hundred winters.

[145] Manuscript: 'son of Ingólfr'.

INDEX

Table of chapters, showing the relationship of the Hauksbók recension to the Sturlubók recension, and of primary settlers:

Chapter in Hauksbók	Chapter in Sturlubók	Primary settlers
H1	S1	*papar*
H2	S2	Time of the discovery of Iceland and location of the island
H3	S4	Garðarr son of Svávarr
H4	S3	Naddoddr the Viking
H5	S5	Flóki son of Vilgerðr
H6	S6	Ingólfr, son of Ǫrn, and Sword-Leifr, son of Hróðmarr
H7	S7	Ingólfr, son of Ǫrn, and Sword-Leifr, son of Hróðmarr
H8	S8	Ingólfr, son of Ǫrn, and Sword-Leifr, son of Hróðmarr
H9	S9	Ingólfr, son of Ǫrn
H10	S9	Ingólfr, son of Ǫrn
H11	S10, S11	Þórðr Shaggy, son of Hrappr
H12	S12	Hallr, son of Þórir
H13	S13	Ketill Flat-Nose, son of Bjǫrn the Ungartered
H14	S14	Helgi *bjóla*, son of Ketill Flat-Nose
H15	S15	Ørlygr, son of Hrappr
H16	S16	Svartkell
H17	S17	Valþjófr, son of Ørlygr
H18	S18	Hvamm-Þórir
H19	S19	Sǫlmundr, son of Þórólfr Butter
H20	S20	Ávangr the Irishman
H21	S22–S24	Þormóðr the Old and Ketill and Kalman, sons of Bresi
H22	S21	Kolgrímr the Old, son of the chieftain Hrólfr
H23	S26	Finnr the Rich, son of Halldórr
H24	S25	Bekan
H25	S27	Harbour-Ormr
H26	S38	Rauðr
H27	S39	Grímr
H28	S40	Þorkell Grain-Hill
H29	S41	Úlfr, son of Grímr the Hálogalander

H30	S42	Kalman the Hebridean
H31	S43	Hallkell, son of Hrosskell
H32	S44	Ásbjǫrn the Rich, son of Hǫrðr
H33	S45	Ǫrnólfr
H34	S46	Hrómundr
H35	S47	Ísleifr and Ísrøðr
H36	S48	Ásgeirr
H37	S49	Arnbjǫrg
H38	S50	Þorbjǫrn, son of Arnbjǫrn
H39	S51	Þorbjǫrn *blesi*
H40	S52	Geirmundr, son of Gunnbjǫrn Enchantment
H41	S53	Ǫrn the Old
H42	S54	Bjǫrn-of-the-Bog-Ore
H43	S55	Karl
H44	S56	Gríss and Grímr
H45	S57	Bálki, son of Blæingr
H46	S58	Sigmundr
H47	S59	Bjǫrn-of-the-Bog-Ore
H48	S60	Þorbjǫrn *krumr* and Þórir *beigaldi*
H49	S61	Þórðr Giant and Þorgeirr Earth-Long and Þorbjǫrg Pole
H50	S62	Áni
H51	S63	Þorfinnr the Hard
H52	S64	Yngvarr
H53	S65	Steinólfr
H54	S66	Þórhaddr, son of Steinn the Swift-Sailing
H55	S67	Þorgils *knappi*
H56	S68	Grímr, son of Ingjaldr and Seal-Þórir
H57	–	Kolbeinn Damaged-Head
H58	S69, S70	Þormóðr the *goði* and Þórðr the Stooping, sons of Oddr the Dog
H59	S71	Guðlaugr
H60	S72	Váli the Strong
H61	S73	Hrólfr the Fat, son of Eyvindr Oaken-Hook
H62	S74	Sǫlvi
H63	S75	Sigmundr, son of Ketill Thistle
H64	S76	Grímkell, son of Úlfr Crow
H65	S77	Álfarinn, son of Váli
H66	S78	Óláfr the Elder
H67	S79	Ormr the Thin
H68	S80	Sigurðr Pig-Head
H69	S81	Vestarr, son of Þórólfr Bladder-Baldhead

H108	S136	Geirþjófr, son of Valþjófr
H109	S137	Eiríkr
H110	S138	Vésteinn, the son of Végeirr
H111	S139	Dýri
H112	S140	Þórðr, son of Víkingr
H113	S141	Ingjaldr, son of Brúni
H114	S144	Hallvarðr Wind-Gust
H115	S143	Qnundr, son of Víkingr
H116	S145	Þuríðr Channel-Filler
H117	S146	Helgi, son of Hrólfr
H118	S147	Þórólfr Brackish-Taste
H119	S148	Eyvindr Knee
H120	S149	Sanctuary-Geirr
H121	S150	Gunnsteinn and Halldórr, sons of Gunnbjǫrn
H122	S151, S152	Snæbjǫrn, son of Eyvindr the Eastman
H123	S153	Óláfr Dye-Head
H124	S154	Þórólfr Fast-Holding
H125	S155	Ørlygr, the son of Bǫðvarr
H126	S156	Hella-Bjǫrn, son of Herfinnr
H127	S157	Geirólfr
H128	S159	Eyvindr and Ófeigr and Ingólfr, sons of Herrøðr *hvikatimbr*
H129	S160	Eiríkr String
H130	S161	Qnundr Wooden-Foot, son of Ófeigr *burlufótr*
H131	S162	Bjǫrn
H132	S163	Steingrímr
H133	S164	Kolli
H134	S165	Þorbjǫrn Bitterness
H135	S166	Bálki, son of Blæingr
H136	S167	Arndís the Rich, daughter of Steinólfr the Humble
H137	S168	Grenjuðr and Þrǫstr, sons of Hermundr *hǫlknir*
H138	S172	Eysteinn *meinfretr*, son of Álfr
H139	S173	Þóroddr
H140	S174	Bjǫrn-of-Furs, son of Skautaðar-Skeggi
H141	S175	Haraldr Ring
H142	S176	Sóti
H143	S177	Auðun Shaft, son of Bjǫrn
H144	S178	Ormr
H145	S179	Ingimundr the Old, son of Þorsteinn
H146	S179	Jǫrundr Neck
H147	S180	Hrolleifr the Big, son of Arnaldr

H188	S222	Galmr
H189	S223	Geirleifr, son of Hrappr
H190	S224	Þórðr the Ripping
H191	S225	Þórir Giants-Burster
H192	S226	Auðólfr
H193	S227	Eysteinn, son of Ráðúlfr
H194	S228	Eyvindr Cock
H195	S229	The sons of Ǫndóttr
H196	S230	Hámundr
H197	S231	Gunnarr, son of Úlfljótr
H198	S232	Auðun the Rotten, son of Þórólfr Butter
H199	S233	Hrólfr, son of Helgi the Skinny
H200	S235	Þorgeirr, son of Þórðr Beam
H201	S236	Skagi, son of Skopti
H202	S237	Þórir Flap, son of Ketill Seal
H203	S238	Þengill the Swift-Sailing
H204	S239	Þormóðr
H205	S240	Þorgeirr
H206	S241	Loðinn Angle
H207	S242	Bárðr, son of Bjǫrn-of-Heyjangr
H208	S243, S244	Þorfiðr Moon [and Þórir, son of Grímr Grey-Coat's-Mull]
H209	S245	Heðinn and Hǫskuldr, sons of Þorsteinn Giant
H210	S246	Vestmaðr and Úlfr
H211	S247	Eyvindr and Ketill, sons of Þorsteinn Headland
H212	S248	Grenjaðr, son of Hrappr
H213	S249	Bǫðólfr, son of Grímr
H214	S250	Skeggi, son of Bǫðólfr
H215	S251	Máni
H216	S252	Ljótr Unwashed
H217	S253	Ǫnundr, son of Blæingr
H218	S254	Þorsteinn, son of Sigmundr
H219	S255	Þorkell the Tall
H220	S256	Geiri
H221	S257	Einarr, son of Þorgeirr Blunderhead
H222	S258	Reistr, son of Ketill-of-Bjarney Island
H223	S259	Arngeirr
H224	S260	Sveinungr and Kolli
H225	S261, S263	Ketill Thistle
H226	S264	Gunnólfr *kroppa*, son of Þórir the Hawk-Nosed
H227	S265	Finni

H266	S305	Firebrand-Ǫnundr
H267	S306	Firebrand-Ǫnundr
H268	S307	Þórðr Shaggy and Úlfljótr, son of Þóra; the pagan laws
H269	S308	Þorsteinn Leg, son of Bjǫrn Blue-Tooth
H270	S309, S310	The illegitimate sons of Jarl Rǫgnvaldr, son of Eysteinn Rattle; Hrollaugr, son of Rǫgnvaldr
H271	S311	Ketill
H272	S312	Auðun the Red
H273	S314	Úlfr the Man of Vǫrs
H274	S313	Þorsteinn the Squinting
H275	S315	Þórðr *illugi*, son of Eyvindr Oaken-Hook
H276	S316	Ásbjǫrn, son of Bjǫrn-of-Heyjangr, and his wife Þorgerðr
H277	S317	Helgi, son of Bjǫrn-of-Heyjangr
H278	S318	Bárðr-of-Gnúpar, son of Bjǫrn-of-Heyjangr
H279	S319	Eyvindr *karpi*
H280	S320	Ketill the Foolish, son of Jórunn Woman-Wisdom's-Slope
H281	S321	Bǫðmóðr
H282	S322	Eysteinn the Fat
H283	S323	Eysteinn, son of Hrani
H284	S328, S329	Vémundr and Molda-Gnúpr, sons of Hrólfr the Hewer
H285	S324	Vilbaldr, son of Dofnak
H286	S325	Leiðólfr the Champion
H287	S326	Ísólfr
H288	S327	Hrafn Haven-Key
H289	S330	Eysteinn, son of Þorsteinn Man-of-the-Rock-Pillars
H290	S330	Ǫlvir, son of Eysteinn
H291	S331	Sigmundr *kleykir*, son of Ǫnundr *bíldr*
H292	S332	Bjǫrn
H293	S333, S334	The children of Loðmundr the Old
H294	S336	The beginning of the settlement in the South Quarter
H295	S337	Þrasi, son of Þórólfr
H296	S338	Hrafn the Stay-at-Home, son of Valgarðr
H297	S339	Ásgeirr Pincers, son of Óleifr the White
H298	S340	Þorgeirr the Hordalander, son of Bárðr Cup-of-Whey-Water
H299	S341	Ófeigr and Ásgerðr, daughter of Askr *enn ómálgi*
H300	S342	Þórólfr
H301	S343	Ásbjǫrn and Steinfiðr, sons of Reyrketill
H302	S351	Herjólfr, son of Bárðr
H303	S344	Ketill Salmon, son of Þorkell
H304	S345	Sighvatr the Red

H343	S389	Hallkell
H344	S390	Þorgrímr *bíldr*, son of Úlfr
H345	S390	Steinrøðr, son of Melpatrekr
H346	S395	Hrolleifr, son of Einarr, and Eyvindr
H347	S391	Ormr the Old, son of Jarl Eyvindr
H348	S392	Álfr the Man-from-Agðir and Þorgrímr, son of Grímólfr
H349	S393	Þórir Autumn-Darkness
H350	S394	Steinunnr the Old
H351	S395	Eyvindr
H352	S91	Herjólfr
H353	S396	Ásbjǫrn, son of Ǫzurr
H354	–; S397	Haukr's postscript; most famous settlers
H355	S398	Duration of the settlement period and most prominent chieftains at the point when the land was fully settled
H356	S399	Christianity among the earliest settlers

INDEX OF SELECTED PRIMARY PROTAGONISTS

Given the extremely high number of both personal and place names found in the *Book of Settlements*, no full index is given; such an index would be at least as long as the translation of the text itself and could therefore not be included in the present volume. This material is already presented in an exemplary fashion by Jakob Benediktsson, whose 1968 edition of the *Book of Settlements* contains a conveniently accessible and virtually exhaustive concordance of the persons and places mentioned in the text. The following index is restricted to a comparatively small selection of the most significant protagonists of the *Book of Settlements*. Place names have had to be left aside entirely. Reference is made to chapter numbers.